WEALTH OF NATIONS

ADAM SMITH

An Inquiry into the Nature and Causes of the WEALTH OF NATIONS

Abridged,
with Commentary
and Notes, by

LAURENCE DICKEY

Hackett Publishing Company
Indianapolis/Cambridge

Copyright © 1993 by Hackett Publishing Company, Inc.
All rights reserved
Printed in the United States of America

99 98 97 96 95 94 93   1 2 3 4 5 6 7

Cover design by Listenberger & Associates
Text design by Dan Kirklin

For further information, please address
  Hackett Publishing Company, Inc.
  P.O. Box 44937
  Indianapolis, Indiana 46244-0937

Library of Congress Cataloging-in-Publication Data

Smith, Adam, 1723–1790.
    An inquiry into the nature and causes of the wealth of nations/
  abridged with commentary and notes, by Laurence Dickey.
          p.   cm.
    Includes bibliographical references.
    ISBN 0-87220-205-4   ISBN 0-87220-204-6 (pbk.)
    1. Economics.   I. Dickey, Laurence Winant.   II. Title.
  III. Title: Wealth of nations.
  HB161.S65   1993c
  330.15′3—dc20   93-24370
                                                          CIP

The paper used in this publication meets the minimum
requirements of American National Standard for Information
Sciences—Permanence of Paper for Printed Library
Materials, ANSI Z39.48-1984. ∞

CONTENTS

EDITORIAL PREFACE

How texts are read, "classic" or otherwise, depends very much on the situation in which they are read. In the closing decades of the twentieth century, for example, a lot has happened that will shape the way college students in America read a text like *The Wealth of Nations* (Henceforth *WN*). In light of the boom-and-bust experiences and expectations of the 1980s the inclination to view the *WN* through the lenses of the economic policies of the Reagan-Bush administrations will be strong. That, of course, is because those economic policies were often justified by appealing to the authority of Adam Smith. On the one side, therefore, some will credit Smithian principles for the robust business enterprise of the 1980s. Others will implicate Smith in the spawning of a decade of greed which widened the gap between the rich and just about everybody else in America. Either way, it will be difficult to disassociate Smith from the not so subtle symbolism evoked by those 1980s Washington officials who wore neckties with multiple miniature profiles of Adam Smith imprinted on them.[1]

Given the perception of an ideological connection between recent Republican administrations in Washington and the *WN*, it is not at all improbable that a generation of college students will read Smith's book with the successes and/or failures of the economic policies of the 1980s in mind. More important, though, contemporary views of the *WN* will be influenced by the rhetoric Republicans used throughout the 1980s to make the case for what became known as "supply-side" economics. In doing this, Republicans again invoked the name of Adam Smith, appealing specifically to the (allegedly) "Smithian" idea that self-interest should be allowed to determine society's economic decisions about how its resources will be allocated.[2] Because this idea—so often associated with laissez-faire economics—has occupied center stage in a decade-long public debate over American economic policy, it will require some intellectual agility to contest Republican interpretations of Smith without impugning the principles of the *WN* at the same time.

That the *WN* figured so prominently on one side of the polarized economic debates of the 1980s is ironic from a scholarly point of view. For in the last twenty years Smith scholarship in general and studies of the *WN* in particular have reached new heights of excellence, comprehensiveness, and historical nuance. Important work, for example, has been done on the Scottish Enlightenment—the period of great intellectual achievement in eighteenth-century Scottish history that is associated with the names of Hugh Blair, Adam Ferguson, David Hume, Lord Kames, John Millar, William Robertson, and James Steuart, as well as Adam Smith.[3] Knowing more about the Scottish Enlightenment, in turn, has helped us understand how Smith's uniquely Scottish context shaped his thinking in ways that would not have occurred had Smith lived in France or even England.[4]

Concurrent with these scholarly developments has been a growing appreciation of what scholars today call the "civic," "civil," and "natural jurisprudential" aspects of Smith's thinking.[5] Some fine recent studies in the intellectual history of economics have also corrected many misconceptions we have long held about Smith's position in the history of economic thinking.[6] Especially important here has been a new awareness of the many "liberalizing" tendencies in mercantilist thinking in the late seventeenth and early eighteenth centuries. As a result of this recent work, more precise questions are now being asked as to what kind of breakthrough in economic thinking occurred with the publication of the *WN* in 1776.

Dozens of other recent and equally important studies of Smith's thought, economic and otherwise, provide incontestable proof of the vast scope and richly textured quality of Smith's writings.[7] All this, however, is happening at a time when the *WN* is being ideologically pigeonholed as the book of what one well-known Smith scholar has called "right-wing politicians."[8] So, instead of the exciting prospect of explaining the *WN* to students with the help of this excellent new scholarship, teachers of the *WN* today are faced with the task of extricating Smith from the ideological tangles of the 1980s before they can do anything else.

I would very much like to say that misconceptions of Adam Smith as a thinker and of the *WN* as a book could be resolved simply by having students read the *WN* for themselves. But a work of over one thousand pages does not lend itself to that kind of scrutiny, even in college courses that devote a week or two of study to Smith or to topics that may be related to Smith. In addition, it would be presumptuous to assume that even highly motivated students could negotiate their own way through even a small segment of the rapidly expanding body of new Smith scholarship. Thus, if students need to read the *WN* themselves in order to avoid thinking and speaking about it in clichés, the teachers of those students need to develop a strategy for making that task more manageable for them.

This abridged volume of the *WN* has been designed with the reading needs of today's students in mind. To achieve this purpose, I have set two objectives for this edition. First of all, text selections and editorial commentary have been coordinated so as to alert students to certain strategic turning points in the argument of the *WN*. More specifically, my text selections draw attention to long stretches of the *WN* in which Smith skillfully works high-minded moral arguments into economic discussions. Indeed, by illustrating and detailing what role Smith thought morality played in fostering and sustaining economic growth, the selections deliberately challenge the prevailing wisdom that the *WN* justifies self-interested economic behavior, narrowly (i.e., selfishly) understood.[9]

Second of all, and in order to avoid imposing preconceptions on students as to how to read and interpret Smith's text, I have relegated to four Appendices my own views both on how the argument of the *WN* unfolds and on what I take to be the point of the argument's unfolding the way it does. For pedagogic purposes, I have focused the discussion in each Appendix on themes developed more or less discretely in each of the five books that delineate the *WN*'s internal structure. The material in Appendix IV is an exception to this procedure, insofar as I try there (among other things) to offer an explanation of the different positions Smith seems to take in Books I and Books V on the division of labor. Yet, I do that within a framework of interpretation that has been elucidated in Appendices I–III.[10]

Two final and related points. A guiding premise of this volume has been that the *WN* raises so many challenging problems of interpretation for students in its own right that questions about the text's relationship to Smith's biography and to his other writings, especially *The Theory of Moral Sentiments* (Henceforth *TMS*), need not be entered into here. As a Smith scholar, I certainly know how important examining these relations are for a full understanding of Smith as a thinker. Still, it seems to me that asking students to immerse themselves in the *WN* is the best way to introduce the profundity of Adam Smith to them. There is, after all, little in Smith's "placid" and "reclusive" life to grab students' attention,[11] and to ask them to grapple with the complex moral philosophy of the *TMS* at the same time they are reading the *WN* (probably) for the first time strikes me as unwise, for educational reasons.[12] Therefore, my commentary in the Appendices deals almost exclusively with themes internal to the *WN* itself.

On a personal note, I would like to add that my first encounter with Smith occurred in 1980 at Columbia University. As an instructor in Columbia's justly renowned Contemporary Civilization course, I was required to teach the *WN* to Columbia College's undergraduates. To prepare for that, I studied Smith and worked on the scholarship of the Scottish Enlightenment, with the result that I gradually came to appreciate the role political economy played in eighteenth-century European intellectual history. Since I stumbled around in Smith scholarship for several years before I finally got my bearings, I would like to dedicate this volume to my Contemporary Civilization students, who showed great patience and understanding in allowing me to experiment with different ways of teaching the *WN* to them.

Notes to the Editorial Preface

1. The use made of Smith by Republicans in the 1980s was hardly new. Since at least early in the nineteenth century a broad cross-section of European thinkers had expressed grave concerns about the antisocial implications of Smith's (alleged) materialism. In many ways, therefore, recent exchanges among professional economists over the social and ethical implications of Smith's thinking mirror divergent long-term tendencies in the debate about the meaning of the *WN*. For a perspective on both sides of the debate, see A. Sen (1987, pp. 1–27). That the turn to Smith in America had been gaining momentum before the 1980s is evident from comments made by two famous economists, P. Samuelson and G. Stigler, in *The New York Times*'s bicentenary celebration of the publication of the *WN* (March 9, 1976). As Samuelson, for example, stated: "In a simplistic way, Adam Smith's ideas are near those of the Ford Administration."

2. See, e.g., G. Stigler's "Preface" to the 1976 Chicago reissue of E. Cannan's edition of the *WN*. Stigler's view of the role of "self-interest" in Smith's thinking has been contested by D. Winch (1978, pp. 165ff), B. Mazlich and N. Goodwin (1983), and A. Sen (1986, p. 31f).

3. For starters, see the essays in I. Hont and M. Ignatieff (1983).

4. N. Phillipson (1981) provides a useful introduction to the pecularities of the Scottish milieu and outlook in the eighteenth century. I should probably note here that recent scholarly efforts to dissociate the Scottish from the French Enlightenment often entails an attempt to rescue Adam Smith from the charge either of antisocial individualism or of social engineering. In that historiographical framework, Smith as well as other Scottish thinkers are presented as having a more social and less atomistic view of the individual than their French counterparts. See, e.g., I. Kristol (1983, pp. 142–44), J. Peil (1991, pp. 283–84), and D. Forbes (1982).

5. For an overview, consult J.G.A. Pocock (1983).

6. T. Hutchison (1988) is exemplary here.

7. See the essays collected in A. Skinner and T. Wilson (1975) and in G. O'Driscoll (1979).

8. D. D. Raphael (1985, p. 1).

9. On how the narrow view of self-interest has permeated interpretations of Smith's work, see D. Winch (1978, pp. 1–27).

10. The decision to organize my commentary around the individual books of the *WN* grows out of a conviction that Smith scholarship has avoided asking probing questions about the *WN*'s structure. Indeed, in my judgment the more the issue of continuity and change between the *WN*'s various books is analyzed, the more complex the argument of the *WN* becomes.

11. Stigler (1976, p. xiii) and R. H. Campbell and A. Skinner (1982, p. 7) use such terms to describe Smith's uneventful life. As the latter show (p. 131), D. Hume drew attention to Smith's "sedentary reclusive life" in a letter of July 1766.

12. In an Appendix written for, but not included in this edition, I discuss the so-called "Adam Smith Problem" as it developed over the last two hundred years. I argue that modern renderings of that problem—all of which deal with the problem in terms of the relationship between *TMS* and the *WN*—fail to acknowledge that from 1790 to late in the nineteenth century the Adam Smith Problem had nothing to do with *TMS* at all. Indeed, the question about the relationship between the ethical and economic aspects of Smith's thinking focused almost exclusively on issues internal to the *WN* itself (e.g., the relationship between Books I and II on the one hand and Books III–V on the other; and on the relationship between induction and deduction in Smith's argument). It is not at all insignificant that *TMS* became part of the debate under the auspices of French thinkers (e.g., V. Cousin) who, wishing to rescue Smith from misguided materialistic disciples in Britain, spiritualized Smith's economics by reminding readers of the *WN* that Smith was first and foremost a moral philosopher (Consult Winch 1978, p. 10, for the dangers of doing this).

Basic Biographical Information on Smith's Life

1723   Born in Kirkcaldy, Scotland, into a well-established family of some affluence, his father had died shortly before. Receives quality education at the town school there.

1737–1740   Enrolled at the University of Glasgow. F. Hutcheson, an important eighteenth-century philosopher and the key figure in the so-called Glasgow school of moral philosophy, is one of Smith's teachers.

1740–1746   Awarded Snell Fellowship for Scottish students to study at Oxford University in England. Expected to pursue a career in the Scottish church. Spends six unhappy years there—at Balliol College.

1746–1748   Lives in Kirkcaldy with his mother. Seeks an academic alternative to a church career. Henry Home (later Lord Kames) arranges lecture series for Smith at Edinburgh, though not under the auspices of the university.

1748–1751   Lectures on various topics in Edinburgh. Much scholarly conjecture about the economic content of these lectures. Resigns Snell Fellowship and is free to pursue an academic career. Receives appointment to the Chair in Logic at the University of Glasgow early in 1751. Shifts to Chair in Moral Philosophy, 1752.

1751–1763   Lectures on a variety of subjects at Glasgow. Active in various literary societies with members of the church, business, and university communities. Publishes *The Theory of Moral Sentiments* in 1759, which is well received throughout Europe. In the early 1760s, Smith devotes increasing attention to economic topics—the division of labor, the critique of monopolies, and more. We have evidence from these years—the so-called "Early Draft" of the *Wealth of Nations* and the *Lectures on Jurisprudence*—that attest to Smith's emerging economic interests. Scholars continue to debate how this evidence anticipates the *Wealth of Nations*.

1764–1766   For financial reasons Smith accepts a proposal to tutor the Duke of Buccleuch while the latter takes a Continental tour. Smith lives in France for the better part of three years. Meets several important French economic thinkers, Turgot and Quesnay among them. Evidence that important aspects of the *Wealth of Nations* derive from Smith's experience in

France. Tour ends in late 1766 when the Duke's brother, traveling with the group, suddenly dies.

1767–1777   While living in Kirkcaldy (1767–1773) and London (1766–1767 and 1773–1777), Smith writes the *Wealth of Nations*. Publishes the *Wealth of Nations* March 9, 1776. Off and on during these years Smith is asked for advice on British policy toward America. Applies for a position in the Scottish Customs office in Edinburgh.

1778–1790   Assumes Custom's position in early 1778. Duties basically involve administering mercantile regulations of the sort he criticizes in the *Wealth of Nations*. Enjoys this work and is considered to be a "good bureaucrat." In 1784 he adds much new material to the third edition of the *Wealth of Nations*. Some evidence that his views on free trade figure in the British-French trade agreement of 1786. Though his health is not good, he begins in 1786 to rework *The Theory of Moral Sentiments*. In 1790 the sixth edition of that book is published. Smith dies that year. In accordance with his wishes, all his manuscript material is burned, thus the difficulty of reconstructing how he came to write what he did.

Suggestions for Further Reading

I. Smith's Collected Works:
   The Glasgow Edition of the Works and Correspondence of Adam Smith,
      published by Oxford University Press, 6 vol., (1976–1983)
II. Biographical Information about Smith's Life and Times:
   Campbell, R. H. and A. Skinner, *Adam Smith*, 1982
   Fay, C. R., *Adam Smith and the Scotland of His Day*, 1956
   Rae, J. *Life of Adam Smith*, 1896
   Scott, W. R., *Adam Smith as Student and Professor*, 1937
   Viner, J., "Guide to John Rae's *Life of Adam Smith*," 1965
   West, E. G., *Adam Smith*, 1969
III. The Scottish Enlightenment:
   Hont, I. and M. Ignatieff, eds., *Wealth and Virtue*, 1983
   Hope, V., ed., *Philosophers of the Scottish Enlightenment*, Edinburgh,
      1984
   Sher, R., *Church and University in the Scottish Enlightenment*, 1985
   Skinner, A. and R. Campbell, eds., *The Origins and Nature of the
      Scottish Enlightenment*, 1982
   Stewart, M. A., ed., *Studies in the Philosophy of the Scottish Enlighten-
      ment*, 1990
IV. Smith, Mercantilism, and the History of Economic Thinking:
   Coats, A. W., "Adam Smith and Mercantilism", in *Essays on Adam
      Smith*, A. Skinner and T. Wilson, eds., 1975
   Coleman, D. C., ed., *Revisions in Mercantilism*, 1969
   _____, "Mercantilism Revisited," in *Historical Journal*,
      vol. 23, 1980
   Hutchison, T., *Before Adam Smith*, 1988
   Johnson, E.A.J., *Predecessors of Adam Smith*, 1937
   Schumpeter, J., *History of Economic Analysis*, 1954
   Viner, J., *Studies in the Theory of International Trade*, 1937
   Wilson, C., "Mercantilism: Some Vicissitudes of an Idea," *Economic
      History Review*, vol. 10, 1957
V. Essay Collections on Adam Smith's Work:
   Blaug, M., ed., *Pioneers in Economics*, vol. 12: Adam Smith
      (1723–1790), 1991
   Elliott, N., ed., *Adam Smith's Legacy*, 1990
   Fry, M., ed., *Adam Smith's Legacy*, 1992
   Macfie, A. L., *The Individual in Society*, 1967
   O'Driscoll, G., ed., *Adam Smith and Modern Political Economy*, 1979
   Skinner, A., *A System of Social Science*, 1979
   _____ and Wilson, T., eds., *Essays on Adam Smith*, 1975
   Wilson, T. and Skinner, A., eds., *The Market and the State*, 1976
   Wood, J. C., ed., *Adam Smith: Critical Assessments*, 1984

VI. Reader's Guides to the *Wealth of Nations*:

Blaug, M., *Economic Theory in Retrospect*, rev. ed., pp. 40–61, 1968

Hutchison, T., *Before Adam Smith*, pp. 352–71, 1988

Letwin, W., "The 'Wealth of Nations' ", in *Adam Smith's Legacy*, ed. N. Elliott, pp. 29–40, 1990

Schumpeter, J., *History of Economic Analysis*, pp. 181–94, 1954

Viner, J., *Essays on the Intellectual History of Economics*, ed. D. Irwin, 1991

VII. Major Interpretations:

Cropsey, J., *Polity and Economy: An Interpretation of the Principles of Adam Smith*, 1957

Forbes, D., 1954. "Scientific Whiggism: Adam Smith and John Millar" *Cambridge Journal* 7: 643–70

Haakonssen, K., *The Science of the Legislator*, 1981

Morrow, G., *The Ethical and Economic Theories of Adam Smith: A Study of the Social Philosophy of the 18th Century*, 1923

Raphael, D. D., *Adam Smith*, 1985

Viner, J., "Adam Smith and Laissez-Faire", in *Essays on the Intellectual History of Economics*, 1991

Winch, D., *Adam Smith's Politics*, 1978

——————————, "Adam Smith and the Liberal Tradition," in *Traditions of Liberalism*, ed. K. Haakonssen, 1988

Note on the Text

This abridgment is based on the corrected version of Edwin Cannan's edition of the *WN*. Originally published in 1904, the Cannan text has long been the standard edition of the *WN*. Cannan himself was a diligent and resourceful student of the history of economic thinking; his edition therefore contains much important editorial commentary on the argument of the *WN*. Since Cannan's critical notes are not included in this abridgment, students wishing access to Cannan's notes will have to consult the original.

Relatively recently, a definitive text of the *WN* has been published by Oxford University Press in connection with the University of Glasgow's celebration of the bicentenary of the publication of the *WN* in 1776. That celebration inaugurated publication of a complete six-volume edition of Smith's works and correspondence—the only such scholarly edition of Smith's works that we have. The *WN* is the second volume in that series and was published in two volumes. The critical scholarly apparatus that buttresses the Glasgow edition skillfully incorporates much of modern Smith scholarship.

In order to produce a manageable abridgment, I have not included in this edition the index in the Cannan volume. The lengthy Cannan index includes the index Smith attached to the third edition of the *WN* in 1784, as well as Cannan's own numerous entries. Cannan also appended to his edition a second index in which references to authorities referred to in Smith's text were listed. That, too, is absent from this abridgment. Following the example of other abridgments of the *WN*, I have also not included in this volume Smith's own notes to the text or any of his tables.

The *WN* was originally published in March 1776, in two volumes. Volume one contained Books I–III; volume two, Books IV–V. According to Cannan, the page count of the original came to 1097. Major changes in the third edition of 1784 included expansion to three volumes, the second of which ran from Book II, Chapter III, to Book IV, Chapter VIII. Cannan's text is based on the three-volume fifth edition of 1789, the last edition corrected by Smith himself. Although the *WN* was published in Smith's lifetime in two-volume and three-volume sets, the Cannan and Oxford editions appear in two-volume sets, which themselves divide in different places. To avoid adding to the confusion on this score, the selections from the *WN* listed in the table of contents to this abridgment refer only to book-chapter sequences. These remained constant through the various editions.

In an abridgment of this size, which produces roughly 25% of Smith's text, deletions from the original have been extensive. To give readers a sense of the scope of the cuts, they should know that this abridgment follows Schumpeter in breaking down the original to percentage totals for each of the *WN*'s five books: This abridgment produces approximately 25% of Book I, 50% of II, 100% of III, 25% of IV, and 20% of V. Bracketed material has been inserted into the text by the current editor.

Selections from
WEALTH OF
NATIONS

INTRODUCTION AND PLAN OF THE WORK

The annual labour of every nation is the fund which originally supplies it with all the necessaries and conveniencies of life which it annually consumes, and which consist always either in the immediate produce of that labour, or in what is purchased with that produce from other nations.

According therefore, as this produce, or what is purchased with it, bears a greater or smaller proportion to the number of those who are to consume it, the nation will be better or worse supplied with all the necessaries and conveniencies for which it has occasion.

But this proportion must in every nation be regulated by two different circumstances; first, by the skill, dexterity, and judgment with which its labour is generally applied; and, secondly, by the proportion between the number of those who are employed in useful labour, and that of those who are not so employed. Whatever be the soil, climate, or extent of territory of any particular nation, the abundance or scantiness of its annual supply must, in that particular situation, depend upon those two circumstances.

The abundance or scantiness of this supply too seems to depend more upon the former of those two circumstances than upon the latter. Among the savage nations of hunters and fishers, every individual who is able to work, is more or less employed in useful labour, and endeavours to provide, as well as he can, the necessaries and conveniencies of life, for himself, or such of his family or tribe as are either too old, or too young, or too infirm to go a hunting and fishing. Such nations, however, are so miserably poor, that from mere want, they are frequently reduced, or, at least, think themselves reduced, to the necessity sometimes of directly destroying, and sometimes of abandoning their infants, their old people, and those afflicted with lingering diseases, to perish with hunger, or to be devoured by wild beasts. Among civilized and thriving nations, on the contrary, though a great number of people do not labour at all, many of whom consume the produce of ten times, frequently of a hundred times more labour than the greater part of those who work; yet the produce of the whole labour of the society is so great, that all are often abundantly supplied, and a workman, even of the lowest and poorest order, if he is frugal and industrious, may enjoy a greater share of the necessaries and conveniencies of life than it is possible for any savage to acquire.

The causes of this improvement, in the productive powers of labour, and the order, according to which its produce is naturally distributed among the different ranks and conditions of men in the society, make the subject of the First Book of this Inquiry.

Whatever be the actual state of the skill, dexterity, and judgment with which labour is applied in any nation, the abundance or scantiness of its annual supply must depend, during the continuance of that state, upon the proportion between the number of those who are annually employed in useful labour, and that of those who are not so employed. The number of useful and productive labourers, it will hereafter appear, is every where in proportion to the quantity of capital stock which is employed in setting them to work, and to the particular way in which it is so employed. The Second Book, therefore, treats of the nature of capital stock, of the manner in which it is gradually accumulated, and of the different quantities of labour which it puts into motion, according to the different ways in which it is employed.

Nations tolerably well advanced as to skill, dexterity, and judgment, in the application of labour, have followed very different plans in the general conduct or direction of it; and those plans have not all been equally favourable to the greatness of its produce. The policy of some nations has given extraordinary encouragement to the industry of the country; that of others to the industry of towns. Scarce any nation has dealt equally and impartially with every sort of industry. Since the downfall of the Roman empire, the policy of Europe has been more favourable to arts, manufactures, and commerce, the industry of towns; than to agriculture, the industry of the country. The circumstances which seem to have introduced and established this policy are explained in the Third Book.

Though those different plans were, perhaps, first introduced by the private interests and prejudices of particular orders of men, without any regard to, or foresight of, their consequences upon the general welfare of the society; yet they have given occasion to very different theories of political oeconomy; of which some magnify the importance of that industry which is carried on in towns, others of that which is carried on in the country. Those theories have had a considerable influence, not only upon the opinions of men of learning, but upon the public conduct of princes and sovereign states. I have endeavoured, in the Fourth Book, to explain, as fully and distinctly as I can, those different theories, and the principal effects which they have produced in different ages and nations.

To explain in what has consisted the revenue of the great body of the people, or what has been the nature of those funds, which, in different ages and nations, have supplied their annual consumption, is the object of these Four first Books. The Fifth and last Book treats of the revenue of the sovereign, or commonwealth. In this book I have endeavoured to show; first, what are the necessary expences of the sovereign, or commonwealth; which of those expences ought to be defrayed by the general contribution of the whole society; and which of them, by that of some particular part only, or of some particular members of it: secondly, what are the different methods in which the whole society may be made to contribute towards defraying the expences incumbent on the whole society, and what are the principal advantages and inconveniencies of each of those methods: and, thirdly and lastly, what are the reasons and causes which have induced almost all modern governments to mortgage some part of this revenue, or to contract debts, and what have been the effects of those debts upon the real wealth, the annual produce of the land and labour of the society.

BOOK I

Of the Causes of Improvement in the productive Powers of Labour, and of the Order according to which its Produce is naturally distributed among the different Ranks of the People.

[The opening four chapters of Book I argue the case for the division of labor as an organizational devise for enhancing the productive power of labor. In conjunction with that, Smith also identifies conditions that are conducive to the extension of the division of labor to wider and wider spheres of economic and social organization. At a key point in all this, Smith's discussion becomes socially focused in that the division of labor is designated a force not only of economic mutualism but also of social co-operation. In that respect, especially in Chapters I–IV, Smith may be said to have economized social relations by having monetarized persuasion.]

CHAPTER I

OF THE DIVISION OF LABOUR

The greatest improvement in the productive powers of labour, and the greater part of the skill, dexterity, and judgment with which it is any where directed, or applied, seem to have been the effects of the division of labour.

The effects of the division of labour, in the general business of society, will be more easily understood, by considering in what manner it operates in some particular manufactures. It is commonly supposed to be carried furthest in some very trifling ones; not perhaps that it really is carried further in them than in others of more importance: but in those trifling manufactures which are destined to supply the small wants of but a small number of people, the whole number of workmen must necessarily be small; and those employed in every different branch of the work can often be collected into the same workhouse, and placed at once under the view of the spectator. In those great manufactures, on the contrary, which are destined to supply the great wants of the great body of the people, every different branch of the work employs so great a number of workmen, that it is impossible to collect them all into the same workhouse. We can seldom see more, at one time, than those employed in one single branch. Though in such manufactures, therefore, the work may really be divided into a much greater number of parts, than in those of a more trifling nature, the division is not near so obvious, and has accordingly been much less observed.

To take an example, therefore, from a very trifling manufacture; but one in which the division of labour has been very often taken notice of, the trade of the pin-maker; a workman not educated to this business (which the division of labour has rendered a distinct trade), nor acquainted with the use of the machinery employed in it (to the invention of which the same division of labour has probably given occasion), could scarce, perhaps, with his utmost industry, make one pin in a day, and certainly could not make twenty. But in the way in which this business is now carried on, not only the whole work is a peculiar trade, but it is divided into a number of branches, of which the greater part are likewise peculiar trades. One man draws out the wire, another straights it, a third cuts it, a fourth points it, a fifth grinds it at the top for receiving the head; to make the head requires two or three distinct operations; to put it on, is a peculiar business, to whiten the pins is another; it is even a trade by itself to put them into the paper; and the important business of making a pin is, in this manner, divided into about eighteen distinct operations, which, in some manufactories, are all performed by distinct hands, though in others the same man will sometimes perform two or three of them. I have seen a small manufactory of this kind where ten men only were employed, and where some of them consequently performed two or three distinct operations. But though they were very poor, and therefore but indifferently accommodated with the necessary machinery, they could, when they exerted themselves, make among them about twelve pounds of pins in a day. There are in a pound upwards of four thousand pins of a middling size. Those ten persons, therefore, could make among them upwards of forty-eight thousand pins in a day. Each person, therefore, making a tenth part of forty-eight thousand pins, might be considered as making four thousand eight hundred pins in a day. But if they had all wrought separately and independently, and without any of them having been educated to this peculiar business, they certainly could not each of them have made twenty, perhaps not one pin in a day; that is, certainly, not the two hundred and fortieth, perhaps not the four thousand eight hundredth part of what they are at present capable of performing, in consequence of a proper division and combination of their different operations.

In every other art and manufacture, the effects of the division of labour are similar to what they are in this very trifling one; though, in many of them, the labour can neither be so much subdivided, nor reduced to so great a simplicity of operation. The division of labour, however, so far as it can be introduced, occasions, in every art, a proportionable increase of the productive powers of labour. The separation of different trades and employments from one another, seems to have taken place, in consequence of this advantage. This separation too is generally carried furthest in those countries which enjoy the highest degree of industry and improvement; what is the work of one man in a rude state of society, being generally that of several in an improved one. In every improved society, the farmer is generally nothing but a farmer; the manufacturer, nothing but a manufacturer. The labour too which is necessary to produce any one complete manufacture, is almost always divided among a great number of hands. How many different trades are employed in each branch of the linen and woollen manufactures, from the growers of the flax and the wool, to the bleachers and smoothers of the linen, or to the dyers and dressers of the cloth! The nature of agriculture, indeed, does not admit of so many subdivisions of labour, nor of so complete a separation of one business from another, as manufactures. It is impossible to separate so entirely, the business of the grazier from that of the corn-farmer, as the trade of the carpenter is commonly separated from that of the smith. The spinner is almost always a distinct person from the weaver; but the ploughman, the harrower, the sower of the seed, and the reaper of the corn, are often the same. The occasions for those different sorts of labour returning with the different seasons of the year, it is impossible that one man should be constantly employed in any one of them. This impossibility of making so complete and entire a separation of all the different branches of labour employed in agriculture, is perhaps the reason why the improvement of the productive powers of labour in this art, does not always keep pace with their improvement in manufactures. The most opulent nations, indeed, generally excel all their neighbours in agriculture as well as in manufactures; but they are commonly more distinguished by their superiority in the latter than in the former. Their lands are in general better cultivated, and having more labour and expence bestowed upon them, produce more in proportion to the extent and natural fertility of the ground. But this superiority of produce is seldom much more than in proportion to the superiority of labour and expence. In agriculture, the labour of the rich country is not always much more productive than that of the poor; or, at least, it is never so much more productive, as it commonly is in manufactures. The corn of the rich country, therefore, will not always, in the same degree of goodness, come cheaper to market than that of the poor. The corn of Poland, in the same degree of goodness, is as cheap as that of France, notwithstanding the superior opulence and improvement of the latter country. The corn of France is, in the corn provinces, fully as good, and in most years nearly about the same price with the corn of England, though, in opulence and improvement, France is perhaps inferior to England. The corn-lands of England, however, are better cultivated than those of France, and the corn-lands of France are said to be much better cultivated than those of Poland. But though the poor country, notwithstanding the inferiority of its cultivation, can, in some measure, rival the rich in the cheapness and goodness of its corn, it can pretend to no such competition in its manufactures; at least if those manufactures suit the soil, climate, and situation of the rich country. The silks of France are better and cheaper than those of England, because the silk manufacture, at least under the present high duties upon the importation of raw silk, does not so well suit the climate of England as that of France. But the hard-ware and the coarse woollens of England are beyond all comparison superior to those of France, and much cheaper too in the same degree of goodness. In Poland there are said to be scarce any manufactures of any kind, a few of those coarser household manufactures excepted, without which no country can well subsist.

This great increase of the quantity of work, which, in consequence of the division of labour, the same number of people are capable of performing, is owing to three different circumstances; first, to the increase of dexterity in every particular workman; secondly, to the saving of the time which is commonly lost in passing from one species of work to another; and lastly, to the invention of a great number of machines which facilitate and abridge labour, and enable one man to do the work of many.

First, the improvement of the dexterity of the workman necessarily increases the quantity of the work he can perform; and the division of labour, by reducing every man's business to some one simple operation, and by making this operation the sole employment of his life, necessarily increases very much the dexterity of the workman. A common smith, who, though accustomed to handle the hammer, has never been used to make nails, if upon some particular occasion he is obliged to attempt it, will scarce, I am assured, be able to make above two or three hundred nails in a day, and those too very bad ones. A smith who has been accustomed to make nails, but whose sole or principal business has not been that of a nailer, can seldom with his utmost diligence make more than eight hundred or a thousand nails in a day. I have seen several boys under twenty years of age who had never exercised any other trade but that of making nails, and who, when they exerted themselves, could make, each of them, upwards of two thousand three hundred nails in a day. The making of a nail, however, is by no means one of the simplest operations. The same person blows the bellows, stirs or mends the fire as there is occasion, heats the iron, and forges every part of the nail: In forging the head too he is obliged to change his tools. The different operations into which the making of a pin, or of a metal button, is subdivided, are all of them much more simple, and the dexterity of the person, of whose life it has been the sole business to perform them, is usually much greater. The rapidity with which some of the operations of those manufactures are performed, exceeds what the human hand could, by those who had never seen them, be supposed capable of acquiring.

Secondly, the advantage which is gained by saving the time commonly lost in passing from one sort of work to another, is much greater than we should at first view be apt to imagine it. It is impossible to pass very quickly from one kind of work to another, that is carried on in a different place, and with quite different tools. A country weaver, who cultivates a small farm, must lose a good deal of time in passing from his loom to the field, and from the field to his loom. When the two trades can be carried on in the same workhouse, the loss of time is no doubt much less. It is even in this case, however, very considerable. A man commonly saunters a little in turning his hand from one sort of employment to another. When he first begins the new work he is seldom very keen and hearty; his mind, as they say, does not go to it, and for some time he rather trifles than applies to good purpose. The habit of sauntering and of indolent care-less application, which is naturally, or rather necessarily acquired by every country workman who is obliged to change his work and his tools every half hour, and to apply his hand in twenty different ways almost every day of his life; renders him almost always slothful and lazy, and incapable of any vigorous application even on the most pressing occasions. Independent, therefore, of his deficiency in point of dexterity, this cause alone must always reduce considerably the quantity of work which he is capable of performing.

Thirdly, and lastly, every body must be sensible how much labour is facilitated and abridged by the application of proper machinery. It is unnecessary to give any example. I shall only observe, therefore, that the invention of all those machines by which labour is so much facilitated and abridged, seems to have been originally owing to the division of labour. Men are much more likely to discover easier and readier methods of attaining any object, when the whole attention of their minds is directed towards that single object, than when it is dissipated among a great variety of things. But in consequence of the division of labour, the whole of every man's attention comes naturally to be directed towards some one very simple object. It is naturally to be expected, therefore, that some one or other of those who are employed in each particular branch of labour should soon find out easier and readier methods of performing their own particular work, wherever the nature of it admits of such improvement. A great part of the machines made use of in those manufactures in which labour is most subdivided, were originally the inventions of common workmen, who, being each of them employed in some very simple operation, naturally turned their thoughts towards finding out easier and readier methods of performing it. Whoever has been much accustomed to visit such manufactures, must frequently have been shewn very pretty machines, which were the inventions of such workmen, in order to facilitate and quicken their own particular part of the work. In the first fire-engines, a boy was constantly employed to open and shut alternately the communication between the boiler and the cylinder, according as the piston either ascended or descended. One of those boys, who loved to play with his companions, observed that, by tying a string from the handle of the valve which opened this communication to another part of the machine, the valve would open and shut without his assistance, and leave him at liberty to divert himself with his play-fellows. One of the greatest improvements that has been made upon this machine, since it was first invented, was in this manner the discovery of a boy who wanted to save his own labour.

All the improvements in machinery, however, have by no means been the inventions of those who had occasion to use the machines. Many improvements have been made by the ingenuity of the makers of the machines, when to make them became the business of a peculiar trade; and some by that of those who are called philosophers or men of speculation, whose trade it is not to do any thing, but to observe every thing; and who, upon that account, are often capable of combining together the powers of the most distant and dissimilar objects. In the progress of society, philosophy or speculation becomes, like every other employment, the principal or sole trade and occupation of a particular class of citizens. Like every other employment too, it is subdivided into a great number of different branches, each of which affords occupation to a peculiar tribe or class of philosophers; and this subdivision of employment in philosophy, as well as in every other business, improves dexterity, and saves time. Each individual becomes more expert in his own peculiar branch, more work is done upon the whole, and the quantity of science is considerably increased by it.

It is the great multiplication of the productions of all the different arts, in consequence of the division of labour, which occasions, in a well-governed society, that universal opulence which extends itself to the lowest ranks of the people. Every workman has a great quantity of his own work to dispose of beyond what he himself has occasion for; and every other workman being exactly in the same situation, he is enabled to exchange a great quantity of his own goods for a great quantity, or, what comes to the same thing, for the price of a great quantity of theirs. He supplies them abundantly with what they have occasion for, and they accommodate him as amply with what he has occasion for, and a general plenty diffuses itself through all the different ranks of the society.

Observe the accommodation of the most common artificer or day-labourer in a civilized and thriving country, and you will perceive that the number of people of whose industry a part, though but a small part, has been employed in procuring him this accommodation, exceeds all computation. The woollen coat, for example, which covers the day-labourer, as coarse and rough as it may appear, is the produce of the joint labour of a great multitude of workmen. The shepherd, the sorter of the wool, the wool-comber or carder, the dyer, the scribbler, the spinner, the weaver, the fuller, the dresser, with many others, must all join their different arts in order to complete even this homely production. How many merchants and carriers, besides, must have been employed in trans-porting the materials from some of those workmen to others who often live in a very distant part of the country! how much commerce and navigation in particular, how many ship-builders, sailors, sail-makers, rope-makers, must have been employed in order to bring together the different drugs made use of by the dyer, which often come from the remotest corners of the world! What a variety of labour too is necessary in order to produce the tools of the meanest of those workmen! To say nothing of such complicated machines as the ship of the sailor, the mill of the fuller, or even the loom of the weaver, let us consider only what a variety of labour is requisite in order to form that very simple machine, the shears with which the shepherd clips the wool. The miner, the builder of the furnace for smelting the ore, the feller of the timber, the burner of the charcoal to be made use of in the smelting-house, the brick-maker, the brick-layer, the workmen who attend the furnace, the mill-wright, the forger, the smith, must all of them join their different arts in order to produce them. Were we to examine, in the same manner, all the different parts of his dress and household furniture, the coarse linen shirt which he wears next his skin, the shoes which cover his feet, the bed which he lies on, and all the different parts which compose it, the kitchen-grate at which he prepares his victuals, the coals which he makes use of for that purpose, dug from the bowels of the earth, and brought to him perhaps by a long sea and a long land carriage, all the other utensils of his kitchen, all the furniture of his table, the knives and forks, the earthen or pewter plates upon which he serves up and divides his victuals, the different hands employed in preparing his bread and his beer, the glass window which lets in the heat and the light, and keeps out the wind and the rain, with all the knowledge and art requisite for preparing that beautiful and happy invention, without which these northern parts of the world could scarce have afforded a very comfortable habitation, together with the tools of all the different workmen employed in producing those different conveniencies; if we examine, I say, all these things, and consider what a variety of labour is employed about each of them, we shall be sensible that without the assistance and co-operation of many thousands, the very meanest person in a civilized country could not be provided, even according to, what we very falsely imagine, the easy and simple manner in which he is commonly accommodated. Compared, indeed, with the more extravagant luxury of the great, his accommodation must no doubt appear extremely simple and easy; and yet it may be true, perhaps, that the accommodation of an European prince does not always so much exceed that of an industrious and frugal peasant, as the accommodation of the latter exceeds that of many an African king, the absolute master of the lives and liberties of ten thousand naked savages.

CHAPTER II

OF THE PRINCIPLE WHICH GIVES OCCASION TO THE DIVISION OF LABOUR

This division of labour, from which so many advantages are derived, is not originally the effect of any human wisdom, which foresees and intends that general opulence to which it gives occasion. It is the necessary, though very slow and gradual, consequence of a certain propensity in human nature which has in view no such extensive utility; the propensity to truck, barter, and exchange one thing for another.

Whether this propensity be one of those original principles in human nature, of which no further account can be given; or whether, as seems more probable, it be the necessary consequence of the faculties of reason and speech, it belongs not to our present subject to enquire. It is common to all men, and to be found in no other race of animals, which seem to know neither this nor any other species of contracts. Two greyhounds, in running down the same hare, have sometimes the appearance of acting in some sort of concert. Each turns her towards his companion, or endeavours to intercept her when his companion turns her towards himself. This, however, is not the effect of any contract, but of the accidental concurrence of their passions in the same object at that particular time. Nobody ever saw a dog make a fair and deliberate exchange of one bone for another with another dog. Nobody ever saw one animal by its gestures and natural cries signify to another, this is mine, that yours; I am willing to give this for that. When an animal wants to obtain something either of a man or of another animal, it has no other means of persuasion but to gain the favour of those whose service it requires. A puppy fawns upon its dam, and a spaniel endeavours by a thousand attractions to engage the attention of its master who is at dinner, when it wants to be fed by him. Man sometimes uses the same arts with his brethren, and when he has no other means of engaging them to act according to his inclinations, endeavours by every servile and fawning attention to obtain their good will. He has not time, however, to do this upon every occasion. In civilized society he stands at all times in need of the co-operation and assistance of great multitudes, while his whole life is scarce sufficient to gain the friendship of a few persons. In almost every other race of animals each individual, when it is grown up to maturity, is entirely independent, and in its natural state has occasion for the assistance of no other living creature. But man has almost constant occasion for the help of his brethren, and it is in vain for him to expect it from their benevolence only. He will be more likely to prevail if he can interest their self-love in his favour, and shew them that it is for their own advantage to do for him what he requires of them. Whoever offers to another a bargain of any kind, proposes to do this. Give me that which I want, and you shall have this which you want, is the meaning of every such offer; and it is in this manner that we obtain from one another the far greater part of those good offices which we stand in need of. It is not from the benevolence of the butcher, the brewer, or the baker, that we expect our dinner, but from their regard to their own interest. We address ourselves, not to their humanity but to their self-love, and never talk to them of our own necessities but of their advantages. Nobody but a beggar chuses to depend chiefly upon the benevolence of his fellow-citizens. Even a beggar does not depend upon it entirely. The charity of well-disposed people, indeed, supplies him with the whole fund of his subsistence. But though this principle ultimately provides him with all the necessaries of life which he has occasion for, it neither does nor can provide him with them as he has occasion for them. The greater part of his occasional wants are supplied in the same manner as those of other people, by treaty, by barter, and by purchase. With the money which one man gives him he purchases food. The old cloaths which another bestows upon him he exchanges for other old cloaths which suit him better, or for lodging, or for food, or for money, with which he can buy either food, cloaths, or lodging, as he has occasion.

As it is by treaty, by barter, and by purchase, that we obtain from one another the greater part of those mutual good offices which we stand in need of, so it is this same trucking disposition which originally gives occasion to the division of labour. In a tribe of hunters or shepherds a particular person makes bows and arrows, for example, with more readiness and dexterity than any other. He frequently exchanges them for cattle or for venison with his companions; and he finds at last that he can in this manner get more cattle and venison, than if he himself went to the field to catch them. From a regard to his own interest, therefore, the making of bows and arrows grows to be his chief business, and he becomes a sort of armourer. Another excels in making the frames and covers of their little huts or moveable houses. He is accustomed to be of use in this way to his neighbours, who reward him in the same manner with cattle and with venison, till at last he finds it his interest to dedicate himself entirely to this employment, and to become a sort of house-carpenter. In the same manner a third becomes a smith or a brazier; a fourth a tanner or dresser of hides or skins, the principal part of the clothing of savages. And thus the certainty of being able to exchange all that surplus part of the produce of his own labour, which is over and above his own consumption, for such parts of the produce of other men's labour as he may have occasion for, encourages every man to apply himself to a particular occupation, and to cultivate and bring to perfection whatever talent or genius he may possess for that particular species of business.

The difference of natural talents in different men is, in reality, much less than we are aware of; and the very different genius which appears to distinguish men of different professions, when grown up to maturity, is not upon many occasions so much the cause, as the effect of the division of labour. The difference between the most dissimilar characters, between a philosopher and a common street porter, for example, seems to arise not so much from nature, as from habit, custom, and education. When they came into the world, and for the first six or eight years of their existence, they were, perhaps, very much alike, and neither their parents nor playfellows could perceive any remarkable difference. About that age, or soon after, they come to be employed in very different occupations. The difference of talents comes then to be taken notice of, and widens by degrees, till at last the vanity of the philosopher is willing to acknowledge scarce any resemblance. But without the disposition to truck, barter, and exchange, every man must have procured to himself every necessary and conveniency of life which he wanted. All must have had the same duties to perform, and the same work to do, and there could have been no such difference of employment as could alone give occasion to any great difference of talents.

As it is this disposition which forms that difference of talents, so remarkable among men of different professions, so it is this same disposition which renders that difference useful. Many tribes of animals acknowledged to be all of the same species, derive from nature a much more remarkable distinction of genius, than what, antecedent to custom and education, appears to take place among men. By nature a philosopher is not in genius and disposition half so different from a street porter, as a mastiff is from a greyhound, or a greyhound from a spaniel, or this last from a shepherd's dog. Those different tribes of animals, however, though all of the same species, are of scarce any use to one another. The strength of the mastiff is not in the least supported either by the swiftness of the greyhound, or by the sagacity of the spaniel, or by the docility of the shepherd's dog. The effects of those different geniuses and talents, for want of the power or disposition to barter and exchange, cannot be brought into a common stock, and do not in the least contribute to the better accommodation and conveniency of the species. Each animal is still obliged to support and defend itself, separately and independently, and derives no sort of advantage from that variety of talents with which nature has distinguished its fellows. Among men, on the contrary, the most dissimilar geniuses are of use to one another; the different produces of their respective talents, by the general disposition to truck, barter, and exchange, being brought, as it were, into a common stock, where every man may purchase whatever part of the produce of other men's talents he has occasion for.

CHAPTER III

THAT THE DIVISION OF LABOUR IS LIMITED BY THE EXTENT OF THE MARKET

As it is the power of exchanging that gives occasion to the division of labour, so the extent of this division must always be limited by the extent of that power, or, in other words, by the extent of the market. When the market is very small, no person can have any encouragement to dedicate himself entirely to one employment, for want of the power to exchange all that surplus part of the produce of his own labour, which is over and above his own consumption, for such parts of the produce of other men's labour as he has occasion for.

There are some sorts of industry, even of the lowest kind, which can be carried on no where but in a great town. A porter, for example, can find employment and subsistence in no other place. A village is by much too narrow a sphere for him; even an ordinary market town is scarce large enough to afford him constant occupation. In the lone houses and very small villages which are scattered about in so desert a country as the Highlands of Scotland, every farmer must be butcher, baker and brewer for his own family. In such situations we can scarce expect to find even a smith, a carpenter, or a mason, within less than twenty miles of another of the same trade. The scattered families that live at eight or ten miles distance from the nearest of them, must learn to perform themselves a great number of little pieces of work, for which, in more populous countries, they would call in the assistance of those workmen. Country workmen are almost every where obliged to apply themselves to all the different branches of industry that have so much affinity to one another as to be employed about the same sort of materials. A country carpenter deals in every sort of work that is made of wood: a country smith in every sort of work that is made of iron. The former is not only a carpenter, but a joiner, a cabinet maker, and even a carver in wood, as well as a wheelwright, a ploughwright, a cart and waggon maker. The employments of the latter are still more various. It is impossible there should be such a trade as even that of a nailer in the remote and inland parts of the Highlands of Scotland. Such a workman at the rate of a thousand nails a day, and three hundred working days in the year, will make three hundred thousand nails in the year. But in such a situation it would be impossible to dispose of one thousand, that is, of one day's work in the year.

As by means of water-carriage a more extensive market is opened to every sort of industry than what land-carriage alone can afford it, so it is upon the sea-coast, and along the banks of navigable rivers, that industry of every kind naturally begins to subdivide and improve itself, and it is frequently not till a long time after that those improvements extend themselves to the inland parts of the country. A broad-wheeled waggon, attended by two men, and drawn by eight horses, in about six weeks time carries and brings back between London and Edinburgh near four ton weight of goods. In about the same time a ship navigated by six or eight men, and sailing between the ports of London and Leith, frequently carries and brings back two hundred ton weight of goods. Six or eight men, therefore, by the help of water-carriage, can carry and bring back in the same time the same quantity of goods between London and Edinburgh, as fifty broad-wheeled waggons, attended by a hundred men, and drawn by four hundred horses. Upon two hundred tons of goods, therefore, carried by the cheapest land-carriage from London to Edinburgh, there must be charged the maintenance of a hundred men for three weeks, and both the maintenance, and, what is nearly equal to the maintenance, the wear and tear of four hundred horses as well as of fifty great waggons. Whereas, upon the same quantity of goods carried by water, there is to be charged only the maintenance of six or eight men, and the wear and tear of a ship of two hundred tons burthen, together with the value of the superior risk, or the difference of the insurance between land and water-carriage. Were there no other communication between those two places, therefore, but by land-carriage, as no goods could be transported from the one to the other, except such whose price was very considerable in proportion to their weight, they could carry on but a small part of that commerce which at present subsists between them, and consequently could give but a small part of that encouragement which they at present mutually afford to each other's industry. There could be little or no commerce of any kind between the distant parts of the world. What goods could bear the expence of land-carriage between London and Calcutta? Or if there were any so precious as to be able to support this expence, with what safety could they be transported through the territories of so many barbarous nations? Those two cities, however, at present carry on a very considerable commerce with each other, and by mutually affording a market, give a good deal of encouragement to each other's industry.

Since such, therefore, are the advantages of water-carriage, it is natural that the first improvements of art and industry should be made where this conveniency opens the whole world for a market to the produce of every sort of labour, and that they should always be much later in extending themselves into the inland parts of the country. The inland parts of the country can for a long time have no other market for the greater part of their goods, but the country which lies round about them, and separates them from the seacoast, and the great navigable rivers. The extent of their market, therefore, must for a long time be in proportion to the riches and populousness of that country, and consequently their improvement must always be posterior to the improvement of that country. In our North American colonies the plantations have constantly followed either the sea-coast or the banks of navigable rivers, and have scarce any where extended themselves to any considerable distance from both.

The nations that, according to the best authenticated history, appear to have been first civilized, were those that dwelt round the coast of the Mediterranean sea. That sea, by far the greatest inlet that is known in the world, having no tides, nor consequently any waves except such as are caused by the wind only, was, by the smoothness of its surface, as well as by the multitude of its islands, and the proximity of its neighbouring shores, extremely favourable to the infant navigation of the world; when, from their ignorance of the compass, men were afraid to quit the view of the coast, and from the imperfection of the art of ship-building, to abandon themselves to the boisterous waves of the ocean. To pass beyond the pillars of Hercules, that is, to sail out of the Streights of Gibraltar, was, in the ancient world, long considered as a most wonderful and dangerous exploit of navigation. It was late before even the Phenicians and Carthaginians, the most skilful navigators and ship-builders of those old times, attempted it, and they were for a long time the only nations that did attempt it.

Of all the countries on the coast of the Mediterranean sea, Egypt seems to have been the first in which either agriculture or manufactures were cultivated and improved to any considerable degree. Upper Egypt extends itself nowhere above a few miles from the Nile, and in Lower Egypt that great river breaks itself into many different canals, which, with the assistance of a little art, seem to have afforded a communication by water-carriage, not only between all the great towns, but between all the considerable villages, and even to many farm-houses in the country; nearly in the same manner as the Rhine and the Maese do in Holland at present. The extent and easiness of this inland navigation was probably one of the principal causes of the early improvement of Egypt.

The improvements in agriculture and manufactures seem likewise to have been of very great antiquity in the provinces of Bengal in the East Indies, and in some of the eastern provinces of China; though the great extent of this antiquity is not authenticated by any histories of whose authority we, in this part of the world, are well assured. In Bengal the Ganges and several other great rivers form a great number of navigable canals in the same manner as the Nile does in Egypt. In the Eastern provinces of China too, several great rivers form, by their different branches, a multitude of canals, and by communicating with one another afford an inland navigation much more extensive than that either of the Nile or the Ganges, or perhaps than both of them put together. It is remarkable that neither the ancient Egyptians, nor the Indians, nor the Chinese, encouraged foreign commerce, but seem all to have derived their great opulence from this inland navigation.

All the inland parts of Africa, and all that part of Asia which lies any considerable way north of the Euxine and Caspian seas, the ancient Scythia, the modern Tartary and Siberia, seem in all ages of the world to have been in the same barbarous and uncivilized state in which we find them at present. The sea of Tartary is the frozen ocean which admits of no navigation, and though some of the greatest rivers in the world run through that country, they are at too great a distance from one another to carry commerce and communication through the greater part of it. There are in Africa none of those great inlets, such as the Baltic and

Adriatic seas in Europe, the Mediterranean and Euxine seas in both Europe and Asia, and the gulphs of Arabia, Persia, India, Bengal, and Siam, in Asia, to carry maritime commerce into the interior parts of that great continent: and the great rivers of Africa are at too great a distance from one another to give occasion to any considerable inland navigation. The commerce besides which any nation can carry on by means of a river which does not break itself into any great number of branches or canals, and which runs into another territory before it reaches the sea, can never be very considerable; because it is always in the power of the nations who possess that other territory to obstruct the communication between the upper country and the sea. The navigation of the Danube is of very little use to the different states of Bavaria, Austria and Hungary, in comparison of what it would be if any of them possessed the whole of its course till it falls into the Black Sea.

CHAPTER IV

OF THE ORIGIN AND USE OF MONEY

When the division of labour has been once thoroughly established, it is but a very small part of a man's wants which the produce of his own labour can supply. He supplies the far greater part of them by exchanging that surplus part of the produce of his own labour, which is over and above his own consumption, for such parts of the produce of other men's labour as he has occasion for. Every man thus lives by exchanging, or becomes in some measure a merchant, and the society itself grows to be what is properly a commercial society.

But when the division of labour first began to take place, this power of exchanging must frequently have been very much clogged and embarrassed in its operations. One man, we shall suppose, has more of a certain commodity than he himself has occasion for, while another has less. The former consequently would be glad to dispose of, and the latter to purchase, a part of this superfluity. But if this latter should chance to have nothing that the former stands in need of, no exchange can be made between them. The butcher has more meat in his shop than he himself can consume, and the brewer and the baker would each of them be willing to purchase a part of it. But they have nothing to offer in exchange, except the different productions of their respective trades, and the butcher is already provided with all the bread and beer which he has immediate occasion for. No exchange can, in this case, be made between them. He cannot be their merchant, nor they his customers; and they are all of them thus mutually less serviceable to one another. In order to avoid the inconveniency of such situations, every prudent man in every period of society, after the first establishment of the division of labour, must naturally have endeavoured to manage his affairs in such a manner, as to have at all times by him, besides the peculiar produce of his own industry, a certain quantity of some one commodity or other, such as he imagined few people would be likely to refuse in exchange for the produce of their industry.

Many different commodities, it is probable, were successively both thought of and employed for this purpose. In the rude ages of society, cattle are said to have been the common instrument of commerce; and, though they must have been a most inconvenient one, yet in old times we find things were frequently valued according to the number of cattle which had been given in exchange for them. The armour of Diomede, says Homer, cost only nine oxen; but that of Glaucus cost an hundred oxen. Salt is said to be the common instrument of commerce and exchanges in Abyssinia; a species of shells in some parts of the coast of India; dried cod at Newfoundland; tobacco in Virginia; sugar in some of our West India colonies; hides or dressed leather in some other countries; and there is at this day a village in Scotland where it is not uncommon, I am told, for a workman to carry nails instead of money to the baker's shop or the ale-house.

In all countries, however, men seem at last to have been determined by irresistible reasons to give the preference, for this employment, to metals above every other commodity. Metals can not only be kept with as little loss as any other commodity, scarce any thing being less perishable than they are, but they can likewise, without any loss, be divided into any number of parts, as by fusion those parts can easily be reunited again; a quality which no other equally durable commodities possess, and which more than any other quality renders them fit to be the instruments of commerce and circulation. The man who wanted to buy salt, for example, and had nothing but cattle to give in exchange for it, must have been obliged to buy salt to the value of a whole ox, or a whole sheep, at a time. He could seldom buy less than this, because what he was to give for it could seldom be divided without loss; and if he had a mind to buy more, he must, for the same reasons, have been obliged to buy double or triple the quantity, the value, to wit, of two or three oxen, or of two or three sheep. If, on the contrary, instead of sheep or oxen, he had metals to give in exchange for it, he could easily proportion the quantity of the metal to the precise quantity of the commodity which he had immediate occasion for.

Different metals have been made use of by different nations for this purpose. Iron was the common instrument of commerce among the ancient Spartans; copper among the ancient Romans; and gold and silver among all rich and commercial nations.

Those metals seem originally to have been made use of for this purpose in rude bars, without any stamp or coinage. Thus we are told by Pliny, upon the authority of Timæus, an ancient historian, that, till the time of Servius Tullius, the Romans had no coined money, but made use of unstamped bars of copper, to purchase whatever they had occasion for. These rude bars, therefore, performed at this time the function of money.

The use of metals in this rude state was attended with two very considerable inconveniencies; first with the trouble of weighing; and, secondly, with that of assaying them. In the precious metals, where a small difference in the quantity makes a great difference in the value, even the business of weighing, with proper exactness, requires at least very accurate weights and scales. The weighing of gold in particular is an operation of some nicety. In the coarser metals, indeed, where a small error would be of little consequence, less accuracy would, no doubt, be necessary. Yet we should find it excessively troublesome, if every time a poor man had occasion either to buy or sell a farthing's worth of goods, he was obliged to weigh the farthing. The operation of assaying is still more difficult, still more tedious, and, unless a part of the metal is fairly melted in the crucible, with proper dissolvents, any conclusion that can be drawn from it, is extremely uncertain. Before the institution of coined money, however, unless they went through this tedious and difficult operation, people must always have been liable to the grossest frauds and impositions, and instead of a pound weight of pure silver, or pure copper, might receive in exchange for their goods, an adulterated composition of the coarsest and cheapest materials, which had, however, in their outward appearance, been made to resemble those metals. To prevent such abuses, to facilitate exchanges, and thereby to encourage all sorts of industry and commerce, it had been found necessary, in all countries that have made any considerable advances towards improvement, to affix a public stamp upon certain quantities of such particular metals, as were in those countries commonly made use of to purchase goods. Hence the origin of coined money, and of those public offices called mints; institutions exactly of the same nature with those of the aulnagers and stampmasters of woollen and linen cloth. All of them are equally meant to ascertain, by means of a public stamp, the quantity and uniform goodness of those different commodities when brought to market.

The first public stamps of this kind that were affixed to the current metals, seem in many cases to have been intended to ascertain, what it was both most difficult and most important to ascertain, the goodness or fineness of the metal, and to have resembled the sterling mark which is at present affixed to plate and bars of silver, or the Spanish mark which is sometimes affixed to ingots of gold, and which being struck only upon one side of the piece, and not covering the whole surface, ascertains the fineness, but not the weight of the metal. Abraham weighs to Ephron the four hundred shekels of silver which he had agreed to pay for the field of Machpelah. They are said however to be the current money of the merchant, and yet are received by weight and not by tale, in the same manner as ingots of gold and bars of silver are at present. The revenues of the ancient Saxon kings of England are said to have been paid, not in money but in kind, that is, in victuals and provisions of all sorts. William the Conqueror introduced the custom of paying them in money. This money, however, was, for a long time, received at the exchequer, by weight and not by tale.

The inconveniency and difficulty of weighing those metals with exact-ness gave occasion to the institution of coins, of which the stamp, covering entirely both sides of the piece and sometimes the edges too, was supposed to ascertain not only the fineness, but the weight of the metal. Such coins, therefore, were received by tale as at present, without the trouble of weighing.

The denominations of those coins seem originally to have expressed the weight or quantity of metal contained in them. In the time of Servius Tullius, who first coined money at Rome, the Roman As or Pondo con-tained a Roman pound of good copper. It was divided in the same manner as our Troyes pound, into twelve ounces, each of which contained a real ounce of good copper. The English pound sterling in the time of Edward I., contained a pound, Tower weight, of silver of a known fineness. The Tower pound seems to have been something more than the Roman pound, and something less than the Troyes pound. This last was not introduced into the mint of England till the 18th of Henry VIII. The French livre contained in the time of Charlemagne a pound, Troyes weight, of silver of a known fineness. The fair of Troyes in Champaign was at that time frequented by all the nations of Europe, and the weights and measures of so famous a market were generally known and esteemed. The Scots money pound contained, from the time of Alexander the First to that of Robert Bruce, a pound of silver of the same weight and fineness with the English pound sterling. English, French, and Scots pennies too, contained all of them originally a real pennyweight of silver, the twentieth part of an ounce, and the two-hundred-and-fortieth part of a pound. The shilling too seems originally to have been the denomination of a weight. *When wheat is at twelve shillings the quarter,* says an ancient statute of Henry III. *then wastel bread of a farthing shall weigh eleven shillings and four pence.* The proportion, however, between the shilling and either the penny on the one hand, or the pound on the other, seems not to have been so constant and uniform as that between the penny and the pound. During the first race of the kings of France, the French sou or shilling appears upon different occasions to have contained five, twelve, twenty, and forty pennies. Among the ancient Saxons a shilling appears at one time to have contained only five pennies, and it is not improbable that it may have been as variable among them as among their neighbours, the ancient Franks. From the time of Charlemagne among the French, and from that of William the Conqueror among the English, the proportion between the pound, the shilling, and the penny, seems to have been uniformly the same as at present, though the value of each has been very different. For in every country of the world, I believe, the avarice and injustice of princes and sovereign states, abusing the confidence of their subjects, have by degrees diminished the real quantity of metal, which had been originally contained in their coins. The Roman As, in the latter ages of the Republic, was reduced to the twenty-fourth part of its original value, and, instead of weighing a pound, came to weigh only half an ounce. The English pound and penny contain at present about a third only; the Scots pound and penny about a thirty-sixth; and the French pound and penny about a sixty-sixth part of their original value. By means of those operations the princes and sovereign states which performed them were enabled, in appearance, to pay their debts and to fulfil their engagements with a smaller quantity of silver than would otherwise have been requisite. It was indeed in appearance only; for their creditors were really defrauded of a part of what was due to them. All other debtors in the state were allowed the same privilege, and might pay with the same nominal sum of the new and debased coin whatever they had borrowed in the old. Such operations, therefore, have always proved favourable to the debtor, and ruinous to the creditor, and have sometimes produced a greater and more universal revolution in the fortunes of private persons, than could have been occasioned by a very great public calamity.

It is in this manner that money has become in all civilized nations the universal instrument of commerce, by the intervention of which goods of all kinds are bought and sold, or exchanged for one another.

What are the rules which men naturally observe in exchanging them either for money or for one another, I shall now proceed to examine. These rules determine what may be called the relative or exchangeable value of goods.

The word VALUE, it is to be observed, has two different meanings, and sometimes expresses the utility of some particular object, and sometimes the power of purchasing other goods which the possession of that object conveys. The one may be called "value in use;" the other, "value in exchange." The things which have the greatest value in use have frequently little or no value in exchange; and on the contrary, those which have the greatest value in exchange have frequently little or no value in use. Nothing is more useful than water: but it will purchase scarce any thing; scarce any thing can be had in exchange for it. A diamond, on the contrary, has scarce any value in use; but a very great quantity of other goods may frequently be had in exchange for it.

In order to investigate the principles which regulate the exchangeable value of commodities, I shall endeavour to shew,

First, what is the real measure of this exchangeable value; or, wherein consists the real price of all commodities.

Secondly, what are the different parts of which this real price is composed or made up.

And, lastly, what are the different circumstances which sometimes raise some or all of these different parts of price above, and sometimes sink them below their natural or ordinary rate; or, what are the causes which sometimes hinder the market price, that is, the actual price of commodities, from coinciding exactly with what may be called their natural price.

I shall endeavour to explain, as fully and distinctly as I can, those three subjects in the three following chapters, for which I must very earnestly entreat both the patience and attention of the reader: his patience in order to examine a detail which may perhaps in some places appear unnecessarily tedious; and his attention in order to understand what may, perhaps, after the fullest explication which I am capable of giving of it, appear still in some degree obscure. I am always willing to run some hazard of being tedious in order to be sure that I am perspicuous; and after taking the utmost pains that I can to be perspicuous, some obscurity may still appear to remain upon a subject in its own nature extremely abstracted.

[In Chapters V and VI, Smith talks about how prices are set in market contexts. Although the discussion is not "tedious", the main outlines of the discussion are reiterated in Chapter VII, where we pick-up the text. Of special importance here is the connection Smith draws between monopolies and artificially high prices—a theme he develops in greater detail in Book IV, Chapter VII. In Chapter VIII, Book II, Smith seems to measure the "progressive state" in terms of the wage scale of workers not the profits of employers. To that end, he is concerned with how to keep the demand for labor rising.]

CHAPTER VII

OF THE NATURAL AND MARKET PRICE OF COMMODITIES

There is in every society or neighbourhood an ordinary or average rate both of wages and profit in every different employment of labour and stock. This rate is naturally regulated, as I shall show hereafter, partly by the general circumstances of the society, their riches or poverty, their advancing, stationary, or declining condition; and partly by the particular nature of each employment.

There is likewise in every society or neighbourhood an ordinary or average rate of rent, which is regulated too, as I shall show hereafter, partly by the general circumstances of the society or neighbourhood in which the land is situated, and partly by the natural or improved fertility of the land.

These ordinary or average rates may be called the natural rates of wages, profit, and rent, at the time and place in which they commonly prevail.

When the price of any commodity is neither more nor less than what is sufficient to pay the rent of the land, the wages of the labour, and the profits of the stock employed in raising, preparing, and bringing it to market, according to their natural rates, the commodity is then sold for what may be called its natural price.

The commodity is then sold precisely for what it is worth, or for what it really costs the person who brings it to market; for though in common language what is called the prime cost of any commodity does not comprehend the profit of the person who is to sell it again, yet if he sells it at a price which does not allow him the ordinary rate of profit in his neighbourhood, he is evidently a loser by the trade; since by employing his stock in some other way he might have made that profit. His profit, besides, is his revenue, the proper fund of his subsistence. As, while he is preparing and bringing the goods to market, he advances to his workmen their wages, or their subsistence; so he advances to himself, in the same manner, his own subsistence, which is generally suitable to the profit which he may reasonably expect from the sale of his goods. Unless they yield him this profit, therefore, they do not repay him what they may very properly be said to have really cost him.

Though the price, therefore, which leaves him this profit, is not always the lowest at which a dealer may sometimes sell his goods, it is the lowest at which he is likely to sell them for any considerable time; at least where there is perfect liberty, or where he may change his trade as often as he pleases.

The actual price at which any commodity is commonly sold is called its market price. It may either be above, or below, or exactly the same with its natural price.

The market price of every particular commodity is regulated by the proportion between the quantity which is actually brought to market, and the demand of those who are willing to pay the natural price of the commodity, or the whole value of the rent, labour, and profit, which must be paid in order to bring it thither. Such people may be called the effectual demanders, and their demand the effectual demand; since it may be sufficient to effectuate the bringing of the commodity to market. It is different from the absolute demand. A very poor man may be said in some sense to have a demand for a coach and six; he might like to have it; but his demand is not an effectual demand, as the commodity can never be brought to market in order to satisfy it.

When the quantity of any commodity which is brought to market falls short of the effectual demand, all those who are willing to pay the whole value of the rent, wages, and profit, which must be paid in order to bring it thither, cannot be supplied with the quantity which they want. Rather than want it altogether, some of them will be willing to give more. A competition will immediately begin among them, and the market price will rise more or less above the natural price, according as either the greatness of the deficiency, or the wealth and wanton luxury of the competitors, happen to animate more or less the eagerness of the competition. Among competitors of equal wealth and luxury the same deficiency will generally occasion a more or less eager competition, according as the acquisition of the commodity happens to be of more or less importance to them. Hence the exorbitant price of the necessaries of life during the blockade of a town or in a famine.

When the quantity brought to market exceeds the effectual demand, it cannot be all sold to those who are willing to pay the whole value of the rent, wages and profit, which must be paid in order to bring it thither. Some part must be sold to those who are willing to pay less, and the low price which they give for it must reduce the price of the whole. The market price will sink more or less below the natural price, according as the greatness of the excess increases more or less the competition of the sellers, or according as it happens to be more or less important to them to get immediately rid of the commodity. The same excess in the importation of perishable, will occasion a much greater competition than in that of durable commodities; in the importation of oranges, for example, than in that of old iron.

When the quantity brought to market is just sufficient to supply the effectual demand and no more, the market price naturally comes to be either exactly, or as nearly as can be judged of, the same with the natural price. The whole quantity upon hand can be disposed of for this price, and cannot be disposed of for more. The competition of the different dealers obliges them all to accept of this price, but does not oblige them to accept of less.

The quantity of every commodity brought to market naturally suits itself to the effectual demand. It is the interest of all those who employ their land, labour, or stock, in bringing any commodity to market, that the quantity never should exceed the effectual demand; and it is the interest of all other people that it never should fall short of that demand.

If at any time it exceeds the effectual demand, some of the component parts of its price must be paid below their natural rate. If it is rent, the interest of the landlords will immediately prompt them to withdraw a part of their land; and if it is wages or profit, the interest of the labourers in the one case, and of their employers in the other, will prompt them to withdraw a part of their labour or stock from this employment. The quantity brought to market will soon be no more than sufficient to supply the effectual demand. All the different parts of its price will rise to their natural rate, and the whole price to its natural price.

If, on the contrary, the quantity brought to market should at any time fall short of the effectual demand, some of the component parts of its price must rise above their natural rate. If it is rent, the interest of all other landlords will naturally prompt them to prepare more land for the raising of this commodity; if it is wages or profit, the interest of all other labourers and dealers will soon prompt them to employ more labour and stock in preparing and bringing it to market. The quantity brought thither will soon be sufficient to supply the effectual demand. All the different parts of its price will soon sink to their natural rate, and the whole price to its natural price.

The natural price, therefore, is, as it were, the central price, to which the prices of all commodities are continually gravitating. Different accidents may sometimes keep them suspended a good deal above it, and sometimes force them down even somewhat below it. But whatever may be the obstacles which hinder them from settling in this center of repose and continuance, they are constantly tending towards it.

The whole quantity of industry annually employed in order to bring any commodity to market, naturally suits itself in this manner to the effectual demand. It naturally aims at bringing always that precise quantity thither which may be sufficient to supply, and no more than supply, that demand.

But in some employments the same quantity of industry will in different years produce very different quantities of commodities; while in others it will produce always the same, or very nearly the same. The same number of labourers in husbandry will, in different years, produce very different quantities of corn, wine, oil, hops, &c. But the same number of spinners and weavers will every year produce the same or very nearly the same quantity of linen and woollen cloth. It is only the average produce of the one species of industry which can be suited in any respect to the effectual demand; and as its actual produce is frequently much greater and frequently much less than its average produce, the quantity of the commodities brought to market will sometimes exceed a good deal, and sometimes fall short a good deal, of the effectual demand. Even though that demand therefore should continue always the same, their market price will be liable to great fluctuations, will sometimes fall a good deal below, and sometimes rise a good deal above, their natural price. In the other species of industry, the produce of equal quantities of labour being always the same, or very nearly the same, it can be more exactly suited to the effectual demand. While that demand continues the same, therefore, the market price of the commodities is likely to do so too, and to be either altogether, or as nearly as can be judged of, the same with the natural price. That the price of linen and woollen cloth is liable neither to such frequent nor to such great variations as the price of corn, every man's experience will inform him. The price of the one species of commodities varies only with the variations in the demand: That of the other varies not only with the variations in the demand, but with the much greater and more frequent variations in the quantity of what is brought to market in order to supply that demand.

The occasional and temporary fluctuations in the market price of any commodity fall chiefly upon those parts of its price which resolve themselves into wages and profit. That part which resolves itself into rent is less affected by them. A rent certain in money is not in the least affected by them either in its rate or in its value. A rent which consists either in a certain proportion or in a certain quantity of the rude produce, is no doubt affected in its yearly value by all the occasional and temporary fluctuations in the market price of that rude produce; but it is seldom affected by them in its yearly rate. In settling the terms of the lease, the landlord and farmer endeavour, according to their best judgment, to adjust that rate, not to the temporary and occasional, but to the average and ordinary price of the produce.

Such fluctuations affect both the value and the rate either of wages or of profit, according as the market happens to be either over-stocked or under-stocked with commodities or with labour; with work done, or with work to be done. A public mourning raises the price of black cloth (with which the market is almost always under-stocked upon such occasions), and augments the profits of the merchants who possess any considerable quantity of it. It has no effect upon the wages of the weavers. The market is under-stocked with commodities, not with labour; with work done, not with work to be done. It raises the wages of journeymen taylors. The market is here under-stocked with labour. There is an effectual demand for more labour, for more work to be done than can be had. It sinks the price of coloured silks and cloths, and thereby reduces the profits of the merchants who have any considerable quantity of them upon hand. It sinks too the wages of the workmen employed in preparing such commodities, for which all demand is stopped for six months, perhaps for a twelvemonth. The market is here over-stocked both with commodities and with labour.

But though the market price of every particular commodity is in this manner continually gravitating, if one may say so, towards the natural price, yet sometimes particular accidents, sometimes natural causes, and sometimes particular regulations of police, may, in many commodities, keep up the market price, for a long time together, a good deal above the natural price.

When by an increase in the effectual demand, the market price of some particular commodity happens to rise a good deal above the natural price, those who employ their stocks in supplying that market are generally careful to conceal this change. If it was commonly known, their great profit would tempt so many new rivals to employ their stocks in the same way, that, the effectual demand being fully supplied, the market price would soon be reduced to the natural price, and perhaps for some time even below it. If the market is at a great distance from the residence of those who supply it, they may sometimes be able to keep the secret for several years together, and may so long enjoy their extraordinary profits without any new rivals. Secrets of this kind, however, it must be acknowledged, can seldom be long kept; and the extraordinary profit can last very little longer than they are kept.

Secrets in manufactures are capable of being longer kept than secrets in trade. A dyer who has found the means of producing a particular colour with materials which cost only half the price of those commonly made use of, may, with good management, enjoy the advantage of his discovery as long as he lives, and even leave it as a legacy to his posterity. His extraordinary gains arise from the high price which is paid for his private labour. They properly consist in the high wages of that labour. But as they are repeated upon every part of his stock, and as their whole amount bears, upon that account, a regular proportion to it, they are commonly considered as extraordinary profits of stock.

Such enhancements of the market price are evidently the effects of particular accidents, of which, however, the operation may sometimes last for many years together.

Some natural productions require such a singularity of soil and situation, that all the land in a great country, which is fit for producing them, may not be sufficient to supply the effectual demand. The whole quantity brought to market, therefore, may be disposed of to those who are willing to give more than what is sufficient to pay the rent of the land which produced them, together with the wages of the labour, and the profits of the stock which were employed in preparing and bringing them to market, according to their natural rates. Such commodities may continue for whole centuries together to be sold at this high price; and that part of it which resolves itself into the rent of land is in this case the part which is generally paid above its natural rate. The rent of the land which affords such singular and esteemed productions, like the rent of some vineyards in France of a peculiarly happy soil and situation, bears no regular proportion to the rent of other equally fertile and equally well-cultivated land in its neighbourhood. The wages of the labour and the profits of the stock employed in bringing such commodities to market, on the contrary, are seldom out of their natural proportion to those of the other employments of labour and stock in their neighbourhood.

Such enhancements of the market price are evidently the effect of natural causes which may hinder the effectual demand from ever being fully supplied, and which may continue, therefore, to operate for ever.

A monopoly granted either to an individual or to a trading company has the same effect as a secret in trade or manufactures. The monopolists, by keeping the market constantly under-stocked, by never fully supplying the effectual demand, sell their commodities much above the natural price, and raise their emoluments, whether they consist in wages or profit, greatly above their natural rate.

The price of monopoly is upon every occasion the highest which can be got. The natural price, or the price of free competition, on the contrary, is the lowest which can be taken, not upon every occasion indeed, but for any considerable time together. The one is upon every occasion the highest which can be squeezed out of the buyers, or which, it is supposed, they will consent to give: The other is the lowest which the sellers can commonly afford to take, and at the same time continue their business.

The exclusive privileges of corporations, statutes of apprenticeship, and all those laws which restrain, in particular employments, the competition to a smaller number than might otherwise go into them, have the same tendency, though in a less degree. They are a sort of enlarged monopolies, and may frequently, for ages together, and in whole classes of employments, keep up the market price of particular commodities above the natural price, and maintain both the wages of the labour and the profits of the stock employed about them somewhat above their natural rate.

Such enhancements of the market price may last as long as the regulations of police which give occasion to them.

The market price of any particular commodity, though it may continue long above, can seldom continue long below, its natural price. Whatever part of it was paid below the natural rate, the persons whose interest it affected would immediately feel the loss, and would immediately withdraw either so much land, or so much labour, or so much stock, from being employed about it, that the quantity brought to market would soon be no more than sufficient to supply the effectual demand. Its market price, therefore, would soon rise to the natural price. This at least would be the case where there was perfect liberty.

The same statutes of apprenticeship and other corporation laws indeed, which, when a manufacture is in prosperity, enable the workman to raise his wages a good deal above their natural rate, sometimes oblige him, when it decays, to let them down a good deal below it. As in the one case they exclude many people from his employment, so in the other they exclude him from many employments. The effect of such regulations, however, is not near so durable in sinking the workman's wages below, as in raising them above, their natural rate. Their operation in the one way may endure for many centuries, but in the other it can last no longer than the lives of some of the workmen who were bred to the business in the time of its prosperity. When they are gone, the number of those who are afterwards educated to the trade will naturally suit itself to the effectual demand. The police must be as violent as that of Indostan or ancient Egypt (where every man was bound by a principle of religion to follow the occupation of his father, and was supposed to commit the most horrid sacrilege if he changed it for another), which can in any particular employment, and for several generations together, sink either the wages of labour or the profits of stock below their natural rate.

This is all that I think necessary to be observed at present concerning the deviations, whether occasional or permanent, of the market price of commodities from the natural price.

The natural price itself varies with the natural rate of each of its component parts, of wages, profit, and rent; and in every society this rate varies according to their circumstances, according to their riches or poverty, their advancing, stationary, or declining condition. I shall, in the four following chapters, endeavour to explain, as fully and distinctly as I can, the causes of those different variations.

First, I shall endeavour to explain what are the circumstances which naturally determine the rate of wages, and in what manner those circumstances are affected by the riches or poverty, by the advancing, stationary, or declining state of the society.

Secondly, I shall endeavour to show what are the circumstances which naturally determine the rate of profit, and in what manner too those circumstances are affected by the like variations in the state of the society.

Though pecuniary wages and profit are very different in the different employments of labour and stock; yet a certain proportion seems commonly to take place between both the pecuniary wages in all the different employments of labour, and the pecuniary profits in all the different employments of stock. This proportion, it will appear hereafter, depends partly upon the nature of the different employments, and partly upon the different laws and policy of the society in which they are carried on. But though in many respects dependent upon the laws and policy, this proportion seems to be little affected by the riches or poverty of that society; by its advancing, stationary, or declining condition; but to remain the same or very nearly the same in all those different states. I shall, in the third place, endeavour to explain all the different circumstances which regulate this proportion.

In the fourth and last place, I shall endeavour to show what are the circumstances which regulate the rent of land, and which either raise or lower the real price of all the different substances which it produces.

CHAPTER VIII

OF THE WAGES OF LABOUR

The produce of labour constitutes the natural recompence or wages of labour.

In that original state of things, which precedes both the appropriation of land and the accumulation of stock, the whole produce of labour belongs to the labourer. He has neither landlord nor master to share with him.

Had this state continued, the wages of labour would have augmented with all those improvements in its productive powers, to which the division of labour gives occasion. All things would gradually have become cheaper. They would have been produced by a smaller quantity of labour; and as the commodities produced by equal quantities of labour would naturally in this state of things be exchanged for one another, they would have been purchased likewise with the produce of a smaller quantity.

But though all things would have become cheaper in reality, in appearance many things might have become dearer than before, or have been exchanged for a greater quantity of other goods. Let us suppose, for example, that in the greater part of employments the productive powers of labour had been improved to tenfold, or that a day's labour could produce ten times the quantity of work which it had done originally; but that in a particular employment they had been improved only to double, or that a day's labour could produce only twice the quantity of work which it had done before. In exchanging the produce of a day's labour in the greater part of employments, for that of a day's labour in this particular one, ten times the original quantity of work in them would purchase only twice the original quantity in it. Any particular quantity in it, therefore, a pound weight, for example, would appear to be five times dearer than before. In reality, however, it would be twice as cheap. Though it required five times the quantity of other goods to purchase it, it would require only half the quantity of labour either to purchase or to produce it. The acquisition, therefore, would be twice as easy as before.

But this original state of things, in which the labourer enjoyed the whole produce of his own labour, could not last beyond the first introduction of the appropriation of land and the accumulation of stock. It was at an end, therefore, long before the most considerable improvements were made in the productive powers of labour, and it would be to no purpose to trace further what might have been its effects upon the recompence or wages of labour.

As soon as land becomes private property, the landlord demands a share of almost all the produce which the labourer can either raise, or collect from it. His rent makes the first deduction from the produce of the labour which is employed upon land.

It seldom happens that the person who tills the ground has wherewithal to maintain himself till he reaps the harvest. His maintenance is generally advanced to him from the stock of a master, the farmer who employs him, and who would have no interest to employ him, unless he was to share in the produce of his labour, or unless his stock was to be replaced to him with a profit. This profit makes a second deduction from the produce of the labour which is employed upon land.

The produce of almost all other labour is liable to the like deduction of profit. In all arts and manufactures the greater part of the workmen stand in need of a master to advance them the materials of their work, and their wages and maintenance till it be completed. He shares in the produce of their labour, or in the value which it adds to the materials upon which it is bestowed; and in this share consists his profit.

It sometimes happens, indeed, that a single independent workman has stock sufficient both to purchase the materials of his work, and to maintain himself till it be completed. He is both master and workman, and enjoys the whole produce of his own labour, or the whole value which it adds to the materials upon which it is bestowed. It includes what are usually two distinct revenues, belonging to two distinct persons, the profits of stock, and the wages of labour.

Such cases, however, are not very frequent, and in every part of Europe, twenty workmen serve under a master for one that is independent; and the wages of labour are every where understood to be, what they usually are, when the labourer is one person, and the owner of the stock which employs him another.

What are the common wages of labour, depends every where upon the contract usually made between those two parties, whose interests are by no means the same. The workmen desire to get as much, the masters to give as little as possible. The former are disposed to combine in order to raise, the latter in order to lower the wages of labour.

It is not, however, difficult to foresee which of the two parties must, upon all ordinary occasions, have the advantage in the dispute, and force the other into a compliance with their terms. The masters, being fewer in number, can combine much more easily; and the law, besides, author-ises, or at least does not prohibit their combinations, while it prohibits those of the workmen. We have no acts of parliament against combining to lower the price of work; but many against combining to raise it. In all such disputes the masters can hold out much longer. A landlord, a farmer, a master manufacturer, or merchant, though they did not employ a single workman, could generally live a year or two upon the stocks which they have already acquired. Many workmen could not subsist a week, few could subsist a month, and scarce any a year without employment. In the long-run the workman may be as necessary to his master as his master is to him, but the necessity is not so immediate.

We rarely hear, it has been said, of the combinations of masters, though frequently of those of workmen. But whoever imagines, upon this ac-count, that masters rarely combine, is as ignorant of the world as of the subject. Masters are always and every where in a sort of tacit, but constant and uniform combination, not to raise the wages of labour above their actual rate. To violate this combination is every where a most unpopular action, and a sort of reproach to a master among his neighbours and equals. We seldom, indeed, hear of this combination, because it is the usual, and one may say, the natural state of things which nobody ever hears of. Masters too sometimes enter into particular combinations to sink the wages of labour even below this rate. These are always conducted with the utmost silence and secrecy, till the moment of execution, and when the workmen yield, as they sometimes do, without resistance, though severely felt by them, they are never heard of by other people. Such combinations, however, are frequently resisted by a contrary defensive combination of the workmen; who sometimes too, without any provocation of this kind, combine of their own accord to raise the price of their labour. Their usual pretences are, sometimes the high price of provisions; sometimes the great profit which their masters make by their work. But whether their combinations be offensive or defensive, they are always abundantly heard of. In order to bring the point to a speedy decision, they have always recourse to the loudest clamour, and sometimes to the most shocking violence and outrage. They are desperate, and act with the folly and extravagance of desperate men, who must either starve, or frighten their masters into an immediate compliance with their demands. The masters upon these occasions are just as clamorous upon the other side, and never cease to call aloud for the assistance of the civil magistrate, and the rigorous execution of those laws which have been enacted with so much severity against the combinations of servants, labourers, and journeymen. The workmen, accordingly, very seldom derive any advantage from the violence of those tumultuous combinations, which, partly from the interposition of the civil magistrate, partly from the superior steadiness of the masters, partly from the necessity which the greater part of the workmen are under of submitting for the sake of present subsistence, generally end in nothing, but the punishment or ruin of the ring-leaders.

But though in disputes with their workmen, masters must generally have the advantage, there is however a certain rate below which it seems impossible to reduce, for any considerable time, the ordinary wages even of the lowest species of labour.

A man must always live by his work, and his wages must at least be sufficient to maintain him. They must even upon most occasions be somewhat more; otherwise it would be impossible for him to bring up a family, and the race of such workmen could not last beyond the first generation. Mr. Cantillon seems, upon this account, to suppose that the lowest species of common labourers must every where earn at least double their own maintenance, in order that one with another they may be enabled to bring up two children; the labour of the wife, on account of her necessary attendance on the children, being supposed no more than sufficient to provide for herself. But one-half the children born, it is computed, die before the age of manhood. The poorest labourers, therefore, according to this account, must, one with another, attempt to rear at least four children, in order that two may have an equal chance of living to that age. But the necessary maintenance of four children, it is supposed, may be nearly equal to that of one man. The labour of an able-bodied slave, the same author adds, is computed to be worth double his maintenance; and that of the meanest labourer, he thinks, cannot be worth less than that of an able-bodied slave. Thus far at least seems certain, that, in order to bring up a family, the labour of the husband and wife together must, even in the lowest species of common labour, be able to earn something more than what is precisely necessary for their own maintenance; but in what proportion, whether in that above mentioned, or in any other, I shall not take upon me to determine.

There are certain circumstances, however, which sometimes give the labourers an advantage, and enable them to raise their wages considerably above this rate; evidently the lowest which is consistent with common humanity.

When in any country the demand for those who live by wages; labourers, journeymen, servants of every kind, is continually increasing; when every year furnishes employment for a greater number than had been employed the year before, the workmen have no occasion to combine in order to raise their wages. The scarcity of hands occasions a competition among masters, who bid against one another, in order to get workmen, and thus voluntarily break through the natural combination of masters not to raise wages.

The demand for those who live by wages, it is evident, cannot increase but in proportion to the increase of the funds which are destined for the payment of wages. These funds are of two kinds; first, the revenue which is over and above what is necessary for the maintenance; and, secondly, the stock which is over and above what is necessary for the employment of their masters.

When the landlord, annuitant, or monied man, has a greater revenue than what he judges sufficient to maintain his own family, he employs either the whole or a part of the surplus in maintaining one or more menial servants. Increase this surplus, and he will naturally increase the number of those servants.

When an independent workman, such as a weaver or shoe-maker, has got more stock than what is sufficient to purchase the materials of his own work, and to maintain himself till he can dispose of it, he naturally employs one or more journeymen with the surplus, in order to make a profit by their work. Increase this surplus, and he will naturally increase the number of his journeymen.

The demand for those who live by wages, therefore, necessarily increases with the increase of the revenue and stock of every country, and cannot possibly increase without it. The increase of revenue and stock is the increase of national wealth. The demand for those who live by wages, therefore, naturally increases with the increase of national wealth, and cannot possibly increase without it.

It is not the actual greatness of national wealth, but its continual increase, which occasions a rise in the wages of labour. It is not, accordingly, in the richest countries, but in the most thriving, or in those which are growing rich the fastest, that the wages of labour are highest. England is certainly, in the present times, a much richer country than any part of North America. The wages of labour, however, are much higher in North America than in any part of England. In the province of New York, common labourers earn three shillings and sixpence currency, equal to two shillings sterling, a day; ship carpenters, ten shillings and sixpence currency, with a pint of rum worth sixpence sterling, equal in all to six shillings and sixpence sterling; house carpenters and bricklayers, eight shillings currency, equal to four shillings and sixpence sterling; journeymen taylors, five shillings currency, equal to about two shillings and ten pence sterling. These prices are all above the London price; and wages are said to be as high in the other colonies as in New York. The price of provisions is every where in North America much lower than in England. A dearth has never been known there. In the worst seasons, they have always had a sufficiency for themselves, though less for exportation. If the money price of labour, therefore, be higher than it is any where in the mother country, its real price, the real command of the necessaries and conveniencies of life which it conveys to the labourer, must be higher in a still greater proportion.

But though North America is not yet so rich as England, it is much more thriving, and advancing with much greater rapidity to the further acquisition of riches. The most decisive mark of the prosperity of any country is the increase of the number of its inhabitants. In Great Britain, and most other European countries, they are not supposed to double in less than five hundred years. In the British colonies in North America, it has been found, that they double in twenty or five-and-twenty years. Nor in the present times is this increase principally owing to the continual importation of new inhabitants, but to the great multiplication of the species. Those who live to old age, it is said, frequently see there from fifty to a hundred, and sometimes many more, descendants from their own body. Labour is there so well rewarded that a numerous family of children, instead of being a burthen is a source of opulence and prosperity to the parents. The labour of each child, before it can leave their house, is computed to be worth a hundred pounds clear gain to them. A young widow with four or five young children, who, among the middling or inferior ranks of people in Europe, would have so little chance for a second husband, is there frequently courted as a sort of fortune. The value of children is the greatest of all encouragements to marriage. We cannot, therefore, wonder that the people in North America should generally marry very young. Notwithstanding the great increase occasioned by such early marriages, there is a continual complaint of the scarcity of hands in North America. The demand for labourers, the funds destined for maintaining them, increase, it seems, still faster than they can find labourers to employ.

Though the wealth of a country should be very great, yet if it has been long stationary, we must not expect to find the wages of labour very high in it. The funds destined for the payment of wages, the revenue and stock of its inhabitants, may be of the greatest extent; but if they have continued for several centuries of the same, or very nearly of the same extent, the number of labourers employed every year could easily supply, and even more than supply, the number wanted the following year. There could seldom be any scarcity of hands, nor could the masters be obliged to bid against one another in order to get them. The hands, on the contrary, would, in this case, naturally multiply beyond their employment. There would be a constant scarcity of employment, and the labourers would be obliged to bid against one another in order to get it. If in such a country the wages of labour had ever been more than sufficient to maintain the labourer, and to enable him to bring up a family, the competition of the labourers and the interest of the masters would soon reduce them to this lowest rate which is consistent with common humanity. China has been long one of the richest, that is, one of the most fertile, best cultivated, most industrious, and most populous countries in the world. It seems, however, to have been long stationary. Marco Polo, who visited it more than five hundred years ago, describes its cultivation, industry, and populousness, almost in the same terms in which they are described by travellers in the present times. It had perhaps, even long before his time, acquired that full complement of riches which the nature of its laws and institutions permits it to acquire. The accounts of all travellers, inconsistent in many other respects, agree in the low wages of labour, and in the difficulty which a labourer finds in bringing up a family in China. If by digging the ground a whole day he can get what will purchase a small quantity of rice in the evening, he is contented. The condition of artificers is, if possible, still worse. Instead of waiting indolently in their workhouses, for the calls of their customers, as in Europe, they are continually running about the streets with the tools of their respective trades, offering their service, and as it were begging employment. The poverty of the lower ranks of people in China far surpasses that of the most beggarly nations in Europe. In the neighbourhood of Canton many hundred, it is commonly said, many thousand families have no habitation on the land, but live constantly in little fishing boats upon the rivers and canals. The subsistence which they find there is so scanty that they are eager to fish up the nastiest garbage thrown overboard from any European ship. Any carrion, the carcase of a dead dog or cat, for example, though half putrid and stinking, is as welcome to them as the most wholesome food to the people of other countries. Marriage is encouraged in China, not by the profitableness of children, but by the liberty of destroying them. In all great towns several are every night exposed in the street, or drowned like puppies in the water. The performance of this horrid office is even said to be the avowed business by which some people earn their subsistence.

China, however, though it may perhaps stand still, does not seem to go backwards. Its towns are no-where deserted by their inhabitants. The lands which had once been cultivated are no-where neglected. The same or very nearly the same annual labour must therefore continue to be performed, and the funds destined for maintaining it must not, consequently, be sensibly diminished. The lowest class of labourers, therefore, notwithstanding their scanty subsistence, must some way or another make shift to continue their race so far as to keep up their usual numbers.

But it would be otherwise in a country where the funds destined for the maintenance of labour were sensibly decaying. Every year the demand for servants and labourers would, in all the different classes of employments, be less than it had been the year before. Many who had been bred in the superior classes, not being able to find employment in their own business, would be glad to seek it in the lowest. The lowest class being not only overstocked with its own workmen, but with the overflowings of all the other classes, the competition for employment would be so great in it, as to reduce the wages of labour to the most miserable and scanty subsistence of the labourer. Many would not be able to find employment even upon these hard terms, but would either starve, or be driven to seek a subsistence either by begging, or by the perpetration perhaps of the greatest enormities. Want, famine, and mortality would immediately prevail in that class, and from thence extend themselves to all the superior classes, till the number of inhabitants in the country was reduced to what could easily be maintained by the revenue and stock which remained in it, and which had escaped either the tyranny or calamity which had destroyed the rest. This perhaps is nearly the present state of Bengal, and of some other of the English settlements in the East Indies. In a fertile country which had before been much depopulated, where subsistence, consequently, should not be very difficult, and where, notwithstanding, three or four hundred thousand people die of hunger in one year, we may be assured that the funds destined for the maintenance of the labouring poor are fast decaying. The difference between the genius of the British constitution which protects and governs North America, and that of the mercantile company which oppresses and domineers in the East Indies, cannot perhaps be better illustrated than by the different state of those countries.

The liberal reward of labour, therefore, as it is the necessary effect, so it is the natural symptom of increasing national wealth. The scanty maintenance of the labouring poor, on the other hand, is the natural symptom that things are at a stand, and their starving condition that they are going fast backwards.

In Great Britain the wages of labour seem, in the present times, to be evidently more than what is precisely necessary to enable the labourer to bring up a family. In order to satisfy ourselves upon this point it will not be necessary to enter into any tedious or doubtful calculation of what may be the lowest sum upon which it is possible to do this. There are many plain symptoms that the wages of labour are no-where in this country regulated by this lowest rate which is consistent with common humanity.

First, in almost every part of Great Britain there is a distinction, even in the lowest species of labour, between summer and winter wages. Summer wages are always highest. But on account of the extraordinary expence of fewel, the maintenance of a family is most expensive in winter. Wages, therefore, being highest when this expence is lowest, it seems evident that they are not regulated by what is necessary for this expence; but by the quantity and supposed value of the work. A labourer, it may be said indeed, ought to save part of his summer wages in order to defray his winter expence; and that through the whole year they do not exceed what is necessary to maintain his family through the whole year. A slave, however, or one absolutely dependent on us for immediate subsistence, would not be treated in this manner. His daily subsistence would be proportioned to his daily necessities.

Secondly, the wages of labour do not in Great Britain fluctuate with the price of provisions. These vary every-where from year to year, frequently from month to month. But in many places the money price of labour remains uniformly the same sometimes for half a century together. If in these places, therefore, the labouring poor can maintain their families in dear years, they must be at their ease in times of moderate plenty, and in affluence in those of extraordinary cheapness. The high price of provisions during these ten years past has not in many parts of the kingdom been accompanied with any sensible rise in the money price of labour. It has, indeed, in some; owing probably more to the increase of the demand for labour than to that of the price of provisions.

Thirdly, as the price of provisions varies more from year to year than the wages of labour, so, on the other hand, the wages of labour vary more from place to place than the price of provisions. The prices of bread and butcher's meat are generally the same or very nearly the same through the greater part of the united kingdom. These and most other things which are sold by retail, the way in which the labouring poor buy all things, are generally fully as cheap or cheaper in great towns than in the remoter parts of the country, for reasons which I shall have occasion to explain hereafter. But the wages of labour in a great town and its neighbourhood are frequently a fourth or a fifth part, twenty or five-and-twenty per cent. higher than at a few miles distance. Eighteen pence a day may be reckoned the common price of labour in London and its neighbourhood. At a few miles distance it falls to fourteen and fifteen pence. Ten pence may be reckoned its price in Edinburgh and its neighbourhood. At a few miles distance it falls to eight pence, the usual price of common labour through the greater part of the low country of Scotland, where it varies a good deal less than in England. Such a difference of prices, which it seems is not always sufficient to transport a man from one parish to another, would necessarily occasion so great a transportation of the most bulky commodities, not only from one parish to another, but from one end of the kingdom, almost from one end of the world to the other, as would soon reduce them more nearly to a level. After all that has been said of the levity and inconstancy of human nature, it appears evidently from experience that a man is of all sorts of luggage the most difficult to be transported. If the labouring poor, therefore, can maintain their families in those parts of the kingdom where the price of labour is lowest, they must be in affluence where it is highest.

Fourthly, the variations in the price of labour not only do not correspond either in place or time with those in the price of provisions, but they are frequently quite opposite.

Grain, the food of the common people, is dearer in Scotland than in England, whence Scotland receives almost every year very large supplies. But English corn must be sold dearer in Scotland, the country to which it is brought, than in England, the country from which it comes; and in proportion to its quality it cannot be sold dearer in Scotland than the Scotch corn that comes to the same market in competition with it. The quality of grain depends chiefly upon the quantity of flour or meal which it yields at the mill, and in this respect English grain is so much superior to the Scotch, that, though often dearer in appearance, or in proportion to the measure of its bulk, it is generally cheaper in reality, or in proportion to its quality, or even to the measure of its weight. The price of labour, on the contrary, is dearer in England than in Scotland. If the labouring poor, therefore, can maintain their families in the one part of the united kingdom, they must be in affluence in the other. Oatmeal indeed supplies the common people in Scotland with the greatest and the best part of their food, which is in general much inferior to that of their neighbours of the same rank in England. This difference, however, in the mode of their subsistence is not the cause, but the effect, of the difference in their wages; though, by a strange misapprehension, I have frequently heard it represented as the cause. It is not because one man keeps a coach while his neighbour walks a-foot, that the one is rich and the other poor; but because the one is rich he keeps a coach, and because the other is poor he walks a-foot.

During the course of the last century, taking one year with another, grain was dearer in both parts of the united kingdom than during that of the present. This is a matter of fact which cannot now admit of any reasonable doubt; and the proof of it is, if possible, still more decisive with regard to Scotland than with regard to England. It is in Scotland supported by the evidence of the public fiars, annual valuations made upon oath, according to the actual state of the markets, of all the different sorts of grain in every different county of Scotland. If such direct proof could require any collateral evidence to confirm it, I would observe that this has likewise been the case in France, and probably in most other parts of Europe. With regard to France there is the clearest proof. But though it is certain that in both parts of the united kingdom grain was somewhat dearer in the last century than in the present, it is equally certain that labour was much cheaper. If the labouring poor, therefore, could bring up their families then, they must be much more at their ease now. In the last century, the most usual day-wages of common labour through the greater part of Scotland were sixpence in summer and five-pence in winter. Three shillings a week, the same price very nearly, still continues to be paid in some parts of the Highlands and Western Islands. Through the greater part of the low country the most usual wages of common labour are now eight-pence a day; ten-pence, sometimes a shilling about Edinburgh, in the counties which border upon England, probably on account of that neighbourhood, and in a few other places where there has lately been a considerable rise in the demand for labour, about Glasgow, Carron, Ayr-shire, &c. In England the improvements of agriculture, manufactures and commerce began much earlier than in Scotland. The demand for labour, and consequently its price, must necessarily have increased with those improvements. In the last century, accordingly, as well as in the present, the wages of labour were higher in England than in Scotland. They have risen too considerably since that time, though, on account of the greater variety of wages paid there in different places, it is more difficult to ascertain how much. In 1614, the pay of a foot soldier was the same as in the present times, eight pence a day. When it was first established it would naturally be regulated by the usual wages of common labourers, the rank of people from which foot soldiers are commonly drawn. Lord Chief Justice Hales, who wrote in the time of Charles II. computes the necessary expence of a labourer's family, consisting of six persons, the father and mother, two children able to do something, and two not able, at ten shillings a week, or twenty-six pounds a year. If they cannot earn this by their labour, they must make it up, he supposes, either by begging or stealing. He appears to have enquired very carefully into this subject. In 1688, Mr. Gregory King, whose skill in political arithmetic is so much extolled by Doctor Davenant, computed the ordinary income of labourers and out-servants to be fifteen pounds a year to a family, which he supposed to consist, one with another, of three and a half persons. His calculation, therefore, though different in appearance, corresponds very nearly at bottom with that of judge Hales. Both suppose the weekly expence of such families to be about twenty pence a head. Both the pecuniary income and expence of such families have increased considerably since that time through the greater part of the kingdom; in some places more, and in some less; though perhaps scarce any where so much as some exaggerated accounts of the present wages of labour have lately represented them to the public. The price of labour, it must be observed, cannot be ascertained very accurately any where, different prices being often paid at the same place and for the same sort of labour, not only according to the different abilities of the workmen, but according to the easiness or hardness of the masters. Where wages are not regulated by law, all that we can pretend to determine is what are the most usual; and experience seems to show that law can never regulate them properly, though it has often pretended to do so.

The real recompence of labour, the real quantity of the necessaries and conveniencies of life which it can procure to the labourer, has, during the course of the present century, increased perhaps in a still greater proportion than its money price. Not only grain has become somewhat cheaper, but many other things, from which the industrious poor derive an agreeable and wholesome variety of food, have become a great deal cheaper. Potatoes, for example, do not at present, through the greater part of the kingdom, cost half the price which they used to do thirty or forty years ago. The same thing may be said of turnips, carrots, cabbages; things which were formerly never raised but by the spade, but which are now commonly raised by the plough. All sort of garden stuff too has become cheaper. The greater part of the apples and even of the onions consumed in Great Britain were in the last century imported from Flanders. The great improvements in the coarser manufactures of both linen and woollen cloth furnish the labourers with cheaper and better cloathing; and those in the manufactures of the coarser metals, with cheaper and better instruments of trade, as well as with many agreeable and convenient pieces of household furniture. Soap, salt, candles, leather, and fermented liquors, have, indeed, become a good deal dearer; chiefly from the taxes which have been laid upon them. The quantity of these, however, which the labouring poor are under any necessity of consuming, is so very small, that the increase in their price does not compensate the diminution in that of so many other things. The common complaint that luxury extends itself even to the lowest ranks of the people, and that the labouring poor will not now be contented with the same food, cloathing and lodging which satisfied them in former times, may convince us that it is not the money price of labour only, but its real recompence, which has augmented.

Is this improvement in the circumstances of the lower ranks of the people to be regarded as an advantage or as an inconveniency to the society? The answer seems at first sight abundantly plain. Servants, labourers and workmen of different kinds, make up the far greater part of every great political society. But what improves the circumstances of the greater part can never be regarded as an inconveniency to the whole. No society can surely be flourishing and happy, of which the far greater part of the members are poor and miserable. It is but equity, besides, that they who feed, cloath and lodge the whole body of the people, should have such a share of the produce of their own labour as to be themselves tolerably well fed, cloathed and lodged.

Poverty, though it no doubt discourages, does not always prevent marriage. It seems even to be favourable to generation. A half-starved Highland woman frequently bears more than twenty children, while a pampered fine lady is often incapable of bearing any, and is generally exhausted by two or three. Barrenness, so frequent among women of fashion, is very rare among those of inferior station. Luxury in the fair sex, while it inflames perhaps the passion for enjoyment, seems always to weaken, and frequently to destroy altogether, the powers of generation.

But poverty, though it does not prevent the generation, is extremely unfavourable to the rearing of children. The tender plant is produced, but in so cold a soil, and so severe a climate, soon withers and dies. It is not uncommon, I have been frequently told, in the Highlands of Scotland for a mother who has borne twenty children not to have two alive. Several officers of great experience have assured me, that so far from recruiting their regiment, they have never been able to supply it with drums and fifes from all the soldiers' children that were born in it. A greater number of fine children, however, is seldom seen any where than about a barrack of soldiers. Very few of them, it seems, arrive at the age of thirteen or fourteen. In some places one half the children born die before they are four years of age; in many places before they are seven; and in almost all places before they are nine or ten. This great mortality, however, will every where be found chiefly among the children of the common people, who cannot afford to tend them with the same care as those of better station. Though their marriages are generally more fruitful than those of people of fashion, a smaller proportion of their children arrive at maturity. In foundling hospitals, and among the children brought up by parish charities, the mortality is still greater than among those of the common people.

Every species of animals naturally multiplies in proportion to the means of their subsistence, and no species can ever multiply beyond it. But in civilized society it is only among the inferior ranks of people that the scantiness of subsistence can set limits to the further multiplication of the human species; and it can do so in no other way than by destroying a great part of the children which their fruitful marriages produce.

The liberal reward of labour, by enabling them to provide better for their children, and consequently to bring up a greater number, naturally tends to widen and extend those limits. It deserves to be remarked too, that it necessarily does this as nearly as possible in the proportion which the demand for labour requires. If this demand is continually increasing, the reward of labour must necessarily encourage in such a manner the marriage and multiplication of labourers, as may enable them to supply that continually increasing demand by a continually increasing population. If the reward should at any time be less than what was requisite for this purpose, the deficiency of hands would soon raise it; and if it should at any time be more, their excessive multiplication would soon lower it to this necessary rate. The market would be so much under-stocked with labour in the one case, and so much over-stocked in the other, as would soon force back its price to that proper rate which the circumstances of the society required. It is in this manner that the demand for men, like that for any other commodity, necessarily regulates the production of men; quickens it when it goes on too slowly, and stops it when it advances too fast. It is this demand which regulates and determines the state of propagation in all the different countries of the world, in North America, in Europe, and in China; which renders it rapidly progressive in the first, slow and gradual in the second, and altogether stationary in the last.

The wear and tear of a slave, it has been said, is at the expence of his master; but that of a free servant is at his own expence. The wear and tear of the latter, however, is, in reality, as much at the expence of his master as that of the former. The wages paid to journeymen and servants of every kind must be such as may enable them, one with another, to continue the race of journeymen and servants, according as the increasing, diminishing, or stationary demand of the society may happen to require.

But though the wear and tear of a free servant be equally at the expence of his master, it generally costs him much less than that of a slave. The fund destined for replacing or repairing, if I may say so, the wear and tear of the slave, is commonly managed by a negligent master or careless overseer. That destined for performing the same office with regard to the free man, is managed by the free man himself. The disorders which generally prevail in the oeconomy of the rich, naturally introduce them-selves into the management of the former: The strict frugality and parsi-monious attention of the poor as naturally establish themselves in that of the latter. Under such different management, the same purpose must require very different degrees of expence to execute it. It appears, accord-ingly, from the experience of all ages and nations, I believe, that the work done by freemen comes cheaper in the end than that performed by slaves. It is found to do so even at Boston, New York, and Philadelphia, where the wages of common labour are so very high.

The liberal reward of labour, therefore, as it is the effect of increasing wealth, so it is the cause of increasing population. To complain of it, is to lament over the necessary effect and cause of the greatest public prosperity.

It deserves to be remarked, perhaps, that it is in the progressive state, while the society is advancing to the further acquisition, rather than when it has acquired its full complement of riches, that the condition of the labouring poor, of the great body of the people, seems to be the happiest and the most comfortable. It is hard in the stationary, and miserable in the declining state. The progressive state is in reality the cheerful and the hearty state to all the different orders of the society. The stationary is dull; the declining melancholy.

The liberal reward of labour, as it encourages the propagation, so it increases the industry of the common people. The wages of labour are the encouragement of industry, which, like every other human quality, improves in proportion to the encouragement it receives. A plentiful subsistence increases the bodily strength of the labourer, and the comfort-able hope of bettering his condition, and of ending his days perhaps in ease and plenty, animates him to exert that strength to the utmost. Where wages are high, accordingly, we shall always find the workmen more active, diligent, and expeditious, than where they are low; in England, for example, than in Scotland; in the neighbourhood of great towns, than in remote country places. Some workmen, indeed, when they can earn in four days what will maintain them through the week, will be idle the other three. This, however, is by no means the case with the greater part. Workmen, on the contrary, when they are liberally paid by the piece, are very apt to over-work themselves, and to ruin their health and constitution in a few years. A carpenter in London, and in some other places, is not supposed to last in his utmost vigour above eight years. Something of the same kind happens in many other trades, in which the workmen are paid by the piece; as they generally are in manufactures, and even in country labour, wherever wages are higher than ordinary. Almost every class of artificers is subject to some peculiar infirmity occasioned by excessive application to their peculiar species of work. Ramuzzini, an eminent Italian physician, has written a particular book concerning such diseases. We do not reckon our soldiers the most industrious set of people among us. Yet when soldiers have been employed in some particular sorts of work, and liberally paid by the piece, their officers have frequently been obliged to stipulate with the undertaker, that they should not be allowed to earn above a certain sum every day, according to the rate at which they were paid. Till this stipulation was made, mutual emulation and the desire of greater gain, frequently prompted them to over-work themselves, and to hurt their health by excessive labour. Excessive application during four days of the week, is frequently the real cause of the idleness of the other three, so much and so loudly complained of. Great labour, either of mind or body, continued for several days together, is in most men naturally followed by a great desire of relaxation, which, if not restrained by force or by some strong necessity, is almost irresistible. It is the call of nature, which requires to be relieved by some indulgence, sometimes of ease only, but sometimes too of dissipation and diversion. If it is not complied with, the consequences are often dangerous, and sometimes fatal, and such as almost always, sooner or later, bring on the peculiar infirmity of the trade. If masters would always listen to the dictates of reason and humanity, they have frequently occasion rather to moderate, than to animate the application of many of their workmen. It will be found, I believe, in every sort of trade, that the man who works so moderately, as to be able to work constantly, not only preserves his health the longest, but, in the course of the year, executes the greatest quantity of work.

In cheap years, it is pretended, workmen are generally more idle, and in dear ones more industrious than ordinary. A plentiful subsistence therefore, it has been concluded, relaxes, and a scanty one quickens their industry. That a little more plenty than ordinary may render some workmen idle, cannot well be doubted; but that it should have this effect upon the greater part, or that men in general should work better when they are ill fed than when they are well fed, when they are disheartened than when they are in good spirits, when they are frequently sick than when they are generally in good health, seems not very probable. Years of dearth, it is to be observed, are generally among the common people years of sickness and mortality, which cannot fail to diminish the produce of their industry.

In years of plenty, servants frequently leave their masters, and trust their subsistence to what they can make by their own industry. But the same cheapness of provisions, by increasing the fund which is destined for the maintenance of servants, encourages masters, farmers especially, to employ a greater number. Farmers upon such occasions expect more profit from their corn by maintaining a few more labouring servants, than by selling it at a low price in the market. The demand for servants increases, while the number of those who offer to supply that demand diminishes. The price of labour, therefore, frequently rises in cheap years.

In years of scarcity, the difficulty and uncertainty of subsistence make all such people eager to return to service. But the high price of provisions, by diminishing the funds destined for the maintenance of servants, disposes masters rather to diminish than to increase the number of those they have. In dear years too, poor independent workmen frequently consume the little stocks with which they had used to supply themselves with the materials of their work, and are obliged to become journeymen for subsistence. More people want employment than can easily get it; many are willing to take it upon lower terms than ordinary, and the wages of both servants and journeymen frequently sink in dear years.

Masters of all sorts, therefore, frequently make better bargains with their servants in dear than in cheap years, and find them more humble and dependent in the former than in the latter. They naturally, therefore, commend the former as more favourable to industry. Landlords and farmers, besides, two of the largest classes of masters, have another reason for being pleased with dear years. The rents of the one and the profits of the other depend very much upon the price of provisions. Nothing can be more absurd, however, than to imagine that men in general should work less when they work for themselves, than when they work for other people. A poor independent workman will generally be more industrious than even a journeyman who works by the piece. The one enjoys the whole produce of his own industry; the other shares it with his master. The one, in his separate independent state, is less liable to the temptations of bad company, which in large manufactories so frequently ruin the morals of the other. The superiority of the independent workman over those servants who are hired by the month or by the year, and whose wages and maintenance are the same whether they do much or do little, is likely to be still greater. Cheap years tend to increase the proportion of independent workmen to journeymen and servants of all kinds, and dear years to diminish it.

A French author of great knowledge and ingenuity, Mr. Messance, receiver of the tailles in the election of St. Etienne, endeavours to show that the poor do more work in cheap than in dear years, by comparing the quantity and value of the goods made upon those different occasions in three different manufactures; one of coarse woollens carried on at Elbeuf; one of linen, and another of silk, both which extend through the whole generality of Rouen. It appears from his account, which is copied from the registers of the public offices, that the quantity and value of the goods made in all those three manufactures has generally been greater in cheap than in dear years; and that it has always been greatest in the cheapest, and least in the dearest years. All the three seem to be stationary manufactures, or which, though their produce may vary somewhat from year to year, are upon the whole neither going backwards nor forwards.

The manufacture of linen in Scotland, and that of coarse woollens in the west riding of Yorkshire, are growing manufactures, of which the produce is generally, though with some variations, increasing both in quantity and value. Upon examining, however, the accounts which have been published of their annual produce, I have not been able to observe that its variations have had any sensible connection with the dearness or cheapness of the seasons. In 1740, a year of great scarcity, both manufactures, indeed, appear to have declined very considerably. But in 1756, another year of great scarcity, the Scotch manufacture made more than ordinary advances. The Yorkshire manufacture, indeed, declined, and its produce did not rise to what it had been in 1755 till 1766, after the repeal of the American stamp act. In that and the following year it greatly exceeded what it had ever been before, and it has continued to advance ever since.

The produce of all great manufactures for distant sale must necessarily depend, not so much upon the dearness or cheapness of the seasons in the countries where they are carried on, as upon the circumstances which affect the demand in the countries where they are consumed; upon peace or war, upon the prosperity or declension of other rival manufactures, and upon the good or bad humour of their principal customers. A great part of the extraordinary work, besides, which is probably done in cheap years, never enters the public registers of manufactures. The men servants who leave their masters become independent labourers. The women return to their parents, and commonly spin in order to make cloaths for themselves and their families. Even the independent workmen do not always work for public sale, but are employed by some of their neighbours in manufactures for family use. The produce of their labour, therefore, frequently makes no figure in those public registers of which the records are sometimes published with so much parade, and from which our merchants and manufacturers would often vainly pretend to announce the prosperity or declension of the greatest empires.

Though the variations in the price of labour, not only do not always correspond with those in the price of provisions, but are frequently quite opposite, we must not, upon this account, imagine that the price of provisions has no influence upon that of labour. The money price of labour is necessarily regulated by two circumstances; the demand for labour, and the price of the necessaries and conveniencies of life. The demand for labour, according as it happens to be increasing, stationary, or declining, or to require an increasing, stationary, or declining population, determines the quantity of the necessaries and conveniencies of life which must be given to the labourer; and the money price of labour is determined by what is requisite for purchasing this quantity. Though the money price of labour, therefore, is sometimes high where the price of provisions is low, it would be still higher, the demand continuing the same, if the price of provisions was high.

It is because the demand for labour increases in years of sudden and extraordinary plenty, and diminishes in those of sudden and extraordinary scarcity, that the money price of labour sometimes rises in the one, and sinks in the other.

In a year of sudden and extraordinary plenty, there are funds in the hands of many of the employers of industry, sufficient to maintain and employ a greater number of industrious people than had been employed the year before; and this extraordinary number cannot always be had. Those masters, therefore, who want more workmen, bid against one another, in order to get them, which sometimes raises both the real and the money price of their labour.

The contrary of this happens in a year of sudden and extraordinary scarcity. The funds destined for employing industry are less than they had been the year before. A considerable number of people are thrown out of employment, who bid against one another, in order to get it, which sometimes lowers both the real and the money price of labour. In 1740, a year of extraordinary scarcity, many people were willing to work for bare subsistence. In the succeeding years of plenty, it was more difficult to get labourers and servants.

The scarcity of a dear year, by diminishing the demand for labour, tends to lower its price, as the high price of provisions tends to raise it. The plenty of a cheap year, on the contrary, by increasing the demand, tends to raise the price of labour, as the cheapness of provisions tends to lower it. In the ordinary variations of the price of provisions, those two opposite causes seem to counterbalance one another; which is probably in part the reason why the wages of labour are every-where so much more steady and permanent than the price of provisions.

The increase in the wages of labour necessarily increases the price of many commodities, by increasing that part of it which resolves itself into wages, and so far tends to diminish their consumption both at home and abroad. The same cause, however, which raises the wages of labour, the increase of stock, tends to increase its productive powers, and to make a smaller quantity of labour produce a greater quantity of work. The owner of the stock which employs a great number of labourers, necessarily endeavours, for his own advantage, to make such a proper division and distribution of employment, that they may be enabled to produce the greatest quantity of work possible. For the same reason, he endeavours to supply them with the best machinery which either he or they can think of. What takes place among the labourers in a particular workhouse, takes place, for the same reason, among those of a great society. The greater their number, the more they naturally divide themselves into different classes and subdivisions of employment. More heads are occupied in inventing the most proper machinery for executing the work of each, and it is, therefore, more likely to be invented. There are many commodities, therefore, which, in consequence of these improvements, come to be produced by so much less labour than before, that the increase of its price is more than compensated by the diminution of its quantity.

BOOK II

Of the Nature, Accumulation, and Employment of Stock

[In Chapters VIII and IX of Book I, Smith takes note of the connection between the increasing demand for labor and rising wages. While examining this theme, Smith begins to appreciate the importance of capital accumulation as a force in making labor more productive. As I explain in Appendix I, much of the argument of the *WN* turns on this theme.]

INTRODUCTION

In that rude state of society in which there is no division of labour, in which exchanges are seldom made, and in which every man provides every thing for himself, it is not necessary that any stock should be accumulated or stored up beforehand, in order to carry on the business of the society. Every man endeavours to supply by his own industry his own occasional wants as they occur. When he is hungry, he goes to the forest to hunt; when his coat is worn out, he clothes himself with the skin of the first large animal he kills: and when his hut begins to go to ruin, he repairs it, as well as he can, with the trees and the turf that are nearest it.

But when the division of labour has once been thoroughly introduced, the produce of a man's own labour can supply but a very small part of his occasional wants. The far greater part of them are supplied by the produce of other mens labour, which he purchases with the produce, or what is the same thing, with the price of the produce of his own. But this purchase cannot be made till such time as the produce of his own labour has not only been completed, but sold. A stock of goods of different kinds, therefore, must be stored up somewhere sufficient to maintain him, and to supply him with the materials and tools of his work, till such time, at least, as both these events can be brought about. A weaver cannot apply himself entirely to his peculiar business, unless there is beforehand stored up somewhere, either in his own possession or in that of some other person, a stock sufficient to maintain him, and to supply him with the materials and tools of his work, till he has not only completed, but sold his web. This accumulation must, evidently, be previous to his applying his industry for so long a time to such a peculiar business.

As the accumulation of stock must, in the nature of things, be previous to the division of labour, so labour can be more and more subdivided in proportion only as stock is previously more and more accumulated. The quantity of materials which the same number of people can work up, increases in a great proportion as labour comes to be more and more subdivided; and as the operations of each workman are gradually reduced to a greater degree of simplicity, a variety of new machines come to be invented for facilitating and abridging those operations. As the division of labour advances, therefore, in order to give constant employment to an equal number of workmen, an equal stock of provisions, and a greater stock of materials and tools than what would have been necessary in a ruder state of things, must be accumulated beforehand. But the number of workmen in every branch of business generally increases with the division of labour in that branch, or rather it is the increase of their number which enables them to class and subdivide themselves in this manner.

As the accumulation of stock is previously necessary for carrying on this great improvement in the productive powers of labour, so that accumulation naturally leads to this improvement. The person who employs his stock in maintaining labour, necessarily wishes to employ it in such a manner as to produce as great a quantity of work as possible. He endeavours, therefore, both to make among his workmen the most proper distribution of employment, and to furnish them with the best machines which he can either invent or afford to purchase. His abilities in both these respects are generally in proportion to the extent of his stock, or to the number of people whom it can employ. The quantity of industry, therefore, not only increases in every country with the increase of the stock which employs it, but, in consequence of that increase, the same quantity of industry produces a much greater quantity of work.

Such are in general the effects of the increase of stock upon industry and its productive powers.

In the following book I have endeavoured to explain the nature of stock, the effects of its accumulation into capitals of different kinds, and the effects of the different employments of those capitals. This book is divided into five chapters. In the first chapter, I have endeavoured to show what are the different parts or branches into which the stock, either of an individual, or of a great society, naturally divides itself. In the second, I have endeavoured to explain the nature and operation of money considered as a particular branch of the general stock of the society. The stock which is accumulated into a capital, may either be employed by the person to whom it belongs, or it may be lent to some other person. In the third and fourth chapters, I have endeavoured to examine the manner in which it operates in both these situations. The fifth and last chapter treats Of the different effects which the different employments of capital immediately produce upon the quantity both of national industry, and of the annual produce of land and labour.

CHAPTER I

OF THE DIVISION OF STOCK

When the stock which a man possesses is no more than sufficient to maintain him for a few days or a few weeks, he seldom thinks of deriving any revenue from it. He consumes it as sparingly as he can, and endeavours by his labour to acquire something which may supply its place before it be consumed altogether. His revenue is, in this case, derived from his labour only. This is the state of the greater part of the labouring poor in all countries.

But when he possesses stock sufficient to maintain him for months or years, he naturally endeavours to derive a revenue from the greater part of it; reserving only so much for his immediate consumption as may maintain him till this revenue begins to come in. His whole stock, therefore, is distinguished into two parts. That part which, he expects, is to afford him this revenue, is called his capital. The other is that which supplies his immediate consumption; and which consists either, first, in that portion of his whole stock which was originally reserved for this purpose; or, secondly, in his revenue, from whatever source derived, as it gradually comes in; or, thirdly, in such things as had been purchased by either of these in former years, and which are not yet entirely consumed; such as a stock of clothes, household furniture, and the like. In one, or other, or all of these three articles, consists the stock which men commonly reserve for their own immediate consumption.

There are two different ways in which a capital may be employed so as to yield a revenue or profit to its employer.

First, it may be employed in raising, manufacturing, or purchasing goods, and selling them again with a profit. The capital employed in this manner yields no revenue or profit to its employer, while it either remains in his possession, or continues in the same shape. The goods of the merchant yield him no revenue or profit till he sells them for money, and the money yields him as little till it is again exchanged for goods. His capital is continually going from him in one shape, and returning to him in another, and it is only by means of such circulation, or successive exchanges, that it can yield him any profit. Such capitals, therefore, may very properly be called circulating capitals.

Secondly, it may be employed in the improvement of land, in the purchase of useful machines and instruments of trade, or in suchlike things as yield a revenue or profit without changing masters, or circulating any further. Such capitals, therefore, may very properly be called fixed capitals.

Different occupations require very different proportions between the fixed and circulating capitals employed in them.

The capital of a merchant, for example, is altogether a circulating capital. He has occasion for no machines or instruments of trade, unless his shop, or warehouse, be considered as such.

Some part of the capital of every master artificer or manufacturer must be fixed in the instruments of his trade. This part, however, is very small in some, and very great in others. A master taylor requires no other instruments of trade but a parcel of needles. Those of the master shoemaker are a little, though but a very little, more expensive. Those of the weaver rise a good deal above those of the shoemaker. The far greater part of the capital of all such master artificers, however, is circulated, either in the wages of their workmen, or in the price of their materials, and repaid with a profit by the price of the work.

In other works a much greater fixed capital is required. In a great iron-work, for example, the furnace for melting the ore, the forge, the slitt-mill, are instruments of trade which cannot be erected without a very great expence. In coal-works, and mines of every kind, the machinery necessary both for drawing out the water and for other purposes, is frequently still more expensive.

That part of the capital of the farmer which is employed in the instruments of agriculture is a fixed; that which is employed in the wages and maintenance of his labouring servants, is a circulating capital. He makes a profit of the one by keeping it in his own possession, and of the other by parting with it. The price or value of his labouring cattle is a fixed capital in the same manner as that of the instruments of husbandry: Their maintenance is a circulating capital in the same manner as that of the labouring servants. The farmer makes his profit by keeping the labouring cattle, and by parting with their maintenance. Both the price and the maintenance of the cattle which are bought in and fattened, not for labour, but for sale, are a circulating capital. The farmer makes his profit by parting with them. A flock of sheep or a herd of cattle that, in a breeding country, is bought in, neither for labour, nor for sale, but in order to make a profit by their wool, by their milk, and by their increase, is a fixed capital. The profit is made by keeping them. Their maintenance is a circulating capital. The profit is made by parting with it; and it comes back with both its own profit, and the profit upon the whole price of the cattle, in the price of the wool, the milk, and the increase. The whole value of the seed too is properly a fixed capital. Though it goes backwards and forwards between the ground and the granary, it never changes masters, and therefore does not properly circulate. The farmer makes his profit, not by its sale, but by its increase.

The general stock of any country or society is the same with that of all its inhabitants or members, and therefore naturally divides itself into the same three portions, each of which has a distinct function or office.

The First, is that portion which is reserved for immediate consumption, and of which the characteristic is that it affords no revenue or profit. It consists in the stock of food, clothes, household furniture, &c., which have been purchased by their proper consumers, but which are not yet entirely consumed. The whole stock of mere dwelling houses too subsisting at any one time in the country, make a part of this first portion. The stock that is laid out in a house, if it is to be the dwelling-house of the proprietor, ceases from that moment to serve in the function of a capital, or to afford any revenue to its owner. A dwelling-house, as such, contributes nothing to the revenue of its inhabitant; and though it is, no doubt, extremely useful to him, it is as his clothes and household furniture are useful to him, which, however, make a part of his expence, and not of his revenue. If it is to be let to a tenant for rent, as the house itself can produce nothing, the tenant must always pay the rent out of some other revenue which he derives either from labour, or stock, or land. Though a house, therefore, may yield a revenue to its proprietor, and thereby serve in the function of a capital to him, it cannot yield any to the public, nor serve in the function of a capital to it, and the revenue of the whole body of the people can never be in the smallest degree increased by it. Clothes, and household furniture, in the same manner, sometimes yield a revenue, and thereby serve in the function of a capital to particular persons. In countries where masquerades are common, it is a trade to let out masquerade dresses for a night. Upholsterers frequently let furniture by the month or by the year. Undertakers let the furniture of funerals by the day and by the week. Many people let furnished houses, and get a rent, not only for the use of the house, but for that of the furniture. The revenue, however, which is derived from such things, must always be ultimately drawn from some other source of revenue. Of all parts of the stock, either of an individual, or of a society, reserved for immediate consumption, what is laid out in houses is most slowly consumed. A stock of clothes may last several years: a stock of furniture half a century or a century: but a stock of houses, well built and properly taken care of, may last many centuries. Though the period of their total consumption, however, is more distant, they are still as really a stock reserved for immediate consumption as either clothes or household furniture.

The Second of the three portions into which the general stock of the society divides itself, is the fixed capital; of which the characteristic is, that it affords a revenue or profit without circulating or changing masters. It consists chiefly of the four following articles:

First, of all useful machines and instruments of trade which facilitate and abridge labour:

Secondly, of all those profitable buildings which are the means of procuring a revenue, not only to their proprietor who lets them for a rent, but to the person who possesses them and pays that rent for them; such as shops, warehouses, workhouses, farmhouses, with all their necessary buildings; stables, granaries, &c. These are very different from mere dwelling houses. They are a sort of instruments of trade, and may be considered in the same light:

Thirdly, of the improvements of land, of what has been profitably laid out in clearing, draining, enclosing, manuring, and reducing it into the condition most proper for tillage and culture. An improved farm may very justly be regarded in the same light as those useful machines which facilitate and abridge labour, and by means of which, an equal circulating capital can afford a much greater revenue to its employer. An improved farm is equally advantageous and more durable than any of those machines, frequently requiring no other repairs than the most profitable application of the farmer's capital employed in cultivating it:

Fourthly, of the acquired and useful abilities of all the inhabitants or members of the society. The acquisition of such talents, by the maintenance of the acquirer during his education, study, or apprenticeship, always costs a real expence, which is a capital fixed and realized, as it were, in his person. Those talents, as they make a part of his fortune, so do they likewise of that of the society to which he belongs. The improved dexterity of a workman may be considered in the same light as a machine or instrument of trade which facilitates and abridges labour, and which, though it costs a certain expence, repays that expence with a profit.

The Third and last of the three portions into which the general stock of the society naturally divides itself, is the circulating capital; of which the characteristic is, that it affords a revenue only by circulating or changing masters. It is composed likewise of four parts:

First, of the money by means of which all the other three are circulated and distributed to their proper consumers:

Secondly, of the stock of provisions which are in the possession of the butcher, the grazier, the farmer, the corn-merchant, the brewer, &c. and from the sale of which they expect to derive a profit:

Thirdly, of the materials, whether altogether rude, or more or less manufactured, of clothes, furniture and building, which are not yet made up into any of those three shapes, but which remain in the hands of the growers, the manufacturers, the mercers, and drapers, the timber-merchants, the carpenters and joiners, the brick-makers, &c.

Fourthly, and lastly, of the work which is made up and completed, but which is still in the hands of the merchant or manufacturer, and not yet disposed of or distributed to the proper consumers; such as the finished work which we frequently find ready-made in the shops of the smith, the cabinet-maker, the goldsmith, the jeweller, the china-merchant, &c. The circulating capital consists in this manner, of the provisions, materials, and finished work of all kinds that are in the hands of their respective dealers, and of the money that is necessary for circulating and distributing them to those who are finally to use, or to consume them.

Of these four parts three, provisions, materials, and finished work, are, either annually, or in a longer or shorter period, regularly withdrawn from it, and placed either in the fixed capital or in the stock reserved for immediate consumption.

Every fixed capital is both originally derived from, and requires to be continually supported by a circulating capital. All useful machines and instruments of trade are originally derived from a circulating capital, which furnishes the materials of which they are made, and the maintenance of the workmen who make them. They require too a capital of the same kind to keep them in constant repair.

No fixed capital can yield any revenue but by means of a circulating capital. The most useful machines and instruments of trade will produce nothing without the circulating capital which affords the materials they are employed upon, and the maintenance of the workmen who employ them. Land, however improved, will yield no revenue without a circulating capital, which maintains the labourers who cultivate and collect its produce.

To maintain and augment the stock which may be reserved for immediate consumption, is the sole end and purpose both of the fixed and circulating capitals. It is this stock which feeds, clothes, and lodges the people. Their riches or poverty depends upon the abundant or sparing supplies which those two capitals can afford to the stock reserved for immediate consumption.

So great a part of the circulating capital being continually withdrawn from it, in order to be placed in the other two branches of the general stock of the society; it must in its turn require continual supplies, without which it would soon cease to exist. These supplies are principally drawn from three sources, the produce of land, of mines, and of fisheries. These afford continual supplies of provisions and materials, of which part is afterwards wrought up into finished work, and by which are replaced the provisions, materials and finished work continually withdrawn from the circulating capital. From mines too is drawn what is necessary for maintaining and augmenting that part of it which consists in money. For though, in the ordinary course of business, this part is not, like the other three, necessarily withdrawn from it, in order to be placed in the other two branches of the general stock of the society, it must, however, like all other things, be wasted and worn out at last, and sometimes too be either lost or sent abroad, and must, therefore, require continual, though, no doubt, much smaller supplies.

Land, mines, and fisheries, require all both a fixed and a circulating capital to cultivate them: and their produce replaces with a profit, not only those capitals, but all the others in the society. Thus the farmer annually replaces to the manufacturer the provisions which he had consumed and the materials which he had wrought up the year before; and the manufacturer replaces to the farmer the finished work which he had wasted and worn out in the same time. This is the real exchange that is annually made between those two orders of people, though it seldom happens that the rude produce of the one and the manufactured produce of the other, are directly bartered for one another; because it seldom happens that the farmer sells his corn and his cattle, his flax and his wool, to the very same person of whom he chuses to purchase the clothes, furniture, and instruments of trade which he wants. He sells, therefore, his rude produce for money, with which he can purchase, wherever it is to be had, the manufactured produce he has occasion for. Land even replaces, in part at least, the capitals with which fisheries and mines are cultivated. It is the produce of land which draws the fish from the waters; and it is the produce of the surface of the earth which extracts the minerals from its bowels.

The produce of land, mines, and fisheries, when their natural fertility is equal, is in proportion to the extent and proper application of the capitals employed about them. When the capitals are equal and equally well applied, it is in proportion to their natural fertility.

In all countries where there is tolerable security, every man of common understanding will endeavour to employ whatever stock he can command, in procuring either present enjoyment or future profit. If it is employed in procuring present enjoyment, it is a stock reserved for immediate consumption. If it is employed in procuring future profit, it must procure this profit either by staying with him, or by going from him. In the one case it is a fixed, in the other it is a circulating capital. A man must be perfectly crazy who, where there is tolerable security, does not employ all the stock which he commands, whether it be his own or borrowed of other people, in some one or other of those three ways.

In those unfortunate countries, indeed, where men are continually afraid of the violence of their superiors, they frequently bury and conceal a great part of their stock, in order to have it always at hand to carry with them to some place of safety, in case of their being threatened with any of those disasters to which they consider themselves as at all times exposed. This is said to be a common practice in Turkey, in Indostan, and, I believe, in most other governments of Asia. It seems to have been a common practice among our ancestors during the violence of the feudal government. Treasure-trove was in those times considered as no contemptible part of the revenue of the greatest sovereigns in Europe. It consisted in such treasure as was found concealed in the earth, and to which no particular person could prove any right. This was regarded in those times as so important an object, that it was always considered as belonging to the sovereign, and neither to the finder nor to the proprietor of the land, unless the right to it had been conveyed to the latter by an express clause in his charter. It was put upon the same footing with gold and silver mines, which, without a special clause in the charter, were never supposed to be comprehended in the general grant of the lands, though mines of lead, copper, tin, and coal were, as things of smaller consequence.

CHAPTER II

OF MONEY CONSIDERED AS A PARTICULAR BRANCH OF THE GENERAL STOCK OF THE SOCIETY, OR OF THE EXPENCE OF MAINTAINING THE NATIONAL CAPITAL

It has been shewn in the first Book, that the price of the greater part of commodities resolves itself into three parts, of which one pays the wages of the labour, another the profits of the stock, and a third the rent of the land which had been employed in producing and bringing them to market: that there are, indeed, some commodities of which the price is made up of two of those parts only, the wages of labour, and the profits of stock: and a very few in which it consists altogether in one, the wages of labour: but that the price of every commodity necessarily resolves itself into some one, or other, or all of these three parts; every part of it which goes neither to rent nor to wages, being necessarily profit to somebody.

Since this is the case, it has been observed, with regard to every particular commodity, taken separately; it must be so with regard to all the commodities which compose the whole annual produce of the land and labour of every country, taken complexly. The whole price or exchangeable value of that annual produce, must resolve itself into the same three parts, and be parcelled out among the different inhabitants of the country, either as the wages of their labour, the profits of their stock, or the rent of their land.

But though the whole value of the annual produce of the land and labour of every country is thus divided among and constitutes a revenue to its different inhabitants; yet as in the rent of a private estate we distinguish between the gross rent and the neat rent, so may we likewise in the revenue of all the inhabitants of a great country.

The gross rent of a private estate comprehends whatever is paid by the farmer; the neat rent, what remains free to the landlord, after deducting the expence of management, of repairs, and all other necessary charges; or what, without hurting his estate, he can afford to place in his stock reserved for immediate consumption, or to spend upon his table, equipage, the ornaments of his house and furniture, his private enjoyments and amusements. His real wealth is in proportion, not to his gross, but to his neat rent.

The gross revenue of all the inhabitants of a great country, comprehends the whole annual produce of their land and labour; the neat revenue, what remains free to them after deducting the expence of maintaining; first, their fixed; and, secondly, their circulating capital; or what, without encroaching upon their capital, they can place in their stock reserved for immediate consumption, or spend upon their subsistence, conveniences, and amusements. Their real wealth too is in proportion, not to their gross, but to their neat revenue.

The whole expence of maintaining the fixed capital, must evidently be excluded from the neat revenue of the society. Neither the materials necessary for supporting their useful machines and instruments of trade, their profitable buildings, &c. nor the produce of the labour necessary for fashioning those materials into the proper form, can ever make any part of it. The price of that labour may indeed make a part of it; as the workmen so employed may place the whole value of their wages in their stock reserved for immediate consumption. But in other sorts of labour, both the price and the produce go to this stock, the price to that of the workmen, the produce to that of other people, whose subsistence, conveniencies, and amusements, are augmented by the labour of those workmen.

The intention of the fixed capital is to increase the productive powers of labour, or to enable the same number of labourers to perform a much greater quantity of work. In a farm where all the necessary buildings, fences, drains, communications, &c. are in the most perfect good order, the same number of labourers and labouring cattle will raise a much greater produce, than in one of equal extent and equally good ground, but not furnished with equal conveniencies. In manufactures the same number of hands, assisted with the best machinery, will work up a much greater quantity of goods than with more imperfect instruments of trade. The expence which is properly laid out upon a fixed capital of any kind, is always repaid with great profit, and increases the annual produce by a much greater value than that of the support which such improvements require. This support, however, still requires a certain portion of that produce. A certain quantity of materials, and the labour of a certain number of workmen, both of which might have been immediately employed to augment the food, clothing and lodging, the subsistence and conveniencies of the society, are thus diverted to another employment, highly advantageous indeed, but still different from this one. It is upon this account that all such improvements in mechanics, as enable the same number of workmen to perform an equal quantity of work with cheaper and simpler machinery than had been usual before, are always regarded as advantageous to every society. A certain quantity of materials, and the labour of a certain number of workmen, which had before been employed in supporting a more complex and expensive machinery, can afterwards be applied to augment the quantity of work which that or any other machinery is useful only for performing. The undertaker of some great manufactory who employs a thousand a-year in the maintenance of his machinery, if he can reduce this expence to five hundred, will naturally employ the other five hundred in purchasing an additional quantity of materials to be wrought up by an additional number of workmen. The quantity of that work, therefore, which his machinery was useful only for performing, will naturally be augmented, and with it all the advantage and conveniency which the society can derive from that work.

The expence of maintaining the fixed capital in a great country, may very properly be compared to that of repairs in a private estate. The expence of repairs may frequently be necessary for supporting the produce of the estate, and consequently both the gross and the neat rent of the landlord. When by a more proper direction, however, it can be diminished without occasioning any diminution of produce, the gross rent remains at least the same as before, and the neat rent is necessarily augmented.

But though the whole expence of maintaining the fixed capital is thus necessarily excluded from the neat revenue of the society, it is not the same case with that of maintaining the circulating capital. Of the four parts of which this latter capital is composed, money, provisions, materials, and finished work, the three last, it has already been observed, are regularly withdrawn from it, and placed either in the fixed capital of the society, or in their stock reserved for immediate consumption. Whatever portion of those consumable goods is not employed in maintaining the former, goes all to the latter, and makes a part of the neat revenue of the society. The maintenance of those three parts of the circulating capital, therefore, withdraws no portion of the annual produce from the neat revenue of the society, besides what is necessary for maintaining the fixed capital.

The circulating capital of a society is in this respect different from that of an individual. That of an individual is totally excluded from making any part of his neat revenue, which must consist altogether in his profits. But though the circulating capital of every individual makes a part of that of the society to which he belongs, it is not upon that account totally excluded from making a part likewise of their neat revenue. Though the whole goods in a merchant's shop must by no means be placed in his own stock reserved for immediate consumption, they may in that of other people, who, from a revenue derived from other funds, may regularly replace their value to him, together with its profits, without occasioning any diminution either of his capital or of theirs.

Money, therefore, is the only part of the circulating capital of a society, of which the maintenance can occasion any diminution in their neat revenue.

The fixed capital, and that part of the circulating capital which consists in money, so far as they affect the revenue of the society, bear a very great resemblance to one another.

First, as those machines and instruments of trade, &c. require a certain expence, first to erect them, and afterwards to support them, both which expences, though they make a part of the gross, are deductions from the neat revenue of the society; so the stock of money which circulates in any country must require a certain expence, first to collect it, and afterwards to support it, both which expences, though they make a part of the gross, are, in the same manner, deductions from the neat revenue of the society. A certain quantity of very valuable materials, gold and silver, and of very curious labour, instead of augmenting the stock reserved for immediate consumption, the subsistence, conveniencies, and amusements of individuals, is employed in supporting that great but expensive instrument of commerce, by means of which every individual in the society has his subsistence, conveniencies, and amusements, regularly distributed to him in their proper proportion.

Secondly, as the machines and instruments of trade, &c. which compose the fixed capital either of an individual or of a society, make no part either of the gross or of the neat revenue of either; so money, by means of which the whole revenue of the society is regularly distributed among all its different members, makes itself no part of that revenue. The great wheel of circulation is altogether different from the goods which are circulated by means of it. The revenue of the society consists altogether in those goods, and not in the wheel which circulates them. In computing either the gross or the neat revenue of any society, we must always, from their whole annual circulation of money and goods, deduct the whole value of the money, of which not a single farthing can ever make any part of either.

It is the ambiguity of language only which can make this proposition appear either doubtful or paradoxical. When properly explained and understood, it is almost self-evident.

When we talk of any particular sum of money, we sometimes mean nothing but the metal pieces of which it is composed; and sometimes we include in our meaning some obscure reference to the goods which can be had in exchange for it, or to the power of purchasing which the possession of it conveys. Thus when we say, that the circulating money of England has been computed at eighteen millions, we mean only to express the amount of the metal pieces, which some writers have computed, or rather have supposed to circulate in that country. But when we say that a man is worth fifty or a hundred pounds a-year, we mean commonly to express not only the amount of the metal pieces which are annually paid to him, but the value of the goods which he can annually purchase or consume. We mean commonly to ascertain what is or ought to be his way of living, or the quantity and quality of the necessaries and conveniencies of life in which he can with propriety indulge himself.

When, by any particular sum of money, we mean not only to express the amount of the metal pieces of which it is composed, but to include in its signification some obscure reference to the goods which can be had in exchange for them, the wealth or revenue which it in this case denotes, is equal only to one of the two values which are thus intimated somewhat ambiguously by the same word, and to the latter more properly than to the former, to the money's worth more properly than to the money.

Thus if a guinea be the weekly pension of a particular person, he can in the course of the week purchase with it a certain quantity of subsistence, conveniencies, and amusements. In proportion as this quantity is great or small, so are his real riches, his real weekly revenue. His weekly revenue is certainly not equal both to the guinea, and to what can be purchased with it, but only to one or other of those two equal values; and to the latter more properly than to the former, to the guinea's worth rather than to the guinea.

If the pension of such a person was paid to him, not in gold, but in a weekly bill for a guinea, his revenue surely would not so properly consist in the piece of paper, as in what he could get for it. A guinea may be considered as a bill for a certain quantity of necessaries and conveniences upon all the tradesmen in the neighbourhood. The revenue of the person to whom it is paid, does not so properly consist in the piece of gold, as in what he can get for it, or in what he can exchange it for. If it could be exchanged for nothing, it would, like a bill upon a bankrupt, be of no more value than the most useless piece of paper.

Though the weekly or yearly revenue of all the different inhabitants of any country, in the same manner, may be, and in reality frequently is paid to them in money, their real riches, however, the real weekly or yearly revenue of all of them taken together, must always be great or small in proportion to the quantity of consumable goods which they can all of them purchase with this money. The whole revenue of all of them taken together is evidently not equal to both the money and the consumable goods; but only to one or other of those two values, and to the latter more properly than to the former.

Though we frequently, therefore, express a person's revenue by the metal pieces which are annually paid to him, it is because the amount of those pieces regulates the extent of his power of purchasing, or the value of the goods which he can annually afford to consume. We still consider his revenue as consisting in this power of purchasing or consuming, and not in the pieces which convey it.

But if this is sufficiently evident even with regard to an individual, it is still more so with regard to a society. The amount of the metal pieces which are annually paid to an individual, is often precisely equal to his revenue, and is upon that account the shortest and best expression of its value. But the amount of the metal pieces which circulate in a society, can never be equal to the revenue of all its members. As the same guinea which pays the weekly pension of one man to-day, may pay that of another to-morrow, and that of a third the day thereafter, the amount of the metal pieces which annually circulate in any country, must always be of much less value than the whole money pensions annually paid with them. But the power of purchasing, or the goods which can successively be bought with the whole of those money pensions as they are successively paid, must always be precisely of the same value with those pensions; as must likewise be the revenue of the different persons to whom they are paid. That revenue, therefore, cannot consist in those metal pieces, of which the amount is so much inferior to its value, but in the power of purchasing, in the goods which can successively be bought with them as they circulate from hand to hand.

Money, therefore, the great wheel of circulation, the great instrument of commerce, like all other instruments of trade, though it makes a part and a very valuable part of the capital, makes no part of the revenue of the society to which it belongs; and though the metal pieces of which it is composed, in the course of their annual circulation, distribute to every man the revenue which properly belongs to him, they make themselves no part of that revenue.

Thirdly, and lastly, the machines and instruments of trade, &c. which compose the fixed capital, bear this further resemblance to that part of the circulating capital which consists in money; that as every saving in the expence of erecting and supporting those machines, which does not diminish the productive powers of labour, is an improvement of the neat revenue of the society; so every saving in the expence of collecting and supporting that part of the circulating capital which consists in money, is an improvement of exactly the same kind.

It is sufficiently obvious, and it has partly too been explained already, in what manner every saving in the expence of supporting the fixed capital is an improvement of the neat revenue of the society. The whole capital of the undertaker of every work is necessarily divided between his fixed and his circulating capital. While his whole capital remains the same, the smaller the one part, the greater must necessarily be the other. It is the circulating capital which furnishes the materials and wages of labour, and puts industry into motion. Every saving, therefore, in the expence of maintaining the fixed capital, which does not diminish the productive powers of labour, must increase the fund which puts industry into motion, and consequently the annual produce of land and labour, the real revenue of every society.

The substitution of paper in the room of gold and silver money, replaces a very expensive instrument of commerce with one much less costly, and sometimes equally convenient. Circulation comes to be carried on by a new wheel, which it costs less both to erect and to maintain than the old one. But in what manner this operation is performed, and in what manner it tends to increase either the gross or the neat revenue of the society, is not altogether so obvious, and may therefore require some further explication.

There are several different sorts of paper money; but the circulating notes of banks and bankers are the species which is best known, and which seems best adapted for this purpose.

When the people of any particular country have such confidence in the fortune, probity, and prudence of a particular banker, as to believe that he is always ready to pay upon demand such of his promissory notes as are likely to be at any time presented to him; those notes come to have the same currency as gold and silver money, from the confidence that such money can at any time be had for them.

A particular banker lends among his customers his own promissory notes, to the extent, we shall suppose, of a hundred thousand pounds. As those notes serve all the purposes of money, his debtors pay him the same interest as if he had lent them so much money. This interest is the source of his gain. Though some of those notes are continually coming back upon him for payment, part of them continue to circulate for months and years together. Though he has generally in circulation, therefore, notes to the extent of a hundred thousand pounds, twenty thousand pounds in gold and silver may, frequently, be a sufficient provision for answering occasional demands. By this operation, therefore, twenty thousand pounds in gold and silver perform all the functions which a hundred thousand could otherwise have performed. The same exchanges may be made, the same quantity of consumable goods may be circulated and distributed to their proper consumers, by means of his promissory notes, to the value of a hundred thousand pounds, as by an equal value of gold and silver money. Eighty thousand pounds of gold and silver, therefore, can, in this manner, be spared from the circulation of the country; and if different operations of the same kind should, at the same time, be carried on by many different banks and bankers, the whole circulation may thus be conducted with a fifth part only of the gold and silver which would otherwise have been requisite.

Let us suppose, for example, that the whole circulating money of some particular country amounted, at a particular time, to one million sterling, that sum being then sufficient for circulating the whole annual produce of their land and labour. Let us suppose too, that some time thereafter, different banks and bankers issued promissory notes, payable to the bearer, to the extent of one million, reserving in their different coffers two hundred thousand pounds for answering occasional demands. There would remain, therefore, in circulation, eight hundred thousand pounds in gold and silver, and a million of bank notes, or eighteen hundred thousand pounds of paper and money together. But the annual produce of the land and labour of the country had before required only one million to circulate and distribute it to its proper consumers, and that annual produce cannot be immediately augmented by those operations of banking. One million, therefore, will be sufficient to circulate it after them. The goods to be bought and sold being precisely the same as before, the same quantity of money will be sufficient for buying and selling them. The channel of circulation, if I may be allowed such an expression, will remain precisely the same as before. One million we have supposed sufficient to fill that channel. Whatever, therefore, is poured into it beyond this sum, cannot run in it, but must overflow. One million eight hundred thousand pounds are poured into it. Eight hundred thousand pounds, therefore, must overflow, that sum being over and above what can be employed in the circulation of the country. But though this sum cannot be employed at home, it is too valuable to be allowed to lie idle. It will, therefore, be sent abroad, in order to seek that profitable employment which it cannot find at home. But the paper cannot go abroad; because at a distance from the banks which issue it, and from the country in which payment of it can be exacted by law, it will not be received in common payments. Gold and silver, therefore, to the amount of eight hundred thousand pounds will be sent abroad, and the channel of home circulation will remain filled with a million of paper, instead of the million of those metals which filled it before.

But though so great a quantity of gold and silver is thus sent abroad, we must not imagine that it is sent abroad for nothing, or that its proprietors make a present of it to foreign nations. They will exchange it for foreign goods of some kind or another, in order to supply the consumption either of some other foreign country, or of their own.

If they employ it in purchasing goods in one foreign country in order to supply the consumption of another, or in what is called the carrying trade, whatever profit they make will be an addition to the neat revenue of their own country. It is like a new fund, created for carrying on a new trade; domestic business being now transacted by paper, and the gold and silver being converted into a fund for this new trade.

If they employ it in purchasing foreign goods for home consumption, they may either, first, purchase such goods as are likely to be consumed by idle people who produce nothing, such as foreign wines, foreign silks, &c.; or, secondly, they may purchase an additional stock of materials, tools, and provisions, in order to maintain and employ an additional number of industrious people, who reproduce, with a profit, the value of their annual consumption.

So far as it is employed in the first way, it promotes prodigality, increases expence and consumption without increasing production, or establishing any permanent fund for supporting that expence, and is in every respect hurtful to the society.

So far as it is employed in the second way, it promotes industry; and though it increases the consumption of the society, it provides a permanent fund for supporting that consumption, the people who consume re-producing, with a profit, the whole value of their annual consumption. The gross revenue of the society, the annual produce of their land and labour, is increased by the whole value which the labour of those workmen adds to the materials upon which they are employed; and their neat revenue by what remains of this value, after deducting what is necessary for supporting the tools and instruments of their trade.

That the greater part of the gold and silver which, being forced abroad by those operations of banking, is employed in purchasing foreign goods for home consumption, is and must be employed in purchasing those of this second kind, seems not only probable but almost unavoidable. Though some particular men may sometimes increase their expence very considerably though their revenue does not increase at all, we may be assured that no class or order of men ever does so; because, though the principles of common prudence do not always govern the conduct of every individual, they always influence that of the majority of every class or order. But the revenue of idle people, considered as a class or order, cannot, in the smallest degree, be increased by those operations of banking. Their expence in general, therefore, cannot be much increased by them, though that of a few individuals among them may, and in reality sometimes is. The demand of idle people, therefore, for foreign goods, being the same, or very nearly the same, as before, a very small part of the money, which being forced abroad by those operations of banking, is employed in purchasing foreign goods for home consumption, is likely to be employed in purchasing those for their use. The greater part of it will naturally be destined for the employment of industry, and not for the maintenance of idleness.

[The phrase "will be naturally destined" in the sentence above tells us a lot about Smith as a thinker and about how the argument of

the *WN* works. At several places in Chapter III below, he uses the
words "destined" or "destination" to explain why capital is invested
in productive labor. Along the way, however, Smith identifies a
certain type of person as the agent of capital's destiny. The ethical
qualities of that person are vital to the overall argument of the
WN. As I point out in Appendix I, this is where Smith begins to
"moralise" about how people should spend their money.]

CHAPTER III

OF THE ACCUMULATION OF CAPITAL, OR OF PRODUCTIVE AND UNPRODUCTIVE LABOUR

There is one sort of labour which adds to the value of the subject upon
which it is bestowed: there is another which has no such effect. The
former, as it produces a value, may be called productive; the latter, unproductive labour. Thus the labour of a manufacturer adds, generally, to the
value of the materials which he works upon, that of his own maintenance,
and of his master's profit. The labour of a menial servant, on the contrary,
adds to the value of nothing. Though the manufacturer has his wages
advanced to him by his master, he, in reality, costs him no expence, the
value of those wages being generally restored, together with a profit, in
the improved value of the subject upon which his labour is bestowed. But
the maintenance of a menial servant never is restored. A man grows rich by
employing a multitude of manufacturers: he grows poor, by maintaining a
multitude of menial servants. The labour of the latter, however, has its
value, and deserves its reward as well as that of the former. But the labour
of the manufacturer fixes and realizes itself in some particular subject or
vendible commodity, which lasts for some time at least after that labour
is past. It is, as it were, a certain quantity of labour stocked and stored
up to be employed, if necessary, upon some other occasion. That subject,
or what is the same thing, the price of that subject, can afterwards, if
necessary, put into motion a quantity of labour equal to that which had
originally produced it. The labour of the menial servant, on the contrary,
does not fix or realize itself in any particular subject or vendible commodity. His services generally perish in the very instant of their performance,
and seldom leave any trace or value behind them, for which an equal
quantity of service could afterwards be procured.

The labour of some of the most respectable orders in the society is,
like that of menial servants, unproductive of any value, and does not fix
or realize itself in any permanent subject, or vendible commodity, which

endures after that labour is past, and for which an equal quantity of labour could afterwards be procured. The sovereign, for example, with all the officers both of justice and war who serve under him, the whole army and navy, are unproductive labourers. They are the servants of the public, and are maintained by a part of the annual produce of the industry of other people. Their service, how honourable, how useful, or how necessary soever, produces nothing for which an equal quantity of service can afterwards be procured. The protection, security, and defence of the commonwealth, the effect of their labour this year, will not purchase its protection, security, and defence for the year to come. In the same class must be ranked, some both of the gravest and most important, and some of the most frivolous professions: churchmen, lawyers, physicians, men of letters of all kinds; players, buffoons, musicians, opera-singers, opera-dancers, &c. The labour of the meanest of these has a certain value, regulated by the very same principles which regulate that of every other sort of labour; and that of the noblest and most useful, produces nothing which could afterwards purchase or procure an equal quantity of labour. Like the declamation of the actor, the harangue of the orator, or the tune of the musician, the work of all of them perishes in the very instant of its production.

Both productive and unproductive labourers, and those who do not labour at all, are all equally maintained by the annual produce of the land and labour of the country. This produce, how great soever, can never be infinite, but must have certain limits. According, therefore, as a smaller or greater proportion of it is in any one year employed in maintaining unproductive hands, the more in the one case and the less in the other will remain for the productive, and the next year's produce will be greater or smaller accordingly; the whole annual produce, if we except the spontaneous productions of the earth, being the effect of productive labour.

Though the whole annual produce of the land and labour of every country, is, no doubt, ultimately destined for supplying the consumption of its inhabitants, and for procuring a revenue to them; yet when it first comes either from the ground, or from the hands of the productive labourers, it naturally divides itself into two parts. One of them, and frequently the largest, is, in the first place, destined for replacing a capital, or for renewing the provisions, materials, and finished work, which had been withdrawn from a capital; the other for constituting a revenue either to the owner of this capital, as the profit of his stock; or to some other person, as the rent of his land. Thus, of the produce of land, one part replaces the capital of the farmer; the other pays his profit and the rent of the landlord; and thus constitutes a revenue both to the owner of this capital, as the profits of his stock; and to some other person, as the rent of his land. Of the produce of a great manufactory, in the same manner, one part, and that always the largest, replaces the capital of the undertaker of the work; the other pays his profit, and thus constitutes a revenue to the owner of this capital.

That part of the annual produce of the land and labour of any country which replaces a capital, never is immediately employed to maintain any but productive hands. It pays the wages of productive labour only. That which is immediately destined for constituting a revenue either as profit or as rent, may maintain indifferently either productive or unproductive hands.

Whatever part of his stock a man employs as a capital, he always expects is to be replaced to him with a profit. He employs it, therefore, in maintaining productive hands only; and after having served in the function of a capital to him, it constitutes a revenue to them. Whenever he employs any part of it in maintaining unproductive hands of any kind, that part is, from that moment, withdrawn from his capital, and placed in his stock reserved for immediate consumption.

Unproductive labourers, and those who do not labour at all, are all maintained by revenue; either, first, by that part of the annual produce which is originally destined for constituting a revenue to some particular persons, either as the rent of land or as the profits of stock; or, secondly, by that part which, though originally destined for replacing a capital and for maintaining productive labourers only, yet when it comes into their hands, whatever part of it is over and above their necessary subsistence, may be employed in maintaining indifferently either productive or unproductive hands. Thus, not only the great landlord or the rich merchant, but even the common workman, if his wages are considerable, may maintain a menial servant; or he may sometimes go to a play or a puppet-show, and so contribute his share towards maintaining one set of unproductive labourers; or he may pay some taxes, and thus help to maintain another set, more honourable and useful, indeed, but equally unproductive. No part of the annual produce, however, which had been originally destined to replace a capital, is ever directed towards maintaining unproductive hands, till after it has put into motion its full complement of productive labour, or all that it could put into motion in the way in which it was employed. The workman must have earned his wages by work done, before he can employ any part of them in this manner. That part too is generally but a small one. It is his spare revenue only, of which productive labourers have seldom a great deal. They generally have some, however; and in the payment of taxes the greatness of their number may compensate, in some measure, the smallness of their contribution. The rent of land and the profits of stock are every-where, therefore, the principal sources from which unproductive hands derive their subsistence. These are the two sorts of revenue of which the owners have generally most to spare. They might both maintain indifferently either productive or unproductive hands. They seem, however, to have some predilection for the latter. The expence of a great lord feeds generally more idle than industrious people. The rich merchant, though with his capital he maintains industrious people only, yet by his expence, that is, by the employment of his revenue, he feeds commonly the very same sort as the great lord.

The proportion, therefore, between the productive and unproductive hands, depends very much in every country upon the proportion between that part of the annual produce, which, as soon as it comes either from the ground or from the hands of the productive labourers, is destined for replacing a capital, and that which is destined for constituting a revenue, either as rent, or as profit. This proportion is very different in rich from what it is in poor countries.

Thus, at present, in the opulent countries of Europe, a very large, frequently the largest portion of the produce of the land, is destined for replacing the capital of the rich and independent farmer; the other for paying his profits, and the rent of the landlord. But anciently, during the prevalency of the feudal government, a very small portion of the produce was sufficient to replace the capital employed in cultivation. It consisted commonly in a few wretched cattle, maintained altogether by the spontaneous produce of uncultivated land, and which might, therefore, be considered as a part of that spontaneous produce. It generally too belonged to the landlord, and was by him advanced to the occupiers of the land. All the rest of the produce properly belonged to him too, either as rent for his land, or as profit upon this paultry capital. The occupiers of land were generally bondmen, whose persons and effects were equally his property. Those who were not bondmen were tenants at will, and though the rent which they paid was often nominally little more than a quit-rent, it really amounted to the whole produce of the land. Their lord could at all times command their labour in peace, and their service in war. Though they lived at a distance from his house, they were equally dependent upon him as his retainers who lived in it. But the whole produce of the land undoubtedly belongs to him, who can dispose of the labour and service of all those whom it maintains. In the present state of Europe, the share of the landlord seldom exceeds a third, sometimes not a fourth part of the whole produce of the land. The rent of land, however, in all the improved parts of the country, has been tripled and quadrupled since those ancient times; and this third or fourth part of the annual produce is, it seems, three or four times greater than the whole had been before.

In the progress of improvement, rent, though it increases in proportion to the extent, diminishes in proportion to the produce of the land.

In the opulent countries of Europe, great capitals are at present employed in trade and manufactures. In the ancient state, the little trade that was stirring, and the few homely and coarse manufactures that were carried on, required but very small capitals. These, however, must have yielded very large profits. The rate of interest was no-where less than ten per cent. and their profits must have been sufficient to afford this great interest. At present the rate of interest, in the improved parts of Europe, is no-where higher than six per cent. and in some of the most improved it is so low as four, three, and two per cent. Though that part of the revenue of the inhabitants which is derived from the profits of stock is always much greater in rich than in poor countries, it is because the stock is much greater: in proportion to the stock the profits are generally much less.

That part of the annual produce, therefore, which, as soon as it comes either from the ground, or from the hands of the productive labourers, is destined for replacing a capital, is not only much greater in rich than in poor countries, but bears a much greater proportion to that which is immediately destined for constituting a revenue either as rent or as profit. The funds destined for the maintenance of productive labour, are not only much greater in the former than in the latter, but bear a much greater proportion to those which, though they may be employed to maintain either productive or unproductive hands, have generally a predilection for the latter.

The proportion between those different funds necessarily determines in every country the general character of the inhabitants as to industry or idleness. We are more industrious than our forefathers; because in the present times the funds destined for the maintenance of industry, are much greater in proportion to those which are likely to be employed in the maintenance of idleness, than they were two or three centuries ago. Our ancestors were idle for want of a sufficient encouragement to industry. It is better, says the proverb, to play for nothing, than to work for nothing. In mercantile and manufacturing towns, where the inferior ranks of people are chiefly maintained by the employment of capital, they are in general industrious, sober, and thriving; as in many English, and in most Dutch towns. In those towns which are principally supported by the constant or occasional residence of a court, and in which the inferior ranks of people are chiefly maintained by the spending of revenue, they are in general idle, dissolute, and poor; as at Rome, Versailles, Compiegne, and Fontainbleau. If you except Rouen and Bourdeaux, there is little trade or industry in any of the parliament towns of France; and the inferior ranks of people, being chiefly maintained by the expence of the members of the courts of justice, and of those who come to plead before them, are in general idle and poor. The great trade of Rouen and Bourdeaux seems to be altogether the effect of their situation. Rouen is necessarily the entrepot of almost all the goods which are brought either from foreign countries, or from the maritime provinces of France, for the consumption of the great city of Paris. Bourdeaux is in the same manner the entrepôt of the wines which grow upon the banks of the Garonne, and of the rivers which run into it, one of the richest wine countries in the world, and which seems to produce the wine fittest for exportation, or best suited to the taste of foreign nations. Such advantageous situations necessarily attract a great capital by the great employment which they afford it; and the employment of this capital is the cause of the industry of those two cities. In the other parliament towns of France, very little more capital seems to be employed than what is necessary for supplying their own consumption; that is, little more than the smallest capital which can be employed in them. The same thing may be said of Paris, Madrid, and Vienna. Of those three cities, Paris is by far the most industrious: but Paris itself is the principal market of all the manufactures established at Paris, and its own consumption is the principal object of all the trade which it carries on. London, Lisbon, and Copenhagen, are, perhaps, the only three cities in Europe, which are both the constant residence of a court, and can at the same time be considered as trading cities, or as cities which trade not only for their own consumption, but for that of other cities and countries. The situation of all the three is extremely advantageous, and naturally fits them to be the entrepôts of a great part of the goods destined for the consumption of distant places. In a city where a great revenue is spent, to employ with advantage a capital for any other purpose than for supplying the consumption of that city, is probably more difficult than in one in which the inferior ranks of people have no other maintenance but what they derive from the employment of such a capital. The idleness of the greater part of the people who are maintained by the expence of revenue, corrupts, it is probable, the industry of those who ought to be maintained by the employment of capital, and renders it less advantageous to employ a capital there than in other places. There was little trade or industry in Edinburgh before the union. When the Scotch parliament was no longer to be assembled in it, when it ceased to be the necessary residence of the principal nobility and gentry of Scotland, it became a city of some trade and industry. It still continues, however, to be the residence of the principal courts of justice in Scotland, of the boards of customs and excise, &c. A considerable revenue, therefore, still continues to be spent in it. In trade and industry it is much inferior to

Glasgow, of which the inhabitants are chiefly maintained by the employment of capital. The inhabitants of a large village, it has sometimes been observed, after having made considerable progress in manufactures, have become idle and poor, in consequence of a great lord's having taken up his residence in their neighbourhood.

The proportion between capital and revenue, therefore, seems everywhere to regulate the proportion between industry and idleness. Wherever capital predominates, industry prevails: wherever revenue, idleness. Every increase or diminution of capital, therefore, naturally tends to increase or diminish the real quantity of industry, the number of productive hands, and consequently the exchangeable value of the annual produce of the land and labour of the country, the real wealth and revenue of all its inhabitants.

Capitals are increased by parsimony, and diminished by prodigality and misconduct.

Whatever a person saves from his revenue he adds to his capital, and either employs it himself in maintaining an additional number of productive hands, or enables some other person to do so, by lending it to him for an interest, that is, for a share of the profits. As the capital of an individual can be increased only by what he saves from his annual revenue or his annual gains, so the capital of a society, which is the same with that of all the individuals who compose it, can be increased only in the same manner.

Parsimony, and not industry, is the immediate cause of the increase of capital. Industry, indeed, provides the subject which parsimony accumulates. But whatever industry might acquire, if parsimony did not save and store up, the capital would never be the greater.

Parsimony, by increasing the fund which is destined for the maintenance of productive hands, tends to increase the number of those hands whose labour adds to the value of the subject upon which it is bestowed. It tends therefore to increase the exchangeable value of the annual produce of the land and labour of the country. It puts into motion an additional quantity of industry, which gives an additional value to the annual produce.

What is annually saved is as regularly consumed as what is annually spent, and nearly in the same time too; but it is consumed by a different set of people. That portion of his revenue which a rich man annually spends, is in most cases consumed by idle guests, and menial servants, who leave nothing behind them in return for their consumption. That portion which he annually saves, as for the sake of the profit it is immediately employed as a capital, is consumed in the same manner, and nearly in the same time too, but by a different set of people, by labourers, manufacturers, and artificers, who re-produce with a profit the value of their annual consumption. His revenue, we shall suppose, is paid him in money. Had he spent the whole, the food, clothing, and lodging, which the whole could have purchased, would have been distributed among the former set of people. By saving a part of it, as that part is for the sake of the profit immediately employed as a capital either by himself or by some other person, the food, clothing, and lodging, which may be purchased with it, are necessarily reserved for the latter. The consumption is the same, but the consumers are different.

By what a frugal man annually saves, he not only affords maintenance to an additional number of productive hands, for that or the ensuing year, but, like the founder of a public workhouse, he establishes as it were a perpetual fund for the maintenance of an equal number in all times to come. The perpetual allotment and destination of this fund, indeed, is not always guarded by any positive law, by any trust-right or deed of mortmain. It is always guarded, however, by a very powerful principle, the plain and evident interest of every individual to whom any share of it shall ever belong. No part of it can ever afterwards be employed to maintain any but productive hands, without an evident loss to the person who thus perverts it from its proper destination.

The prodigal perverts it in this manner. By not confining his expence within his income, he encroaches upon his capital. Like him who perverts the revenues of some pious foundation to profane purposes, he pays the wages of idleness with those funds which the frugality of his forefathers had, as it were, consecrated to the maintenance of industry. By diminishing the funds destined for the employment of productive labour, he necessarily diminishes, so far as it depends upon him, the quantity of that labour which adds a value to the subject upon which it is bestowed, and, consequently, the value of the annual produce of the land and labour of the whole country, the real wealth and revenue of its inhabitants. If the prodigality of some was not compensated by the frugality of others, the conduct of every prodigal, by feeding the idle with the bread of the industrious, tends not only to beggar himself, but to impoverish his country.

Though the expence of the prodigal should be altogether in home-made, and no part of it in foreign commodities, its effect upon the productive funds of the society would still be the same. Every year there would still be a certain quantity of food and clothing, which ought to have maintained productive, employed in maintaining unproductive hands. Every year, therefore, there would still be some diminution in what would otherwise have been the value of the annual produce of the land and labour of the country.

This expence, it may be said indeed, not being in foreign goods, and not occasioning any exportation of gold and silver, the same quantity of money would remain in the country as before. But if the quantity of food and clothing, which were thus consumed by unproductive, had been distributed among productive hands, they would have re-produced, together with a profit, the full value of their consumption. The same quantity of money would in this case equally have remained in the country, and there would besides have been a reproduction of an equal value of consumable goods. There would have been two values instead of one.

The same quantity of money, besides, cannot long remain in any country in which the value of the annual produce diminishes. The sole use of money is to circulate consumable goods. By means of it, provisions, materials, and finished work, are bought and sold, and distributed to their proper consumers. The quantity of money, therefore, which can be annually employed in any country, must be determined by the value of the consumable goods annually circulated within it. These must consist either in the immediate produce of the land and labour of the country itself, or in something which had been purchased with some part of that produce. Their value, therefore, must diminish as the value of that produce diminishes, and along with it the quantity of money which can be employed in circulating them. But the money which by this annual diminution of produce is annually thrown out of domestic circulation, will not be allowed to lie idle. The interest of whoever possesses it, requires that it should be employed. But having no employment at home, it will, in spite of all laws and prohibitions, be sent abroad, and employed in purchasing consumable goods which may be of some use at home. Its annual exportation will in this manner continue for some time to add something to the annual consumption of the country beyond the value of its own annual produce. What in the days of its prosperity had been saved from that annual produce, and employed in purchasing gold and silver, will contribute for some little time to support its consumption in adversity. The exportation of gold and silver is, in this case, not the cause, but the effect of its declension, and may even, for some little time, alleviate the misery of that declension.

The quantity of money, on the contrary, must in every country naturally increase as the value of the annual produce increases. The value of the consumable goods annually circulated within the society being greater, will require a greater quantity of money to circulate them. A part of the increased produce, therefore, will naturally be employed in purchasing, wherever it is to be had, the additional quantity of gold and silver necessary for circulating the rest. The increase of those metals will in this case be the effect, not the cause, of the public prosperity. Gold and silver are purchased every-where in the same manner. The food, clothing, and lodging, the revenue and maintenance of all those whose labour or stock is employed in bringing them from the mine to the market, is the price paid for them in Peru as well as in England. The country which has this price to pay, will never be long without the quantity of those metals which it has occasion for; and no country will ever long retain a quantity which it has no occasion for.

Whatever, therefore, we may imagine the real wealth and revenue of a country to consist in, whether in the value of the annual produce of its land and labour, as plain reason seems to dictate; or in the quantity of the precious metals which circulate within it, as vulgar prejudices suppose; in either view of the matter, every prodigal appears to be a public enemy, and every frugal man a public benefactor.

The effects of misconduct are often the same as those of prodigality. Every injudicious and unsuccessful project in agriculture, mines, fisheries, trade, or manufactures, tends in the same manner to diminish the funds destined for the maintenance of productive labour. In every such project, though the capital is consumed by productive hands only, yet, as by the injudicious manner in which they are employed, they do not reproduce the full value of their consumption, there must always be some diminution in what would otherwise have been the productive funds of the society.

It can seldom happen, indeed, that the circumstances of a great nation can be much affected either by the prodigality or misconduct of individuals; the profusion or imprudence of some, being always more than compensated by the frugality and good conduct of others.

With regard to profusion, the principle which prompts to expence, is the passion for present enjoyment; which, though sometimes violent and very difficult to be restrained, is in general only momentary and occasional. But the principle which prompts to save, is the desire of bettering our condition, a desire which, though generally calm and dispassionate, comes with us from the womb, and never leaves us till we go into the grave. In the whole interval which separates those two moments, there is scarce perhaps a single instant in which any man is so perfectly and completely satisfied with his situation, as to be without any wish of alteration or improvement of any kind. An augmentation of fortune is the means by which the greater part of men propose and wish to better their condition. It is the means the most vulgar and the most obvious; and the most likely way of augmenting their fortune, is to save and accumulate some part of what they acquire, either regularly and annually, or upon some extraordinary occasions. Though the principle of expence, therefore, prevails in almost all men upon some occasions, and in some men upon almost all occasions, yet in the greater part of men, taking the whole course of their life at an average, the principle of frugality seems not only to predominate, but to predominate very greatly.

With regard to misconduct, the number of prudent and successful undertakings is every-where much greater than that of injudicious and unsuccessful ones. After all our complaints of the frequency of bankruptcies, the unhappy men who fall into this misfortune make but a very small part of the whole number engaged in trade, and all other sorts of business; not much more perhaps than one in a thousand. Bankruptcy is perhaps the greatest and most humiliating calamity which can befal an innocent man. The greater part of men, therefore, are sufficiently careful to avoid it. Some, indeed, do not avoid it; as some do not avoid the gallows.

Great nations are never impoverished by private, though they sometimes are by public prodigality and misconduct. The whole, or almost the whole public revenue, is in most countries employed in maintaining unproductive hands. Such are the people who compose a numerous and splendid court, a great ecclesiastical establishment, great fleets and armies, who in time of peace produce nothing, and in time of war acquire nothing which can compensate the expence of maintaining them, even while the war lasts. Such people, as they themselves produce nothing, are all maintained by the produce of other men's labour. When multiplied, therefore, to an unnecessary number, they may in a particular year consume so great a share of this produce, as not to leave a sufficiency for maintaining the productive labourers, who should reproduce it next year. The next year's produce, therefore, will be less than that of the foregoing, and if the same disorder should continue, that of the third year will be still less than that of the second. Those unproductive hands, who should be maintained by a part only of the spare revenue of the people, may consume so great a share of their whole revenue, and therefore oblige so great a number to encroach upon their capitals, upon the funds destined for the maintenance of productive labour, that all the frugality and good conduct of individuals may not be able to compensate the waste and degradation of produce occasioned by this violent and forced encroachment.

This frugality and good conduct, however, is upon most occasions, it appears from experience, sufficient to compensate, not only the private prodigality and misconduct of individuals, but the public extravagance of government. The uniform, constant, and uninterrupted effort of every man to better his condition, the principle from which public and national, as well as private opulence is originally derived, is frequently powerful enough to maintain the natural progress of things toward improvement, in spite both of the extravagance of government, and of the greatest errors of administration. Like the unknown principle of animal life, it frequently restores health and vigour to the constitution, in spite, not only of the disease, but of the absurd prescriptions of the doctor.

The annual produce of the land and labour of any nation can be increased in its value by no other means, but by increasing either the number of its productive labourers, or the productive powers of those labourers who had before been employed. The number of its productive labourers, it is evident, can never be much increased, but in consequence of an increase of capital, or of the funds destined for maintaining them. The productive powers of the same number of labourers cannot be increased, but in consequence either of some addition and improvement to those machines and instruments which facilitate and abridge labour; or of a more proper division and distribution of employment. In either case an additional capital is almost always required. It is by means of an additional capital only, that the undertaker of any work can either provide his workmen with better machinery, or make a more proper distribution of employment among them. When the work to be done consists of a number of parts, to keep every man constantly employed in one way, requires a much greater capital than where every man is occasionally employed in every different part of the work. When we compare, therefore, the state of a nation at two different periods, and find, that the annual produce of its land and labour is evidently greater at the latter than at the former, that its lands are better cultivated, its manufactures more numerous and more flourishing, and its trade more extensive, we may be assured that its capital must have increased during the interval between those two periods, and that more must have been added to it by the good conduct of some, than had been taken from it either by the private misconduct of others, or by the public extravagance of government. But we shall find this to have been the case of almost all nations, in all tolerably quiet and peaceful times, even of those who have not enjoyed the most prudent and parsimonious governments. To form a right judgment of it, indeed, we must compare the state of the country at periods somewhat distant from one another. The progress is frequently so gradual, that, at near periods, the improvement is not only not sensible, but from the declension either of certain branches of industry, or of certain districts of the country, things which sometimes happen though the country in general be in great prosperity, there frequently arises a suspicion, that the riches and industry of the whole are decaying.

The annual produce of the land and labour of England, for example, is certainly much greater than it was, a little more than a century ago, at the restoration of Charles II. Though, at present, few people, I believe, doubt of this, yet during this period, five years have seldom passed away in which some book or pamphlet has not been published, written too with such abilities as to gain some authority with the public, and pretending to demonstrate that the wealth of the nation was fast declining, that the country was depopulated, agriculture neglected, manufactures decaying, and trade undone. Nor have these publications been all party pamphlets, the wretched offspring of falsehood and venality. Many of them have been written by very candid and very intelligent people; who wrote nothing but what they believed, and for no other reason but because they believed it.

The annual produce of the land and labour of England again, was certainly much greater at the restoration, than we can suppose it to have been about an hundred years before, at the accession of Elizabeth. At this period too, we have all reason to believe, the country was much more advanced in improvement, than it had been about a century before, towards the close of the dissensions between the houses of York and Lancaster. Even then it was, probably, in a better condition than it had been at the Norman conquest, and at the Norman conquest, than during the confusion of the Saxon Heptarchy. Even at this early period, it was certainly a more improved country than at the invasion of Julius Cæsar, when its inhabitants were nearly in the same state with the savages in North America.

In each of those periods, however, there was, not only much private and public profusion, many expensive and unnecessary wars, great perversion of the annual produce from maintaining productive to maintain unproductive hands; but sometimes, in the confusion of civil discord, such absolute waste and destruction of stock, as might be supposed, not only to retard, as it certainly did, the natural accumulation of riches, but to have left the country, at the end of the period, poorer than at the beginning. Thus, in the happiest and most fortunate period of them all, that which has passed since the restoration, how many disorders and misfortunes have occurred, which, could they have been foreseen, not only the impoverishment, but the total ruin of the country would have been expected from them? The fire and the plague of London, the two Dutch wars, the disorders of the revolution, the war in Ireland, the four expensive French wars of 1688, 1702, 1742, and 1756, together with the two rebellions of 1715 and 1745. In the course of the four French wars, the nation has contracted more than a hundred and forty-five millions of debt, over and above all the other extraordinary annual expence which they occasioned, so that the whole cannot be computed at less than two hundred millions. So great a share of the annual produce of the land and labour of the country, has, since the revolution, been employed upon different occasions, in maintaining an extraordinary number of unproductive hands. But had not those wars given this particular direction to so large a capital, the greater part of it would naturally have been employed in maintaining productive hands, whose labour would have replaced, with a profit, the whole value of their consumption. The value of the annual produce of the land and labour of the country, would have been considerably increased by it every year, and every year's increase would have augmented still more that of the following year. More houses would have been built, more lands would have been improved, and those which had been improved before would have been better cultivated, more manufactures would have been established, and those which had been established before would have been more extended; and to what height the real wealth and revenue of the country might, by this time, have been raised, it is not perhaps very easy even to imagine.

But though the profusion of government must, undoubtedly, have retarded the natural progress of England towards wealth and improvement, it has not been able to stop it. The annual produce of its land and labour is, undoubtedly, much greater at present than it was either at the restoration or at the revolution. The capital, therefore, annually employed in cultivating this land, and in maintaining this labour, must likewise be much greater. In the midst of all the exactions of government, this capital has been silently and gradually accumulated by the private frugality and good conduct of individuals, by their universal, continual, and uninterrupted effort to better their own condition. It is this effort, protected by law and allowed by liberty to exert itself in the manner that is most advantageous, which has maintained the progress of England towards opulence and improvement in almost all former times, and which, it is to be hoped, will do so in all future times. England, however, as it has never been blessed with a very parsimonious government, so parsimony has at no time been the characteristical virtue of its inhabitants. It is the highest impertinence and presumption, therefore, in kings and ministers, to pretend to watch over the oeconomy of private people, and to restrain their expence, either by sumptuary laws, or by prohibiting the importation of foreign luxuries. They are themselves always, and without any exception, the greatest spendthrifts in the society. Let them look well after their own expence, and they may safely trust private people with theirs. If their own extravagance does not ruin the state, that of their subjects never will.

As frugality increases, and prodigality diminishes the public capital, so the conduct of those whose expence just equals their revenue, without either accumulating or encroaching, neither increases nor diminishes it. Some modes of expence, however, seem to contribute more to the growth of public opulence than others.

The revenue of an individual may be spent, either in things which are consumed immediately, and in which one day's expence can neither alleviate nor support that of another; or it may be spent in things more durable, which can therefore be accumulated, and in which every day's expence may, as he chuses, either alleviate or support and heighten the effect of that of the following day. A man of fortune, for example, may either spend his revenue in a profuse and sumptuous table, and in maintaining a great number of menial servants, and a multitude of dogs and horses; or contenting himself with a frugal table and few attendants, he may lay out the greater part of it in adorning his house or his country villa, in useful or ornamental buildings, in useful or ornamental furniture, in collecting books, statues, pictures; or in things more frivolous, jewels, baubles, ingenious trinkets of different kinds; or, what is most trifling of all, in amassing a great wardrobe of fine clothes, like the favourite and minister of a great prince who died a few years ago. Were two men of equal fortune to spend their revenue, the one chiefly in the one way, the other in the other, the magnificence of the person whose expence had been chiefly in durable commodities, would be continually increasing, every day's expence contributing something to support and heighten the effect of that of the following day: that of the other, on the contrary, would be no greater at the end of the period than at the beginning. The former too would, at the end of the period, be the richer man of the two. He would have a stock of goods of some kind or other, which, though it might not be worth all that it cost, would always be worth something. No trace or vestige of the expence of the latter would remain, and the effects of ten or twenty years profusion would be as completely annihilated as if they had never existed.

As the one mode of expence is more favourable than the other to the opulence of an individual, so is it likewise to that of a nation. The houses, the furniture, the clothing of the rich, in a little time, become useful to the inferior and middling ranks of people. They are able to purchase then when their superiors grow weary of them, and the general accommodation of the whole people is thus gradually improved, when this mode of expence becomes universal among men of fortune. In countries which have long been rich, you will frequently find the inferior ranks of people in possession both of houses and furniture perfectly good and entire, but of which neither the one could have been built, nor the other have been made for their use. What was formerly a seat of the family of Seymour, is now an inn upon the Bath road. The marriage-bed of James the First of Great Britain, which his Queen brought with her from Denmark, as a present fit for a sovereign to make to a sovereign, was, a few years ago, the ornament of an ale-house at Dunfermline. In some ancient cities, which either have been long stationary, or have gone somewhat to decay, you will sometimes scarce find a single house which could have been built for its present inhabitants. If you go into those houses too, you will frequently find many excellent, though antiquated pieces of furniture, which are still very fit for use, and which could as little have been made for them. Noble palaces, magnificent villas, great collections of books, statues, pictures, and other curiosities, are frequently both an ornament and an honour, not only to the neighbourhood, but to the whole country to which they belong. Versailles is an ornament and an honour to France, Stowe and Wilton to England. Italy still continues to command some sort of veneration by the number of monuments of this kind which it possesses, though the wealth which produced them has decayed, and though the genius which planned them seems to be extinguished, perhaps from not having the same employment.

The expence too, which is laid out in durable commodities, is favourable, not only to accumulation, but to frugality. If a person should at any time exceed in it, he can easily reform without exposing himself to the censure of the public. To reduce very much the number of his servants, to reform his table from great profusion to great frugality, to lay down his equipage after he has once set it up, are changes which cannot escape the observation of his neighbours, and which are supposed to imply some acknowledgment of preceding bad conduct. Few, therefore, of those who have once been so unfortunate as to launch out too far into this sort of expence, have afterwards the courage to reform, till ruin and bankruptcy oblige them. But if a person has, at any time, been at too great an expence in building, in furniture, in books or pictures, no imprudence can be inferred from his changing his conduct. These are things in which further expence is frequently rendered unnecessary by former expence; and when a person stops short, he appears to do so, not because he has exceeded his fortune, but because he has satisfied his fancy.

The expence, besides, that is laid out in durable commodities, gives maintenance, commonly, to a greater number of people, than that which is employed in the most profuse hospitality. Of two or three hundred weight of provisions, which may sometimes be served up at a great festival, one-half, perhaps, is thrown to the dunghill, and there is always a great deal wasted and abused. But if the expence of this entertainment had been employed in setting to work masons, carpenters, upholsterers, mechanics, &c. a quantity of provisions, of equal value, would have been distributed among a still greater number of people, who would have bought them in penny-worths and pound weights, and not have lost or thrown away a single ounce of them. In the one way, besides, this expence maintains productive, in the other unproductive hands. In the one way, therefore, it increases, in the other, it does not increase, the exchangeable value of the annual produce of the land and labour of the country.

I would not, however, by all this be understood to mean, that the one species of expence always betokens a more liberal or generous spirit than the other. When a man of fortune spends his revenue chiefly in hospitality, he shares the greater part of it with his friends and companions; but when he employs it in purchasing such durable commodities, he often spends the whole upon his own person, and gives nothing to any body without an equivalent. The latter species of expence, therefore, especially when directed towards frivolous objects, the little ornaments of dress and furniture, jewels, trinkets, gewgaws, frequently indicates, not only a trifling, but a base and selfish disposition. All that I mean is, that the one sort of expence, as it always occasions some accumulation of valuable commodities, as it is more favourable to private frugality, and, consequently, to the increase of the public capital, and as it maintains productive, rather than unproductive hands, conduces more than the other to the growth of public opulence.

BOOK III

Of the different Progress of Opulence in different Nations

[In Chapter V, Book II, Smith explains how and why the "policy of Europe" and feudal conditions combined to hamper investment in productive labor. In this regard, he takes special note of the lack of investment in agriculture. It is crucial to realise that Smith begins to develop his "agrarian bias" here. Clearly, he builds the argument of Book III around that theme. In Appendix II, I discuss some of the wider implications of this important development in Smith's thinking.]

CHAPTER I

OF THE NATURAL PROGRESS OF OPULENCE

The great commerce of every civilized society, is that carried on between the inhabitants of the town and those of the country. It consists in the exchange of rude for manufactured produce, either immediately, or by the intervention of money, or of some sort of paper which represents money. The country supplies the town with the means of subsistence, and the materials of manufacture. The town repays this supply by sending back a part of the manufactured produce to the inhabitants of the country. The town, in which there neither is nor can be any reproduction of substances, may very properly be said to gain its whole wealth and subsistence from the country. We must not, however, upon this account, imagine that the gain of the town is the loss of the country. The gains of both are mutual and reciprocal, and the division of labour is in this, as in all other cases, advantageous to all the different persons employed in the various occupations into which it is subdivided. The inhabitants of the country purchase of the town a greater quantity of manufactured goods, with the produce of a much smaller quantity of their own labour, than they must have employed had they attempted to prepare them themselves. The town affords a market for the surplus produce of the country, or what is over and above the maintenance of the cultivators, and it is there that the inhabitants of the country exchange it for something else which is in demand among them. The greater the number and revenue of the inhabitants of the town, the more extensive is the market which it affords to those of the country; and the more extensive that market, it is always the more advantageous to a great number. The corn which grows within a mile of the town, sells there for the same price with that which comes from twenty miles distance. But the price of the latter must generally, not only pay the expence of raising and bringing it to market, but afford too the ordinary profits of agriculture to the farmer. The proprietors and cultivators of the country, therefore, which lies in the neighbourhood of the town, over and above the ordinary profits of agriculture, gain, in the price of what they sell, the whole value of the carriage of the like produce that is brought from more distant parts, and they save, besides, the whole value of this carriage in the price of what they buy. Compare the cultivation of the lands in the neighbourhood of any considerable town, with that of those which lie at some distance from it, and you will easily satisfy yourself how much the country is benefited by the commerce of the town. Among all the absurd speculations that have been propagated concerning the balance of trade, it has never been pretended that either the country loses by its commerce with the town, or the town by that with the country which maintains it.

As subsistence is, in the nature of things, prior to conveniency and luxury, so the industry which procures the former, must necessarily be prior to that which ministers to the latter. The cultivation and improvement of the country, therefore, which affords subsistence, must, necessarily, be prior to the increase of the town, which furnishes only the means of conveniency and luxury. It is the surplus produce of the country only, or what is over and above the maintenance of the cultivators, that constitutes the subsistence of the town, which can therefore increase only with the increase of this surplus produce. The town, indeed, may not always derive its whole subsistence from the country in its neighbourhood, or even from the territory to which it belongs, but from very distant countries; and this, though it forms no exception from the general rule, has occasioned considerable variations in the progress of opulence in different ages and nations.

That order of things which necessity imposes in general, though not in every particular country, is, in every particular country, promoted by the natural inclinations of man. If human institutions had never thwarted those natural inclinations, the towns could no-where have increased beyond what the improvement and cultivation of the territory in which they were situated could support; till such time, at least, as the whole of that territory was completely cultivated and improved. Upon equal, or nearly equal profits, most men will chuse to employ their capitals rather in the improvement and cultivation of land, than either in manufactures or in foreign trade. The man who employs his capital in land, has it more under his view and command, and his fortune is much less liable to accidents, than that of the trader, who is obliged frequently to commit it, not only to the winds and the waves, but to the more uncertain elements of human folly and injustice, by giving great credits in distant countries to men, with whose character and situation he can seldom be thoroughly acquainted. The capital of the landlord, on the contrary, which is fixed in the improvement of his land, seems to be as well secured as the nature of human affairs can admit of. The beauty of the country besides, the pleasures of a country life, the tranquillity of mind which it promises, and wherever the injustice of human laws does not disturb it, the independency which it really affords, have charms that more or less attract every body; and as to cultivate the ground was the original destination of man, so in every stage of his existence he seems to retain a predilection for this primitive employment.

Without the assistance of some artificers, indeed, the cultivation of land cannot be carried on, but with great inconveniency and continual interruption. Smiths, carpenters, wheel-wrights, and plough-wrights, masons, and bricklayers, tanners, shoemakers, and taylors, are people, whose service the farmer has frequent occasion for. Such artificers too stand, occasionally, in need of the assistance of one another; and as their residence is not, like that of the farmer, necessarily tied down to a precise spot, they naturally settle in the neighbourhood of one another, and thus form a small town or village. The butcher, the brewer, and the baker, soon join them, together with many other artificers and retailers, necessary or useful for supplying their occasional wants, and who contribute still further to augment the town. The inhabitants of the town and those of the country are mutually the servants of one another. The town is a continual fair or market, to which the inhabitants of the country resort, in order to exchange their rude for manufactured produce. It is this commerce which supplies the inhabitants of the town both with the materials of their work, and the means of their subsistence. The quantity of the finished work which they sell to the inhabitants of the country, necessarily regulates the quantity of the materials and provisions which they buy. Neither their employment nor subsistence, therefore, can augment, but in proportion to the augmentation of the demand from the country for finished work; and this demand can augment only in proportion to the extension of improvement and cultivation. Had human institutions, therefore, never disturbed the natural course of things, the progressive wealth and increase of the towns would, in every political society, be consequential, and in proportion to the improvement and cultivation of the territory or country.

In our North American colonies, where uncultivated land is still to be had upon easy terms, no manufactures for distant sale have ever yet been established in any of their towns. When an artificer has acquired a little more stock than is necessary for carrying on his own business in supplying the neighbouring country, he does not, in North America, attempt to establish with it a manufacture for more distant sale, but employs it in the purchase and improvement of uncultivated land. From artificer he becomes planter, and neither the large wages nor the easy subsistence which that country affords to artificers, can bribe him rather to work for other people than for himself. He feels that an artificer is the servant of his customers, from whom he derives his subsistence; but that a planter who cultivates his own land, and derives his necessary subsistence from the labour of his own family, is really a master, and independent of all the world.

In countries, on the contrary, where there is either no uncultivated land, or none that can be had upon easy terms, every artificer who has acquired more stock than he can employ in the occasional jobs of the neighbourhood, endeavours to prepare work for more distant sale. The smith erects some sort of iron, the weaver some sort of linen or woollen manufactory. Those different manufactures come, in process of time, to be gradually subdivided, and thereby improved and refined in a great variety of ways, which may easily be conceived, and which it is therefore unnecessary to explain any further.

In seeking for employment to a capital, manufactures are, upon equal or nearly equal profits, naturally preferred to foreign commerce, for the same reason that agriculture is naturally preferred to manufactures. As the capital of the landlord or farmer is more secure than that of the manufacturer, so the capital of the manufacturer, being at all times more within his view and command, is more secure than that of the foreign merchant. In every period, indeed, of every society, the surplus part both of the rude and manufactured produce, or that for which there is no demand at home, must be sent abroad in order to be exchanged for something for which there is some demand at home. But whether the capital, which carries this surplus produce abroad, be a foreign or a domestic one, is of very little importance. If the society has not acquired sufficient capital both to cultivate all its lands, and to manufacture in the completest manner the whole of its rude produce, there is even a considerable advantage that that rude produce should be exported by a foreign capital, in order that the whole stock of the society may be employed in more useful purposes. The wealth of ancient Egypt, that of China and Indostan, sufficiently demonstrate that a nation may attain a very high degree of opulence, though the greater part of its exportation trade be carried on by foreigners. The progress of our North American and West Indian colonies would have been much less rapid, had not capital but what belonged to themselves been employed in exporting their surplus produce.

According to the natural course of things, therefore, the greater part of the capital of every growing society is, first, directed to agriculture, afterwards to manufactures, and last of all to foreign commerce. This order of things is so very natural, that in every society that had any territory, it has always, I believe, been in some degree observed. Some of their lands must have been cultivated before any considerable towns could be established, and some sort of coarse industry of the manufacturing kind must have been carried on in those towns, before they could well think of employing themselves in foreign commerce.

But though this natural order of things must have taken place in some degree in every such society, it has, in all the modern states of Europe, been, in many respects, entirely inverted. The foreign commerce of some of their cities has introduced all their finer manufactures, or such as were fit for distant sale; and manufactures and foreign commerce together, have given birth to the principal improvements of agriculture. The manners and customs which the nature of their original government introduced, and which remained after that government was greatly altered, necessarily forced them into this unnatural and retrograde order.

CHAPTER II

OF THE DISCOURAGEMENT OF AGRICULTURE IN THE ANCIENT STATE OF EUROPE AFTER THE FALL OF THE ROMAN EMPIRE

When the German and Scythian nations over-ran the western provinces of the Roman empire, the confusions which followed so great a revolution lasted for several centuries. The rapine and violence which the barbarians exercised against the ancient inhabitants, interrupted the commerce between the towns and the country. The towns were deserted, and the country was left uncultivated, and the western provinces of Europe, which had enjoyed a considerable degree of opulence under the Roman empire, sunk into the lowest state of poverty and barbarism. During the continuance of those confusions, the chiefs and principal leaders of those nations, acquired or usurped to themselves the greater part of the lands of those countries. A great part of them was uncultivated; but no part of them, whether cultivated or uncultivated, was left without a proprietor. All of them were engrossed, and the greater part by a few great proprietors.

This original engrossing of uncultivated lands, though a great, might have been but a transitory evil. They might soon have been divided again, and broke into small parcels either by succession or by alienation. The law of primogeniture hindered them from being divided by succession: the introduction of entails prevented their being broke into small parcels by alienation.

When land, like moveables, is considered as the means only of subsistence and enjoyment, the natural law of succession divides it, like them, among all the children of the family; of all of whom the subsistence and enjoyment may be supposed equally dear to the father. This natural law of succession accordingly took place among the Romans, who made no more distinction between elder and younger, between male and female, in the inheritance of lands, than we do in the distribution of moveables. But when land was considered as the means, not of subsistence merely, but of power and protection, it was thought better that it should descend undivided to one. In those disorderly times, every great landlord was a sort of petty prince. His tenants were his subjects. He was their judge, and in some respects their legislator in peace, and their leader in war. He made war according to his own discretion, frequently against his neighbours, and sometimes against his sovereign. The security of a landed estate, therefore, the protection which its owner could afford to those who dwelt on it, depended upon its greatness. To divide it was to ruin it, and to expose every part of it to be oppressed and swallowed up by the incursions of its neighbours. The law of primogeniture, therefore, came to take place, not immediately, indeed, but in process of time, in the succession of landed estates, for the same reason that it has generally taken place in that of monarchies, though not always at their first institution. That the power, and consequently the security of the monarchy, may not be weakened by division, it must descend entire to one of the children. To which of them so important a preference shall be given, must be determined by some general rule, founded not upon the doubtful distinctions of personal merit, but upon some plain and evident difference which can admit of no dispute. Among the children of the same family, there can be no indisputable difference but that of sex, and that of age. The male sex is universally preferred to the female; and when all other things are equal, the elder every-where takes place of the younger. Hence the origin of the right of primogeniture, and of what is called lineal succession.

Laws frequently continue in force long after the circumstances, which first gave occasion to them, and which could alone render them reasonable, are no more. In the present state of Europe, the proprietor of a single acre of land is as perfectly secure of his possession as the proprietor of a hundred thousand. The right of primogeniture, however, still continues to be respected, and as of all institutions it is the fittest to support the pride of family distinctions, it is still likely to endure for many centuries. In every other respect, nothing can be more contrary to the real interest of a numerous family, than a right which in order to enrich one, beggars all the rest of the children.

Entails are the natural consequences of the law of primogeniture. They were introduced to preserve a certain lineal succession, of which the law of primogeniture first gave the idea, and to hinder any part of the original estate from being carried out of the proposed line either by gift, or devise, or alienation; either by the folly, or by the misfortune of any of its successive owners. They were altogether unknown to the Romans. Neither their substitutions nor fideicommisses bear any resemblance to entails, though some French lawyers have thought proper to dress the modern institution in the language and garb of those ancient ones.

When great landed estates were a sort of principalities, entails might not be unreasonable. Like what are called the fundamental laws of some monarchies, they might frequently hinder the security of thousands from being endangered by the caprice or extravagance of one man. But in the present state of Europe, when small as well as great estates derive their security from the laws of their country, nothing can be more completely absurd. They are founded upon the most absurd of all suppositions, the supposition that every successive generation of men have not an equal right to the earth, and to all that it possesses; but that the property of the present generation should be restrained and regulated according to the fancy of those who died perhaps five hundred years ago. Entails, however, are still respected through the greater part of Europe, in those countries particularly in which noble birth is a necessary qualification for the enjoyment either of civil or military honours. Entails are thought necessary for maintaining this exclusive privilege of the nobility to the great offices and honours of their country; and that order having usurped one unjust advantage over the rest of their fellow-citizens, lest their poverty should render it ridiculous, it is thought reasonable that they should have another. The common law of England, indeed, is said to abhor perpetuities, and they are accordingly more restricted there than in any other European monarchy; though even England is not altogether without them. In Scotland more than one-fifth, perhaps more than one-third part of the whole lands of the country, are at present supposed to be under strict entail.

Great tracts of uncultivated land were, in this manner, not only engrossed by particular families, but the possibility of their being divided again was as much as possible precluded for ever. It seldom happens, however, that a great proprietor is a great improver. In the disorderly times which gave birth to those barbarous institutions, the great proprietor was sufficiently employed in defending his own territories, or in extending his jurisdiction and authority over those of his neighbours. He had no leisure to attend to the cultivation and improvement of land. When the establishment of law and order afforded him this leisure, he often wanted the inclination, and almost always the requisite abilities. If the expence of his house and person either equalled or exceeded his revenue, as it did very frequently, he had no stock to employ in this manner. If he was an oeconomist, he generally found it more profitable to employ his annual savings in new purchases, than in the improvement of his old estate. To improve land with profit, like all other commercial projects, requires an exact attention to small savings and small gains, of which a man born to a great fortune, even though naturally frugal, is very seldom capable. The situation of such a person naturally disposes him to attend rather to ornament which pleases his fancy, than to profit for which he has so little occasion. The elegance of his dress, of his equipage, of his house, and household furniture, are objects which from his infancy he has been accustomed to have some anxiety about. The turn of mind which this habit naturally forms, follows him when he comes to think of the improvement of land. He embellishes perhaps four or five hundred acres in the neighbourhood of his house, at ten times the expence which the land is worth after all his improvements; and finds that if he was to improve his whole estate in the same manner, and he has little taste for any other, he would be a bankrupt before he had finished the tenth part of it. There still remain in both parts of the united kingdom some great estates which have continued without interruption in the hands of the same family since the times of feudal anarchy. Compare the present condition of those estates with the possessions of the small proprietors in their neighbourhood, and you will require no other argument to convince you how unfavourable such extensive property is to improvement.

If little improvement was to be expected from such great proprietors, still less was to be hoped for from those who occupied the land under them. In the ancient state of Europe, the occupiers of land were all tenants at will. They were all or almost all slaves; but their slavery was of a milder kind than that known among the ancient Greeks and Romans, or even in our West Indian colonies. They were supposed to belong more directly to the land than to their masters. They could, therefore, be sold with it, but not separately. They could marry, provided it was with the consent of their master; and he could not afterwards dissolve the marriage by selling the man and wife to different persons. If he maimed or murdered any of them, he was liable to some penalty, though generally but to a small one. They were not, however, capable of acquiring property. Whatever they acquired was acquired to their master, and he could take it from them at pleasure. Whatever cultivation and improvement could be carried on by means of such slaves, was properly carried on by their master. It was at his expence. The seed, the cattle, and the instruments of husbandry were all his. It was for his benefit. Such slaves could acquire nothing but their daily maintenance. It was properly the proprietor himself, therefore, that, in this case, occupied his own lands, and cultivated them by his own bondmen. This species of slavery still subsists in Russia, Poland, Hungary, Bohemia, Moravia, and other parts of Germany. It is only in the western and south-western provinces of Europe, that it has gradually been abolished altogether.

But if great improvements are seldom to be expected from great proprietors, they are least of all to be expected when they employ slaves for their workmen. The experience of all ages and nations, I believe, demonstrates that the work done by slaves, though it appears to cost only their maintenance, is in the end the dearest of any. A person who can acquire no property, can have no other interest but to eat as much, and to labour as little as possible. Whatever work he does beyond what is sufficient to purchase his own maintenance, can be squeezed out of him by violence only, and not by any interest of his own. In ancient Italy, how much the cultivation of corn degenerated, how unprofitable it became to the master when it fell under the management of slaves, is remarked by both Pliny and Columella. In the time of Aristotle it had not been much better in ancient Greece. Speaking of the ideal republic described in the laws of Plato, to maintain five thousand idle men (the number of warriors supposed necessary for its defence) together with their women and servants, would require, he says, a territory of boundless extent and fertility, like the plains of Babylon.

The pride of man makes him love to domineer, and nothing mortifies him so much as to be obliged to condescend to persuade his inferiors. Wherever the law allows it, and the nature of the work can afford it, therefore, he will generally prefer the service of slaves to that of freemen.

The planting of sugar and tobacco can afford the expence of slave cultivation. The raising of corn, it seems, in the present times, cannot. In the English colonies, of which the principal produce is corn, the far greater part of the work is done by freemen. The late resolution of the Quakers in Pennsylvania to set at liberty all their negro slaves, may satisfy us that their number cannot be very great. Had they made any considerable part of their property, such a resolution could never have been agreed to. In our sugar colonies, on the contrary, the whole work is done by slaves, and in our tobacco colonies a very great part of it. The profits of a sugar-plantation in any of our West Indian colonies are generally much greater than those of any other cultivation that is known either in Europe or America: And the profits of a tobacco plantation, though inferior to those of sugar, are superior to those of corn, as has already been observed. Both can afford the expence of slave cultivation, but sugar can afford it still better than tobacco. The number of negroes accordingly is much greater, in proportion to that of whites, in our sugar than in our tobacco colonies.

To the slave cultivators of ancient times, gradually succeeded a species of farmers known at present in France by the name of metayers. They are called in Latin, Coloni Partiarii. They have been so long in disuse in England that at present I know no English name for them. The proprietor furnished them with the seed, cattle, and instruments of husbandry, the whole stock, in short, necessary for cultivating the farm. The produce was divided equally between the proprietor and the farmer, after setting aside what was judged necessary for keeping up the stock, which was restored to the proprietor when the farmer either quitted, or was turned out of the farm.

Land occupied by such tenants is properly cultivated at the expence of the proprietor, as much as that occupied by slaves. There is, however, one very essential difference between them. Such tenants, being freemen, are capable of acquiring property, and having a certain proportion of the produce of the land, they have a plain interest that the whole produce should be as great as possible, in order that their own proportion may be so. A slave, on the contrary, who can acquire nothing but his maintenance, consults his own ease by making the land produce as little as possible over and above that maintenance. It is probable that it was partly upon account of this advantage, and partly upon account of the encroachments which the sovereign, always jealous of the great lords, gradually encouraged their villains to make upon their authority, and which seem at last to have been such as rendered this species of servitude altogether inconvenient, that tenure in villanage gradually wore out through the greater part of Europe. The time and manner, however, in which so important a revolution was brought about, is one of the most obscure points in modern history. The church of Rome claims great merit in it; and it is certain that so early as the twelfth century, Alexander III. published a bull for the general emancipation of slaves. It seems, however, to have been rather a pious exhortation, than a law to which exact obedience was required from the faithful. Slavery continued to take place almost universally for several centuries afterwards, till it was gradually abolished by the joint operation of the two interests above mentioned, that of the proprietor on the one hand, and that of the sovereign on the other. A villain enfranchised, and at the same time allowed to continue in possession of the land, having no stock of his own, could cultivate it only by means of what the landlord advanced to him, and must, therefore, have been what the French call a metayer.

It could never, however, be the interest even of this last species of cultivators to lay out, in the further improvement of the land, any part of the little stock which they might save from their own share of the produce, because the lord, who laid out nothing, was to get one-half of whatever it produced. The tithe, which is but a tenth of the produce, is found to be a very great hindrance to improvement. A tax, therefore, which amounted to one-half, must have been an effectual bar to it. It might be the interest of a metayer to make the land produce as much as could be brought out of it by means of the stock furnished by the proprietor; but it could never be his interest to mix any part of his own with it. In France, where five parts out of six of the whole kingdom are said to be still occupied by this species of cultivators, the proprietors complain that their metayers take every opportunity of employing the master's cattle rather in carriage than in cultivation; because in the one case they get the whole profits to themselves, in the other they share them with their landlord. This species of tenants still subsists in some parts of Scotland. They are called steel-bow tenants. Those ancient English tenants, who are said by Chief Baron Gilbert and Doctor Blackstone to have been rather bailiffs of the landlord than farmers properly so called, were probably of the same kind.

To this species of tenancy succeeded, though by very slow degrees, farmers properly so called, who cultivated the land with their own stock, paying a rent certain to the landlord. When such farmers have a lease for a term of years, they may sometimes find it for their interest to lay out part of their capital in the further improvement of the farm; because they may sometimes expect to recover it, with a large profit, before the expiration of the lease. The possession even of such farmers, however, was long extremely precarious, and still is so in many parts of Europe. They could before the expiration of their term be legally outed of their lease, by a new purchaser; in England, even by the fictitious action of a common recovery. If they were turned out illegally by the violence of their master, the action by which they obtained redress was extremely imperfect. It did not always re-instate them in the possession of the land, but gave them damages which never amounted to the real loss. Even in England, the country perhaps of Europe where the yeomanry has always been most respected, it was not till about the 14th of Henry the VIIth that the action of ejectment was invented, by which the tenant recovers, not damages only but possession, and in which his claim is not necessarily concluded by the uncertain decision of a single assize. This action has been found so effectual a remedy that, in the modern practice, when the landlord has occasion to sue for the possession of the land, he seldom makes use of the actions which properly belong to him as landlord, the writ of right or the writ of entry, but sues in the name of his tenant, by the writ of ejectment. In England, therefore, the security of the tenant is equal to that of the proprietor. In England besides a lease for life of forty shillings a year value is a freehold, and entitles the lessee to vote for a member of parliament; and as a great part of the yeomanry have freeholds of this kind, the whole order becomes respectable to their landlords on account of the political consideration which this gives them. There is, I believe, no-where in Europe, except in England, any instance of the tenant building upon the land of which he had no lease, and trusting that the honour of his landlord would take no advantage of so important an improvement. Those laws and customs so favourable to the yeomanry, have perhaps contributed more to the present grandeur of England, than all their boasted regulations of commerce taken together.

The law which secures the longest leases against successors of every kind is, so far as I know, peculiar to Great Britain. It was introduced into Scotland so early as 1449, by a law of James the IId. Its beneficial influence, however, has been much obstructed by entails; the heirs of entail being generally restrained from letting leases for any long term of years, frequently for more than one year. A late act of parliament has, in this respect, somewhat slackened their fetters, though they are still by much too strait. In Scotland, besides, as no leasehold gives a vote for a member of parliament, the yeomanry are upon this account less respectable to their landlords than in England.

In other parts of Europe, after it was found convenient to secure tenants both against heirs and purchasers, the term of their security was still limited to a very short period; in France, for example, to nine years from the commencement of the lease. It has in that country, indeed, been lately extended to twenty-seven, a period still too short to encourage the tenant to make the most important improvements. The proprietors of land were anciently the legislators of every part of Europe. The laws relating to land, therefore, were all calculated for what they supposed the interest of the proprietor. It was for his interest, they had imagined, that no lease granted by any of his predecessors should hinder him from enjoying, during a long term of years, the full value of his land. Avarice and injustice are always shortsighted, and they did not foresee how much this regulation must obstruct improvement, and thereby hurt in the long-run the real interest of the landlord.

The farmers too, besides paying the rent, were anciently, it was supposed, bound to perform a great number of services to the landlord, which were seldom either specified in the lease, or regulated by any precise rule, but by the use and wont of the manor or barony. These services, therefore, being almost entirely arbitrary, subjected the tenant to many vexations. In Scotland the abolition of all services, not precisely stipulated in the lease, has in the course of a few years very much altered for the better the condition of the yeomanry of that country.

The public services to which the yeomanry were bound, were not less arbitrary than the private ones. To make and maintain the high roads, a servitude which still subsists, I believe, every-where, though with different degrees of oppression in different countries, was not the only one. When the king's troops, when his household or his officers of any kind passed through any part of the country, the yeomanry were bound to provide them with horses, carriages, and provisions, at a price regulated by the purveyor. Great Britain is, I believe, the only monarchy in Europe where the oppression of purveyance has been entirely abolished. It still subsists in France and Germany.

The public taxes to which they were subject were as irregular and oppressive as the services. The ancient lords, though extremely unwilling to grant themselves any pecuniary aid to their sovereign, easily allowed him to tallage, as they called it, their tenants, and had not knowledge enough to foresee how much this must in the end affect their own revenue. The taille, as it still subsists in France, may serve as an example of those ancient tallages. It is a tax upon the supposed profits of the farmer, which they estimate by the stock that he has upon the farm. It is his interest, therefore, to appear to have as little as possible, and consequently to employ as little as possible in its cultivation, and none in its improvement. Should any stock happen to accumulate in the hands of a French farmer, the taille is almost equal to a prohibition of its ever being employed upon the land. This tax besides is supposed to dishonour whoever is subject to it, and to degrade him below, not only the rank of a gentleman, but that of a burgher, and whoever rents the lands of another becomes subject to it. No gentleman, nor even any burgher who has stock, will submit to this degradation. This tax, therefore, not only hinders the stock which accumulates upon the land from being employed in its improvement, but drives away all other stock from it. The ancient tenths and fifteenths, so usual in England in former times, seem, so far as they affected the land, to have been taxes of the same nature with the taille.

Under all these discouragements, little improvement could be expected from the occupiers of land. That order of people, with all the liberty and security which law can give, must always improve under great disadvantages. The farmer compared with the proprietor, is as a merchant who trades with borrowed money compared with one who trades with his own. The stock of both may improve, but that of the one, with only equal good conduct, must always improve more slowly than that of the other, on account of the large share of the profits which is consumed by the interest of the loan. The lands cultivated by the farmer must, in the same manner, with only equal good conduct, be improved more slowly than those cultivated by the proprietor; on account of the large share of the produce which is consumed in the rent, and which, had the farmer been proprietor, he might have employed in the further improvement of the land. The station of a farmer besides is, from the nature of things, inferior to that of a proprietor. Through the greater part of Europe the yeomanry are regarded as an inferior rank of people, even to the better sort of tradesmen and mechanics, and in all parts of Europe to the great merchants and master manufacturers. It can seldom happen, therefore, that a man of any considerable stock should quit the superior, in order to place himself in an inferior station. Even in the present state of Europe, therefore, little stock is likely to go from any other profession to the improvement of land in the way of farming. More does perhaps in Great Britain than in any other country, though even there the great stocks which are, in some places, employed in farming, have generally been acquired by farming, the trade, perhaps, in which of all others stock is commonly acquired most slowly. After small proprietors, however, rich and great farmers are, in every country, the principal improvers. There are more such perhaps in England than in any other European monarchy. In the republican governments of Holland and of Berne in Switzerland, the farmers are said to be not inferior to those of England.

The ancient policy of Europe was, over and above all this, unfavourable to the improvement and cultivation of land, whether carried on by the proprietor or by the farmer; first, by the general prohibition of the exportation of corn without a special licence, which seems to have been a very universal regulation; and secondly, by the restraints which were laid upon the inland commerce, not only of corn but of almost every other part of the produce of the farm, by the absurd laws against engrossers, regraters, and forestallers, and by the privileges of fairs and markets. It has already been observed in what manner the prohibition of the exportation of corn, together with some encouragement given to the importation of foreign corn, obstructed the cultivation of ancient Italy, naturally the most fertile country in Europe, and at that time the seat of the greatest empire in the world. To what degree such restraints upon the inland commerce of this commodity, joined to the general prohibition of exportation, must have discouraged the cultivation of countries less fertile, and less favourably circumstanced, it is not perhaps very easy to imagine.

CHAPTER III

OF THE RISE AND PROGRESS OF CITIES AND TOWNS, AFTER THE FALL OF THE ROMAN EMPIRE

The inhabitants of cities and towns were, after the fall of the Roman empire, not more favoured than those of the country. They consisted, indeed, of a very different order of people from the first inhabitants of the ancient republics of Greece and Italy. These last were composed chiefly of the proprietors of lands, among whom the public territory was originally divided, and who found it convenient to build their houses in the neighbourhood of one another, and to surround them with a wall, for the sake of common defence. After the fall of the Roman empire, on the contrary, the proprietors of land seem generally to have lived in fortified castles on their own estates, and in the midst of their own tenants and dependants. The towns were chiefly inhabited by tradesmen and mechanics, who seem in those days to have been of servile, or very nearly of servile condition. The privileges which we find granted by ancient charters to the inhabitants of some of the principal towns in Europe, sufficiently shew what they were before those grants. The people to whom it is granted as a privilege, that they might give away their own daughters in marriage without the consent of their lord, that upon their death their own children, and not their lord, should succeed to their goods, and that they might dispose of their own effects by will, must, before those grants, have been either altogether, or very nearly in the same state of villanage with the occupiers of land in the country.

They seem, indeed, to have been a very poor, mean set of people, who used to travel about with their goods from place to place, and from fair to fair, like the hawkers and pedlars of the present times. In all the different countries of Europe then, in the same manner as in several of the Tartar governments of Asia at present, taxes used to be levied upon the persons and goods of travellers, when they passed through certain manors, when they went over certain bridges, when they carried about their goods from place to place in a fair, when they erected in it a booth or stall to sell them in. These different taxes were known in England by the names of passage, pontage, lastage, and stallage. Sometimes the king, sometimes a great lord, who had, it seems, upon some occasions, authority to do this, would grant to particular traders, to such particularly as lived in their own demesnes, a general exemption from such taxes. Such traders, though in other respects of servile, or very nearly of servile condition, were upon this account called Free-traders. They in return usually paid to their protector a sort of annual poll-tax. In those days protection was seldom granted without a valuable consideration, and this tax might, perhaps, be considered as compensation for what their patrons might lose by their exemption from other taxes. At first, both those poll-taxes and those exemptions seem to have been altogether personal, and to have affected only particular individuals, during either their lives, or the pleasure of their protectors. In the very imperfect accounts which have been published from Domesday-book, of several of the towns of England, mention is frequently made sometimes of the tax which particular burghers paid, each of them, either to the king, or to some other great lord, for this sort of protection; and sometimes of the general amount only of all those taxes.

But how servile soever may have been originally the condition of the inhabitants of the towns, it appears evidently, that they arrived at liberty and independency much earlier than the occupiers of land in the country. That part of the king's revenue which arose from such poll-taxes in any particular town, used commonly to be let in farm, during a term of years for a rent certain, sometimes to the sheriff of the county, and sometimes to other persons. The burghers themselves frequently got credit enough to be admitted to farm the revenues of this sort which arose out of their own town, they becoming jointly and severally answerable for the whole rent. To let a farm in this manner was quite agreeable to the usual oeconomy of, I believe, the sovereigns of all the different countries of Europe; who used frequently to let whole manors to all the tenants of those manors, they becoming jointly and severally answerable for the whole rent; but in return being allowed to collect it in their own way, and to pay it into the king's exchequer by the hands of their own bailiff, and being thus altogether freed from the insolence of the king's officers; a circumstance in those days regarded as of the greatest importance.

At first, the farm of the town was probably let to the burghers, in the same manner as it had been to other farmers, for a term of years only.

In process of time, however, it seems to have become the general practice to grant it to them in fee, that is for ever, reserving a rent certain never afterwards to be augmented. The payment having thus become perpetual, the exemptions, in return for which it was made, naturally became perpetual too. Those exemptions, therefore, ceased to be personal, and could not afterwards be considered as belonging to individuals as individuals, but as burghers of a particular burgh, which upon this account, was called a Free burgh, for the same reason that they had been called Free-burghers or Free-traders.

Along with this grant, the important privileges above mentioned, that they might give away their own daughters in marriage, that their children should succeed to them, and that they might dispose of their own effects by will, were generally bestowed upon the burghers of the town to whom it was given. Whether such privileges had before been usually granted along with the freedom of trade, to particular burghers, as individuals, I know not. I reckon it not improbable that they were, though I cannot produce any direct evidence of it. But however this may have been, the principal attributes of villanage and slavery being thus taken away from them, they now, at least, became really free in our present sense of the word Freedom.

Nor was this all. They were generally at the same time erected into a commonalty or corporation, with the privilege of having magistrates and a town-council of their own, of making bye-laws for their own government, of building walls for their own defence, and of reducing all their inhabitants under a sort of military discipline, by obliging them to watch and ward; that is, as anciently understood, to guard and defend those walls against all attacks and surprises by night as well as by day. In England they were generally exempted from suit to the hundred and county courts; and all such pleas as should arise among them, the pleas of the crown excepted, were left to the decision of their own magistrates. In other countries much greater and more extensive jurisdictions were frequently granted to them.

It might, probably, be necessary to grant to such towns as were admitted to farm their own revenues, some sort of compulsive jurisdiction to oblige their own citizens to make payment. In those disorderly times it might have been extremely inconvenient to have left them to seek this sort of justice from any other tribunal. But it must seem extraordinary that the sovereigns of all the different countries of Europe, should have exchanged in this manner for a rent certain, never more to be augmented, that branch of their revenue, which was, perhaps, of all others the most likely to be improved by the natural course of things, without either expence or attention of their own: and that they should, besides, have in this manner voluntarily erected a sort of independent republics in the heart of their own dominions.

In order to understand this, it must be remembered, that in those days the sovereign of perhaps no country in Europe was able to protect, through the whole extent of his dominions, the weaker part of his subjects from the oppression of the great lords. Those whom the law could not protect, and who were not strong enough to defend themselves, were obliged either to have recourse to the protection of some great lord, and in order to obtain it to become either his slaves or vassals; or to enter into a league of mutual defence for the common protection of one another. The inhabitants of cities and burghs, considered as single individuals, had no power to defend themselves; but by entering into a league of mutual defence with their neighbours, they were capable of making no contemptible resistance. The lords despised the burghers, whom they considered not only as of a different order, but as a parcel of emancipated slaves, almost of a different species from themselves. The wealth of the burghers never failed to provoke their envy and indignation, and they plundered them upon every occasion without mercy or remorse. The burghers naturally hated and feared the lords. The king hated and feared them too; but though perhaps he might despise, he had no reason either to hate or fear the burghers. Mutual interest, therefore, disposed them to support the king, and the king to support them against the lords. They were the enemies of his enemies, and it was his interest to render them as secure and independent of those enemies as he could. By granting them magistrates of their own, the privilege of making bye-laws for their own government, that of building walls for their own defence, and that of reducing all their inhabitants under a sort of military discipline, he gave them all the means of security and independency of the barons which it was in his power to bestow. Without the establishment of some regular government of this kind, without some authority to compel their inhabitants to act according to some certain plan or system, no voluntary league of mutual defence could either have afforded them any permanent security, or have enabled them to give the king any considerable support. By granting them the farm of their town in fee, he took away from those whom he wished to have for his friends, and, if one may say so, for his allies, all ground of jealousy and suspicion that he was ever afterwards to oppress them, either by raising the farm rent of their towns, or by granting it to some other farmer.

The princes who lived upon the worst terms with their barons, seem accordingly to have been the most liberal in grants of this kind to their burghs. King John of England, for example, appears to have been a most munificent benefactor to his towns. Philip the First of France lost all authority over his barons. Towards the end of his reign, his son Lewis, known afterwards by the name of Lewis the Fat, consulted, according to Father Daniel, with the bishops of the royal demesnes, concerning the most proper means of restraining the violence of the great lords. Their advice consisted of two different proposals. One was to erect a new order of jurisdiction by establishing magistrates and a town council in every considerable town of his demesnes. The other was to form a new militia, by making the inhabitants of those towns, under the command of their own magistrates, march out upon proper occasions to the assistance of the king. It is from this period, according to the French antiquarians, that we are to date the institution of the magistrates and councils of cities in France. It was during the unprosperous reigns of the princes of the house of Suabia that the greater part of the free towns of Germany received the first grants of their privileges, and that the famous Hanseatic league first became formidable.

The militia of the cities seems, in those times, not to have been inferior to that of the country, and as they could be more readily assembled upon any sudden occasion, they frequently had the advantage in their disputes with the neighbouring lords. In countries, such as Italy and Switzerland, in which, on account either of their distance from the principal seat of government, of the natural strength of the country itself, or of some other reason, the sovereign came to lose the whole of his authority, the cities generally became independent republics, and conquered all the nobility in their neighbourhood; obliging them to pull down their castles in the country, and to live, like other peaceable inhabitants, in the city. This is the short history of the republic of Berne, as well as of several other cities in Switzerland. If you except Venice, for of that city the history is somewhat different, it is the history of all the considerable Italian republics, of which so great a number arose and perished, between the end of the twelfth and the beginning of the sixteenth century.

In countries such as France or England, where the authority of the sovereign, though frequently very low, never was destroyed altogether, the cities had no opportunity of becoming entirely independent. They became, however, so considerable, that the sovereign could impose no tax upon them, besides the stated farm-rent of the town, without their own consent. They were, therefore, called upon to send deputies to the general assembly of the states of the kingdom, where they might join with the clergy and the barons in granting, upon urgent occasions, some extraordinary aid to the king. Being generally too more favourable to his power, their deputies seem, sometimes, to have been employed by him as a counter-balance in those assemblies to the authority of the great lords. Hence the origin of the representation of burghs in the states general of all the great monarchies in Europe.

Order and good government, and along with them the liberty and security of individuals, were, in this manner, established in cities, at a time when the occupiers of land in the country were exposed to every sort of violence. But men in this defenceless state naturally content themselves with their necessary subsistence; because to acquire more might only tempt the injustice of their oppressors. On the contrary, when they are secure of enjoying the fruits of their industry, they naturally exert it to better their condition and to acquire not only the necessaries, but the conveniencies and elegancies of life. That industry, therefore, which aims at something more than necessary subsistence, was established in cities long before it was commonly practised by the occupiers of land in the country. If in the hands of a poor cultivator, oppressed with the servitude of villanage, some little stock should accumulate, he would naturally conceal it with great care from his master, to whom it would otherwise have belonged, and take the first opportunity of running away to a town. The law was at that time so indulgent to the inhabitants of towns, and so desirous of diminishing the authority of the lords over those of the country, that if he could conceal himself there from the pursuit of his lord for a year, he was free for ever. Whatever stock, therefore, accumulated in the hands of the industrious part of the inhabitants of the country, naturally took refuge in cities, as the only sanctuaries in which it could be secure to the person that acquired it.

The inhabitants of a city, it is true, must always ultimately derive their subsistence, and the whole materials and means of their industry, from the country. But those of a city, situated near either the seacoast or the banks of a navigable river, are not necessarily confined to derive them from the country in their neighbourhood. They have a much wider range, and may draw them from the most remote corners of the world, either in exchange for the manufactured produce of their own industry, or by performing the office of carriers between distant countries, and exchanging the produce of one for that of another. A city might in this manner grow up to great wealth and splendor, while not only the country in its neighbourhood, but all those to which it traded, were in poverty and wretchedness. Each of those countries, perhaps, taken singly, could afford it but a small part, either of its subsistence, or of its employment; but all of them taken together could afford it both a great subsistence and a great employment. There were, however, within the narrow circle of the commerce of those times, some countries that were opulent and industrious. Such was the Greek empire as long as it subsisted, and that of the Saracens during the reigns of the Abassides. Such too was Egypt till it was conquered by the Turks, some part of the coast of Barbary, and all those provinces of Spain which were under the government of the Moors.

The cities of Italy seem to have been the first in Europe which were raised by commerce to any considerable degree of opulence. Italy lay in the centre of what was at that time the improved and civilized part of the world. The crusades, too, though, by the great waste of stock and destruction of inhabitants which they occasioned, they must necessarily have retarded the progress of the greater part of Europe, were extremely favourable to that of some Italian cities. The great armies which marched from all parts to the conquest of the Holy Land, gave extraordinary encouragement to the shipping of Venice, Genoa, and Pisa, sometimes in transporting them thither, and always in supplying them with provisions. They were the commissaries, if one may say so, of those armies; and the most destructive frenzy that ever befel the European nations, was a source of opulence to those republics.

The inhabitants of trading cities, by importing the improved manufactures and expensive luxuries of richer countries, afforded some food to the vanity of the great proprietors, who eagerly purchased them with great quantities of the rude produce of their own lands. The commerce of a great part of Europe in those times, accordingly, consisted chiefly in the exchange of their own rude, for the manufactured produce of more civilized nations. Thus the wool of England used to be exchanged for the wines of France, and the fine cloths of Flanders, in the same manner as the corn of Poland is at this day exchanged for the wines and brandies of France, and for the silks and velvets of France and Italy.

A taste for the finer and more improved manufactures, was in this manner introduced by foreign commerce into countries where no such works were carried on. But when this taste became so general as to occasion a considerable demand, the merchants, in order to save the expence of carriage, naturally endeavoured to establish some manufactures of the same kind in their own country. Hence the origin of the first manufactures for distant sale that seem to have been established in the western provinces of Europe, after the fall of the Roman empire.

No large country, it must be observed, ever did or could subsist without some sort of manufactures being carried on in it; and when it is said of any such country that it has no manufactures, it must always be understood of the finer and more improved, or of such as are fit for distant sale. In every large country, both the clothing and household furniture of the far greater part of the people, are the produce of their own industry. This is even more universally the case in those poor countries which are commonly said to have no manufactures, than in those rich ones that are said to abound in them. In the latter, you will generally find, both in the clothes and household furniture of the lowest rank of people, a much greater proportion of foreign productions than in the former.

Those manufactures which are fit for distant sale, seem to have been introduced into different countries in two different ways.

Sometimes they have been introduced, in the manner above mentioned, by the violent operation, if one may say so, of the stocks of particular merchants and undertakers, who established them in imitation of some foreign manufactures of the same kind. Such manufactures, therefore, are the offspring of foreign commerce, and such seem to have been the ancient manufactures of silks, velvets, and brocades, which flourished in Lucca, during the thirteenth century. They were banished from thence by the tyranny of one of Machiavel's heroes, Castruccio Castracani. In 1310, nine hundred families were driven out of Lucca, of whom thirty-one retired to Venice, and offered to introduce there the silk manufacture. Their offer was accepted; many privileges were conferred upon them, and they began the manufacture with three hundred workmen. Such too seem to have been the manufactures of fine cloths that anciently flourished in Flanders, and which were introduced into England in the beginning of the reign of Elizabeth; and such are the present silk manufactures of Lyons and Spital-fields. Manufactures introduced in this manner are generally employed upon foreign materials, being imitations of foreign manufactures. When the Venetian manufacture was first established, the materials were all brought from Sicily and the Levant. The more ancient manufacture of Lucca was likewise carried on with foreign materials. The cultivation of mulberry trees, and the breeding of silkworms, seem not to have been common in the northern parts of Italy before the sixteenth century. Those arts were not introduced into France till the reign of Charles IX. The manufactures of Flanders were carried on chiefly with Spanish and English wool. Spanish wool was the material, not of the first woollen manufacture of England, but of the first that was fit for distant sale. More than one half the materials of the Lyons manufacture is at this day foreign silk; when it was first established, the whole or very nearly the whole was so. No part of the materials of the Spital-fields manufacture is ever likely to be the produce of England. The seat of such manufactures, as they are generally introduced by the scheme and project of a few individuals, is sometimes established in a maritime city, and sometimes in an inland town, according as their interest, judgment or caprice happen to determine.

At other times manufactures for distant sale grow up naturally, and as it were of their own accord, by the gradual refinement of those household and coarser manufactures which must at all times be carried on even in the poorest and rudest countries. Such manufactures are generally employed upon the materials which the country produces, and they seem frequently to have been first refined and improved in such inland countries as were, not indeed at a very great, but at a considerable distance from the sea coast, and sometimes even from all water carriage. An inland country naturally fertile and easily cultivated, produces a great surplus of provisions beyond what is necessary for maintaining the cultivators, and on account of the expence of land carriage, and inconveniency of river navigation, it may frequently be difficult to send this surplus abroad. Abundance, therefore, renders provisions cheap, and encourages a great number of workmen to settle in the neighbourhood, who find that their industry can there procure them more of the necessaries and conveniencies of life than in other places. They work up the materials of manufacture which the land produces, and exchange their finished work, or what is the same thing the price of it, for more materials and provisions. They give a new value to the surplus part of the rude produce, by saving the expence of carrying it to the water side, or to some distant market; and they furnish the cultivators with something in exchange for it that is either useful or agreeable to them, upon easier terms than they could have obtained it before. The cultivators get a better price for their surplus produce, and can purchase cheaper other conveniencies which they have occasion for. They are thus both encouraged and enabled to increase this surplus produce by a further improvement and better cultivation of the land; and as the fertility of the land had given birth to the manufacture, so the progress of the manufacture reacts upon the land, and increases still further its fertility. The manufacturers first supply the neighbourhood, and afterwards, as their work improves and refines, more distant markets. For though neither the rude produce, nor even the coarse manufacture, could, without the greatest difficulty, support the expence of a considerable land carriage, the refined and improved manufacture easily may. In a small bulk it frequently contains the price of a great quantity of rude produce. A piece of fine cloth, for example, which weighs only eighty pounds, contains in it, the price, not only of eighty pounds weight of wool, but sometimes of several thousand weight of corn, the maintenance of the different working people, and of their immediate employers. The corn, which could with difficulty have been carried abroad in its own shape, is in this manner virtually exported in that of the complete manufacture, and may easily be sent to the remotest corners of the world. In this manner have grown up naturally, and as it were of their own accord, the manufactures of Leeds, Halifax, Sheffield, Birmingham, and Wolverhampton. Such manufactures are the offspring of agriculture. In the modern history of Europe, their extension and improvement have generally been posterior to those which were the offspring of foreign commerce. England was noted for the manufacture of fine cloths made of Spanish wool, more than a century before any of those which now flourish in the places above mentioned were fit for foreign sale. The extension and improvement of these last could not take place but in consequence of the extension and improvement of agriculture, the last and greatest effect of foreign commerce, and of the manufactures immediately introduced by it, and which I shall now proceed to explain.

CHAPTER IV

HOW THE COMMERCE OF THE TOWNS CONTRIBUTED TO THE IMPROVEMENT OF THE COUNTRY

The increase and riches of commercial and manufacturing towns, contributed to the improvement and cultivation of the countries to which they belonged, in three different ways.

First, by affording a great and ready market for the rude produce of the country, they gave encouragement to its cultivation and further improvement. This benefit was not even confined to the countries in which they were situated, but extended more or less to all those with which they had any dealings. To all of them they afforded a market for some part either of their rude or manufactured produce, and consequently gave some encouragement to the industry and improvement of all. Their own country, however, on account of its neighbourhood, necessarily derived the greatest benefit from this market. Its rude produce being charged with less carriage, the traders could pay the growers a better price for it, and yet afford it as cheap to the consumers as that of more distant countries.

Secondly, the wealth acquired by the inhabitants of cities was frequently employed in purchasing such lands as were to be sold, of which a great part would frequently be uncultivated. Merchants are commonly ambitious of becoming country gentlemen, and when they do, they are generally the best of all improvers. A merchant is accustomed to employ his money chiefly in profitable projects; whereas a mere country gentleman is accustomed to employ it chiefly in expence. The one often sees his money go from him and return to him again with a profit: the other, when once he parts with it, very seldom expects to see any more of it. Those different habits naturally affect their temper and disposition in every sort of business. A merchant is commonly a bold; a country gentleman, a timid undertaker. The one is not afraid to lay out at once a large capital upon the improvement of his land, when he has a probable prospect of raising the value of it in proportion to the expence. The other, if he has any capital, which is not always the case, seldom ventures to employ it in this manner. If he improves at all, it is commonly not with a capital, but with what he can save out of his annual revenue. Whoever has had the fortune to live in a mercantile town situated in an unimproved country, must have frequently observed how much more spirited the operations of merchants were in this way, than those of mere country gentlemen. The habits, besides, of order, oeconomy and attention, to which mercantile business naturally forms a merchant, render him much fitter to execute, with profit and success, any project of improvement.

Thirdly, and lastly, commerce and manufactures gradually introduced order and good government, and with them, the liberty and security of individuals, among the inhabitants of the country, who had before lived almost in a continual state of war with their neighbours, and of servile dependency upon their superiors. This, though it has been the least observed, is by far the most important of all their effects. Mr. Hume is the only writer who, so far as I know, has hitherto taken notice of it.

In a country which has neither foreign commerce, nor any of the finer manufactures, a great proprietor, having nothing for which he can exchange the greater part of the produce of his lands which is over and above the maintenance of the cultivators, consumes the whole in rustic hospitality at home. If this surplus produce is sufficient to maintain a hundred or a thousand men, he can make use of it in no other way than by maintaining a hundred or a thousand men. He is at all times, therefore, surrounded with a multitude of retainers and dependants, who having no equivalent to give in return for their maintenance, but being fed entirely by his bounty, must obey him, for the same reason that soldiers must obey the prince who pays them. Before the extension of commerce and manufactures in Europe, the hospitality of the rich and the great, from the sovereign down to the smallest baron, exceeded every thing which in the present times we can easily form a notion of. Westminster hall was the dining-room of William Rufus, and might frequently, perhaps, not be too large for his company. It was reckoned a piece of magnificence in Thomas Becket, that he strowed the floor of his hall with clean hay or rushes in the season, in order that the knights and squires, who could not get seats, might not spoil their fine clothes when they sat down on the floor to eat their dinner. The great earl of Warwick is said to have entertained every day at his different manors, thirty thousand people; and though the number here may have been exaggerated, it must, however, have been very great to admit of such exaggeration. A hospitality nearly of the same kind was exercised not many years ago in many different parts of the highlands of Scotland. It seems to be common in all nations to whom commerce and manufactures are little known. I have seen, says

Doctor Pocock, an Arabian chief dine in the streets of a town where he had
come to sell his cattle, and invite all passengers, even common beggars, to
sit down with him and partake of his banquet.

The occupiers of land were in every respect as dependent upon the
great proprietor as his retainers. Even such of them as were not in a state
of villanage, were tenants at will, who paid a rent in no respect equivalent
to the subsistence which the land afforded them. A crown, half a crown,
a sheep, a lamb, was some years ago in the highlands of Scotland a
common rent for lands which maintained a family. In some places it is
so at this day; nor will money at present purchase a greater quantity of
commodities there than in other places. In a country where the surplus
produce of a large estate must be consumed upon the estate itself, it
will frequently be more convenient for the proprietor, that part of it be
consumed at a distance from his own house, provided they who consume
it are as dependent upon him as either his retainers or his menial servants.
He is thereby saved from the embarrassment of either too large a company
or too large a family. A tenant at will, who possesses land sufficient to
maintain his family for little more than a quit-rent, is as dependent upon
the proprietor as any servant or retainer whatever, and must obey him
with as little reserve. Such a proprietor, as he feeds his servants and
retainers at his own house, so he feeds his tenants at their houses. The
subsistence of both is derived from his bounty, and its continuance depends upon his good pleasure.

Upon the authority which the great proprietors necessarily had in such
a state of things over their tenants and retainers, was founded the power
of the ancient barons. They necessarily became the judges in peace, and
the leaders in war, of all who dwelt upon their estates. They could maintain order and execute the law within their respective demesnes, because
each of them could there turn the whole force of all the inhabitants against
the injustice of any one. No other person had sufficient authority to do
this. The king in particular had not. In those ancient times he was little
more than the greatest proprietor in his dominions, to whom, for the
sake of common defence against their common enemies, the other great
proprietors paid certain respects. To have enforced payment of a small
debt within the lands of a great proprietor, where all the inhabitants were
armed and accustomed to stand by one another, would have cost the king,
had he attempted it by his own authority, almost the same effort as
to extinguish a civil war. He was, therefore, obliged to abandon the
administration of justice through the greater part of the country, to those
who were capable of administering it; and for the same reason to leave
the command of the country militia to those whom that militia would
obey.

It is a mistake to imagine that those territorial jurisdictions took their origin from the feudal law. Not only the highest jurisdictions both civil and criminal, but the power of levying troops, of coining money, and even that of making bye-laws for the government of their own people, were all rights possessed allodially by the great proprietors of land several centuries before even the name of the feudal law was known in Europe. The authority and jurisdiction of the Saxon lords in England, appear to have been as great before the conquest, as that of any of the Norman lords after it. But the feudal law is not supposed to have become the common law of England till after the conquest. That the most extensive authority and jurisdictions were possessed by the great lords in France allodially, long before the feudal law was introduced into that country, is a matter of fact that admits of no doubt. That authority and those jurisdictions all necessarily flowed from the state of property and manners just now described. Without remounting to the remote antiquities of either the French or English monarchies, we may find in much later times many proofs that such effects must always flow from such causes. It is not thirty years ago since Mr. Cameron of Lochiel, a gentleman of Lochabar in Scotland, without any legal warrant whatever, not being what was then called a lord of regality, nor even a tenant in chief, but a vassal of the duke of Argyle, and without being so much as a justice of peace, used, notwithstanding, to exercise the highest criminal jurisdiction over his own people. He is said to have done so with great equity, though without any of the formalities of justice; and it is not improbable that the state of that part of the country at that time made it necessary for him to assume this authority in order to maintain the public peace. That gentleman, whose rent never exceeded five hundred pounds a year, carried, in 1745, eight hundred of his own people into the rebellion with him.

The introduction of the feudal law, so far from extending, may be regarded as an attempt to moderate the authority of the great allodial lords. It established a regular subordination, accompanied with a long train of services and duties, from the king down to the smallest proprietor. During the minority of the proprietor, the rent, together with the management of his lands, fell into the hands of his immediate superior, and, consequently, those of all great proprietors into the hands of the king, who was charged with the maintenance and education of the pupil, and who, from his authority as guardian, was supposed to have a right of disposing of him in marriage, provided it was in a manner not unsuitable to his rank. But though this institution necessarily tended to strengthen the authority of the king, and to weaken that of the great proprietors, it could not do either sufficiently for establishing order and good government among the inhabitants of the country; because it could not alter sufficiently that state of property and manners from which the disorders arose. The authority of government still continued to be, as before, too weak in the head and too strong in the inferior members, and the excessive strength of the inferior members was the cause of the weakness of the head. After the institution of feudal subordination, the king was as incapable of restraining the violence of the great lords as before. They still continued to make war according to their own discretion, almost continually upon one another, and very frequently upon the king; and the open country still continued to be a scene of violence, rapine, and disorder.

But what all the violence of the feudal institutions could never have effected, the silent and insensible operation of foreign commerce and manufactures gradually brought about. These gradually furnished the great proprietors with something for which they could exchange the whole surplus produce of their lands, and which they could consume themselves without sharing it either with tenants or retainers. All for ourselves, and nothing for other people, seems, in every age of the world, to have been the vile maxim of the masters of mankind. As soon, therefore, as they could find a method of consuming the whole value of their rents themselves, they had no disposition to share them with any other persons. For a pair of diamond buckles perhaps, or for something as frivolous and useless, they exchanged the maintenance, or what is the same thing, the price of the maintenance of a thousand men for a year, and with it the whole weight and authority which it could give them. The buckles, however, were to be all their own, and no other human creature was to have any share of them; whereas in the more ancient method of expence they must have shared with at least a thousand people. With the judges that were to determine the preference, this difference was perfectly decisive; and thus, for the gratification of the most childish, the meanest and the most sordid of all vanities, they gradually bartered their whole power and authority.

In a country where there is no foreign commerce, nor any of the finer manufactures, a man of ten thousand a year cannot well employ his revenue in any other way than in maintaining, perhaps, a thousand families, who are all of them necessarily at his command. In the present state of Europe, a man of ten thousand a year can spend his whole revenue, and he generally does so, without directly maintaining twenty people, or being able to command more than ten footmen not worth the commanding. Indirectly, perhaps, he maintains as great or even a greater number of people than he could have done by the ancient method of expence. For though the quantity of precious productions for which he exchanges his whole revenue be very small, the number of workmen employed in collecting and preparing it, must necessarily have been very great. Its great price generally arises from the wages of their labour, and the profits of all their immediate employers. By paying that price he indirectly pays all those wages and profits, and thus indirectly contributes to the maintenance of all the workmen and their employers. He generally contributes, however, but a very small proportion to that of each, to very few perhaps a tenth, to many not a hundredth, and to some not a thousandth, nor even a ten thousandth part of their whole annual maintenance. Though he contributes, therefore, to the maintenance of them all, they are all more or less independent of him, because generally they can all be maintained without him.

When the great proprietors of land spend their rents in maintaining their tenants and retainers, each of them maintains entirely all his own tenants and all his own retainers. But when they spend them in maintaining tradesmen and artificers, they may, all of them taken together, perhaps, maintain as great, or, on account of the waste which attends rustic hospitality, a greater number of people than before. Each of them, however, taken singly, contributes often but a very small share to the maintenance of any individual of this greater number. Each tradesman or artificer derives his subsistence from the employment, not of one, but of a hundred or a thousand different customers. Though in some measure obliged to them all, therefore, he is not absolutely dependent upon any one of them.

The personal expence of the great proprietors having in this manner gradually increased, it was impossible that the number of their retainers should not as gradually diminish, till they were at last dismissed altogether. The same cause gradually led them to dismiss the unnecessary part of their tenants. Farms were enlarged, and the occupiers of land, notwithstanding the complaints of depopulation, reduced to the number necessary for cultivating it, according to the imperfect state of cultivation and improvement in those times. By the removal of the unnecessary mouths, and by exacting from the farmer the full value of the farm, a greater surplus, or what is the same thing, the price of a greater surplus, was obtained for the proprietor, which the merchants and manufacturers soon furnished him with a method of spending upon his own person in the same manner as he had done the rest. The same cause continuing to operate, he was desirous to raise his rents above what his lands, in the actual state of their improvement, could afford. His tenants could agree to this upon one condition only, that they should be secured in their possession, for such a term of years as might give them time to recover with profit whatever they should lay out in the further improvement of the land. The expensive vanity of the landlord made him willing to accept of this condition; and hence the origin of long leases.

Even a tenant at will, who pays the full value of the land, is not altogether dependent upon the landlord. The pecuniary advantages which they receive from one another, are mutual and equal, and such a tenant will expose neither his life nor his fortune in the service of the proprietor. But if he has a lease for a long term of years, he is altogether independent; and his landlord must not expect from him even the most trifling service beyond what is either expressly stipulated in the lease, or imposed upon him by the common and known law of the country.

The tenants having in this manner become independent, and the retainers being dismissed, the great proprietors were no longer capable of interrupting the regular execution of justice, or of disturbing the peace of the country. Having sold their birth-right, not like Esau for a mess of pottage in time of hunger and necessity, but in the wantonness of plenty, for trinkets and baubles, fitter to be the play-things of children than the serious pursuits of men, they became as insignificant as any substantial burgher or tradesman in a city. A regular government was established in the country as well as in the city, nobody having sufficient power to disturb its operations in the one, any more than in the other.

It does not, perhaps, relate to the present subject, but I cannot help remarking it, that very old families, such as have possessed some considerable estate from father to son for many successive generations, are very rare in commercial countries. In countries which have little commerce, on the contrary, such as Wales or the highlands of Scotland, they are very common. The Arabian histories seem to be all full of genealogies, and there is a history written by a Tartar Khan, which has been translated into several European languages, and which contains scarce any thing else; a proof that ancient families are very common among those nations. In countries where a rich man can spend his revenue in no other way than by maintaining as many people as it can maintain, he is not apt to run out, and his benevolence it seems is seldom so violent as to attempt to maintain more than he can afford. But where he can spend the greatest revenue upon his own person, he frequently has no bounds to his expence, because he frequently has no bounds to his vanity, or to his affection for his own person. In commercial countries, therefore, riches, in spite of the most violent regulations of law to prevent their dissipation, very seldom remain long in the same family. Among simple nations, on the contrary, they frequently do without any regulations of law: for among nations of shepherds, such as the Tartars and Arabs, the consumable nature of their property necessarily renders all such regulations impossible.

A revolution of the greatest importance to the public happiness, was in this manner brought about by two different orders of people, who had not the least intention to serve the public. To gratify the most childish vanity was the sole motive of the great proprietors. The merchants and artificers, much less ridiculous, acted merely from a view to their own interest, and in pursuit of their own pedlar principle of turning a penny wherever a penny was to be got. Neither of them had either knowledge or foresight of that great revolution which the folly of the one, and the industry of the other, was gradually bringing about.

It is thus that through the greater part of Europe the commerce and manufactures of cities, instead of being the effect, have been the cause and occasion of the improvement and cultivation of the country.

This order, however, being contrary to the natural course of things, is necessarily both slow and uncertain. Compare the slow progress of those European countries of which the wealth depends very much upon their commerce and manufactures, with the rapid advances of our North American colonies, of which the wealth is founded altogether in agriculture. Through the greater part of Europe, the number of inhabitants is not supposed to double in less than five hundred years. In several of our North American colonies, it is found to double in twenty or five-and-twenty years. In Europe the law of primogeniture, and perpetuities of different kinds, prevent the division of great estates, and thereby hinder the multiplication of small proprietors. A small proprietor, however, who knows every part of his little territory, who views it all with the affection which property, especially small property, naturally inspires, and who upon that account takes pleasure not only in cultivating but in adorning it, is generally of all improvers the most industrious, the most intelligent, and the most successful. The same regulations, besides, keep so much land out of the market, that there are always more capitals to buy than there is land to sell, so that what is sold always sells at a monopoly price. The rent never pays the interest of the purchase-money, and is besides burdened with repairs and other occasional charges, to which the interest of money is not liable. To purchase land is every-where in Europe a most unprofitable employment of a small capital. For the sake of the superior security, indeed, a man of moderate circumstances, when he retires from business, will sometimes chuse to lay out his little capital in land. A man of profession too, whose revenue is derived from another source, often loves to secure his savings in the same way. But a young man, who, instead of applying to trade or to some profession, should employ a capital of two or three thousand pounds in the purchase and cultivation of a small piece of land, might indeed expect to live very happily, and very independently, but must bid adieu, forever, to all hope of either great fortune or great illustration, which by a different employment of his stock he might have had the same chance of acquiring with other people. Such a person too, though he cannot aspire at being proprietor, will often disdain to be a farmer. The small quantity of land, therefore, which is brought to market, and the high price of what is brought thither, prevents a great number of capitals from being employed in its cultivation and improvement which would otherwise have taken that direction. In North America, on the contrary, fifty or sixty pounds is often found a sufficient stock to begin a plantation with. The purchase and improvement of uncultivated land, is there the most profitable employment of the smallest as well as of the greatest capitals, and the most direct road to all the fortune and illustration which can be acquired in that country. Such land, indeed, is in North America to be had almost for nothing, or at a price much below the value of the natural produce; a thing impossible in Europe, or, indeed, in any country where all lands have long been private property. If landed estates, however, were divided equally among all the children, upon the death of any proprietor who left a numerous family, the estate would generally be sold. So much land would come to market, that it could no longer sell at a monopoly price. The free rent of the land would go nearer to pay the interest of the purchase-money, and a small capital might be employed in purchasing land as profitably as in any other way.

England, on account of the natural fertility of the soil, of the great extent of the sea-coast in proportion to that of the whole country, and of the many navigable rivers which run through it, and afford the conveniency of water carriage to some of the most inland parts of it, is perhaps as well fitted by nature as any large country in Europe, to be the seat of foreign commerce, and manufactures for distant sale, and of all the improvements which these can occasion. From the beginning of the reign of Elizabeth too, the English legislature has been peculiarly attentive to the interests of commerce and manufactures, and in reality there is no country in Europe, Holland itself not excepted, of which the law is, upon the whole, more favourable to this sort of industry. Commerce and manufactures have accordingly been continually advancing during all this period. The cultivation and improvement of the country has, no doubt, been gradually advancing too: But it seems to have followed slowly, and at a distance, the more rapid progress of commerce and manufactures. The greater part of the country must probably have been cultivated before the reign of Elizabeth; and a very great part of it still remains cultivated, and the cultivation of the far greater part, much inferior to what it might be. The law of England, however, favours agriculture not only indirectly by the protection of commerce, but by several direct encouragements. Except in times of scarcity, the exportation of corn is not only free, but encouraged by a bounty. In times of moderate plenty, the importation of foreign corn is loaded with duties that amount to a prohibition. The importation of live cattle, except from Ireland, is prohibited at all times, and it is but of late that it was permitted from thence. Those who cultivate the land, therefore, have a monopoly against their countrymen for the two greatest and most important articles of land produce, bread and butcher's meat. These encouragements, though at bottom, perhaps, as I shall endeavour to show hereafter, altogether illusory, sufficiently demonstrate at least the good intention of the legislature to favour agriculture. But what is of much more importance than all of them, the yeomanry of England are rendered as secure, as independent, and as respectable as law can make them. No country, therefore, in which the right of primogeniture takes place, which pays tithes, and where perpetuities, though contrary to the spirit of the law, are admitted in some cases, can give more encouragement to agriculture than England. Such, however, notwithstanding, is the state of its cultivation. What would it have been, had the law given no direct encouragement to agriculture besides what arises indirectly from the progress of commerce, and had left the yeomanry in the same condition as in most other countries of Europe? It is now more than two hundred years since the beginning of the reign of Elizabeth, a period as long as the course of human prosperity usually endures.

France seems to have had a considerable share of foreign commerce near a century before England was distinguished as a commercial country. The marine of France was considerable, according to the notions of the times, before the expedition of Charles the VIIIth to Naples. The cultivation and improvement of France, however, is, upon the whole, inferior to that of England. The law of the country has never given the same direct encouragement to agriculture.

The foreign commerce of Spain and Portugal to the other parts of Europe, though chiefly carried on in foreign ships, is very considerable. That to their colonies is carried on in their own, and is much greater, on account of the great riches and extent of those colonies. But it has never introduced any considerable manufactures for distant sale into either of those countries, and the greater part of both still remains uncultivated. The foreign commerce of Portugal is of older standing than that of any great country in Europe, except Italy.

Italy is the only great country of Europe which seems to have been cultivated and improved in every part, by means of foreign commerce and manufactures for distant sale. Before the invasion of Charles the VIIIth, Italy, according to Guicciardin, was cultivated not less in the most mountainous and barren parts of the country, than in the plainest and most fertile. The advantageous situation of the country, and the great number of independent states which at that time subsisted in it, probably contributed not a little to this general cultivation. It is not impossible too, notwithstanding this general expression of one of the most judicious and reserved of modern historians, that Italy was not at that time better cultivated than England is at present.

The capital, however, that is acquired to any country by commerce and manufactures, is all a very precarious and uncertain possession, till some part of it has been secured and realised in the cultivation and improvement of its lands. A merchant, it has been said very properly, is not necessarily the citizen of any particular country. It is in a great measure indifferent to him from what place he carries on his trade; and a very trifling disgust will make him remove his capital, and together with it all the industry which it supports, from one country to another. No part of it can be said to belong to any particular country, till it has been spread as it were over the face of that country, either in buildings, or in the lasting improvement of lands. No vestige now remains of the great wealth, said to have been possessed by the greater part of the Hans towns, except in the obscure histories of the thirteenth and fourteenth centuries. It is even uncertain where some of them were situated, or to what towns in Europe the Latin names given to some of them belong. But though the misfortunes of Italy in the end of the fifteenth and beginning of the sixteenth centuries greatly diminished the commerce and manufactures of the cities of Lombardy and Tuscany, those countries still continue to be among the most populous and best cultivated in Europe. The civil wars of Flanders, and the Spanish government which succeeded them, chased away the great commerce of Antwerp, Ghent, and Bruges. But Flanders still continues to be one of the richest, best cultivated, and most populous provinces of Europe. The ordinary revolutions of war and government easily dry up the sources of that wealth which arises from commerce only. That which arises from the more solid improvements of agriculture, is much more durable, and cannot be destroyed but by those more violent convulsions occasioned by the depredations of hostile and barbarous nations continued for a century or two together; such as those that happened for some time before and after the fall of the Roman empire in the western provinces of Europe.

BOOK IV

Of Systems of political Oeconomy

[The agrarian investment theme that shapes so much of the argument of Book III carries over into Book IV in the form of a series of criticisms of mercantilism. I discuss some of the complications that arise from this procedure in Appendix III.]

INTRODUCTION

Political oeconomy, considered as a branch of the science of a statesman or legislator, proposes two distinct objects: first, to provide a plentiful revenue or subsistence for the people, or more properly to enable them to provide such a revenue or subsistence for themselves; and secondly, to supply the state or commonwealth with a revenue sufficient for the public services. It proposes to enrich both the people and the sovereign.

The different progress of opulence in different ages and nations, has given occasion to two different systems of political oeconomy, with regard to enriching the people. The one may be called the system of commerce, the other that of agriculture. I shall endeavour to explain both as fully and distinctly as I can, and shall begin with the system of commerce. It is the modern system, and is best understood in our own country and in our own times.

CHAPTER I

OF THE PRINCIPLE OF THE COMMERCIAL OR MERCANTILE SYSTEM

That wealth consists in money, or in gold and silver, is a popular notion which naturally arises from the double function of money, as the instrument of commerce, and as the measure of value. In consequence of its being the instrument of commerce, when we have money we can more readily obtain whatever else we have occasion for, than by means of any other commodity. The great affair, we always find, is to get money. When that is obtained, there is no difficulty in making any subsequent purchase. In consequence of its being the measure of value, we estimate that of all other commodities by the quantity of money which they will exchange for. We say of a rich man that he is worth a great deal, and of a poor man that he is worth very little money. A frugal man, or a man eager to be rich, is said to love money; and a careless, a generous, or a profuse man, is said to be indifferent about it. To grow rich is to get money; and wealth and money, in short, are, in common language, considered as in every respect synonymous.

A rich country, in the same manner as a rich man, is supposed to be a country abounding in money; and to heap up gold and silver in any country is supposed to be the readiest way to enrich it. For some time after the discovery of America, the first enquiry of the Spaniards, when they arrived upon any unknown coast, used to be, if there was any gold or silver to be found in the neighbourhood? By the information which they received, they judged whether it was worth while to make a settlement there, or if the country was worth the conquering. Plano Carpino, a monk sent ambassador from the king of France to one of the sons of the famous Gengis Khan, says that the Tartars used frequently to ask him, if there was plenty of sheep and oxen in the kingdom of France? Their enquiry had the same object with that of the Spaniards. They wanted to know if the country was rich enough to be worth the conquering. Among the Tartars, as among all other nations of shepherds, who are generally ignorant of the use of money, cattle are the instruments of commerce and the measures of value. Wealth, therefore, according to them, consisted in cattle, as according to the Spaniards it consisted in gold and silver. Of the two, the Tartar notion, perhaps, was the nearest to the truth.

Mr. Locke remarks a distinction between money and other moveable goods. All other moveable goods, he says, are of so consumable a nature that the wealth which consists in them cannot be much depended on, and a nation which abounds in them one year may, without any exportation, but merely by their own waste and extravagance, be in great want of them the next. Money, on the contrary, is a steady friend, which, though it may travel about from hand to hand, yet if it can be kept from going out of the country, is not very liable to be wasted and consumed. Gold and silver, therefore, are, according to him, the most solid and substantial part of the moveable wealth of a nation, and to multiply those metals ought, he thinks, upon that account, to be the great object of its political oeconomy.

Others admit that if a nation could be separated from all the world, it would be of no consequence how much, or how little money circulated in it. The consumable goods which were circulated by means of this money, would only be exchanged for a greater or a smaller number of pieces; but the real wealth or poverty of the country, they allow, would depend altogether upon the abundance or scarcity of those consumable goods. But it is otherwise, they think, with countries which have connections with foreign nations, and which are obliged to carry on foreign wars, and to maintain fleets and armies in distant countries. This, they say, cannot be done, but by sending abroad money to pay them with; and a nation cannot send much money abroad, unless it has a good deal at home. Every such nation, therefore, must endeavour in time of peace to accumulate gold and silver, that, when occasion requires, it may have wherewithal to carry on foreign wars.

In consequence of these popular notions, all the different nations of Europe have studied, though to little purpose, every possible means of accumulating gold and silver in their respective countries. Spain and

Portugal, the proprietors of the principal mines which supply Europe with those metals, have either prohibited their exportation under the severest penalties, or subjected it to a considerable duty. The like prohibition seems anciently to have made a part of the policy of most other European nations. It is even to be found, where we should least of all expect to find it, in some old Scotch acts of parliament, which forbid under heavy penalties the carrying gold or silver *forth of the kingdom.* The like policy anciently took place both in France and England.

When those countries became commercial, the merchants found this prohibition, upon many occasions, extremely inconvenient. They could frequently buy more advantageously with gold and silver than with any other commodity, the foreign goods which they wanted, either to import into their own, or to carry to some other foreign country. They remonstrated, therefore, against this prohibition as hurtful to trade.

They represented, first, that the exportation of gold and silver in order to purchase foreign goods, did not always diminish the quantity of those metals in the kingdom. That, on the contrary, it might frequently increase that quantity; because, if the consumption of foreign goods was not thereby increased in the country, those goods might be re-exported to foreign countries, and, being there sold for a large profit, might bring back much more treasure than was originally sent out to purchase them. Mr. Mun compares this operation of foreign trade to the seed-time and harvest of agriculture. "If we only behold," says he, "the actions of the husbandman in the seed-time, when he casteth away much good corn into the ground, we shall account him rather a madman than a husbandman. But when we consider his labours in the harvest, which is the end of his endeavours, we shall find the worth and plentiful increase of his actions."

They represented, secondly, that this prohibition could not hinder the exportation of gold and silver, which, on account of the smallness of their bulk in proportion to their value, could easily be smuggled abroad. That this exportation could only be prevented by a proper attention to, what they called, the balance of trade. That when the country exported to a greater value than it imported, a balance became due to it from foreign nations, which was necessarily paid to it in gold and silver, and thereby increased the quantity of those metals in the kingdom. But that when it imported to a greater value than it exported, a contrary balance became due to foreign nations, which was necessarily paid to them in the same manner, and thereby diminished that quantity. That in this case to prohibit the exportation of those metals could not prevent it, but only by making it more dangerous, render it more expensive. That the exchange was thereby turned more against the country which owed the balance, than it otherwise might have been; the merchant who purchased a bill upon the foreign country being obliged to pay the banker who sold it, not only for the natural risk, trouble and expence of sending the money thither, but for the extraordinary risk arising from the prohibition. But that the more the exchange was against any country, the more the balance of trade became necessarily against it; the money of that country becoming necessarily of so much less value, in comparison with that of the country to which the balance was due. That if the exchange between England and Holland, for example, was five per cent. against England, it would require a hundred and five ounces of silver in England to purchase a bill for a hundred ounces of silver in Holland: that a hundred and five ounces of silver in England, therefore, would be worth only a hundred ounces of silver in Holland, and would purchase only a proportionable quantity of Dutch goods: but that a hundred ounces of silver in Holland, on the contrary, would be worth a hundred and five ounces in England, and would purchase a proportionable quantity of English goods: that the English goods which were sold to Holland would be sold so much cheaper; and the Dutch goods which were sold to England, so much dearer, by the difference of the exchange; that the one would draw so much less Dutch money to England, and the other so much more English money to Holland, as this difference amounted to: and that the balance of trade, therefore, would necessarily be so much more against England, and would require a greater balance of gold and silver to be exported to Holland.

Those arguments were partly solid and partly sophistical. They were solid so far as they asserted that the exportation of gold and silver in trade might frequently be advantageous to the country. They were solid too, in asserting that no prohibition could prevent their exportation, when private people found any advantage in exporting them. But they were sophistical in supposing, that either to preserve or to augment the quantity of those metals required more the attention of government, than to preserve or to augment the quantity of any other useful commodities, which the freedom of trade, without any such attention, never fails to supply in the proper quantity. They were sophistical too, perhaps, in asserting that the high price of exchange necessarily increased, what they called, the unfavourable balance of trade, or occasioned the exportation of a greater quantity of gold and silver. That high price, indeed, was extremely disadvantageous to the merchants who had any money to pay in foreign countries. They paid so much dearer for the bills which their bankers granted them upon those countries. But though the risk arising from the prohibition might occasion some extraordinary expence to the bankers, it would not necessarily carry any more money out of the country. This expence would generally be all laid out in the country, in smuggling the money out of it, and could seldom occasion the exportation of a single six-pence beyond the precise sum drawn for. The high price of exchange too would naturally dispose the merchants to endeavour to make their exports nearly balance their imports, in order that they might have this high exchange to pay upon as small a sum as possible. The high price of exchange, besides, must necessarily have operated as a tax, in raising the price of foreign goods, and thereby diminishing their consumption. It would tend, therefore, not to increase, but to diminish, what they called, the unfavourable balance of trade, and consequently the exportation of gold and silver.

Such as they were, however, those arguments convinced the people to whom they were addressed. They were addressed by merchants to parliaments, and to the councils of princes, to nobles, and to country gentlemen; by those who were supposed to understand trade, to those who were conscious to themselves that they knew nothing about the matter. That foreign trade enriched the country, experience demonstrated to the nobles and country gentlemen, as well as to the merchants; but how, or in what manner, none of them well knew. The merchants knew perfectly in what manner it enriched themselves. It was their business to know it. But to know in what manner it enriched the country, was no part of their business. This subject never came into their consideration, but when they had occasion to apply to their country for some change in the laws relating to foreign trade. It then became necessary to say something about the beneficial effects of foreign trade, and the manner in which those effects were obstructed by the laws as they then stood. To the judges who were to decide the business, it appeared a most satisfactory account of the matter, when they were told that foreign trade brought money into the country, but that the laws in question hindered it from bringing so much as it otherwise would do. Those arguments therefore produced the wished-for effect. The prohibition of exporting gold and silver was in France and England confined to the coin of those respective countries. The exportation of foreign coin and of bullion was made free. In Holland, and in some other places, this liberty was extended even to the coin of the country. The attention of government was turned away from guarding against the exportation of gold and silver, to watch over the balance of trade, as the only cause which could occasion any augmentation or diminution of those metals. From one fruitless care it was turned away to another care much more intricate, much more embarrassing, and just equally fruitless. The title of Mun's book, England's Treasure in Foreign Trade, became a fundamental maxim in the political oeconomy, not of England only, but of all other commercial countries. The inland or home trade, the most important of all, the trade in which an equal capital affords the greatest revenue, and creates the greatest employment to the people of the country, was considered as subsidiary only to foreign trade. It neither brought money into the country, it was said, nor carried any out of it. The country therefore could never become either richer or poorer by means of it, except so far as its prosperity or decay might indirectly influence the state of foreign trade.

A country that has no mines of its own must undoubtedly draw its gold and silver from foreign countries, in the same manner as one that has no vineyards of its own must draw its wines. It does not seem necessary, however, that the attention of government should be more turned towards the one than towards the other object. A country that has wherewithal to buy wine, will always get the wine which it has occasion for; and a country that has wherewithal to buy gold and silver, will never be in want of those metals. They are to be bought for a certain price like all other commodities, and as they are the price of all other commodities, so all other commodities are the price of those metals. We trust with perfect security that the freedom of trade, without any attention of government, will always supply us with the wine which we have occasion for: and we may trust with equal security that it will always supply us with all the gold and silver which we can afford to purchase or to employ, either in circulating our commodities, or in other uses.

[In the four sections that follow—from Chapters I, II, III, and VII of Book IV—Smith explains how erroneous mercantilistic trade policy impeded the emergence of mutually advantageous trade relations between Europe and the rest of the world, especially in America. Of special rhetorical importance for Smith's polemical purposes is the connection he draws between mercantilist policy and increasing "animosity" and "jealousy" between the nations of the world. In Appendix IV, I explain how in doing this Smith developed what we call a *doux-commerce* (gentle commerce) perspective on how the civilizing process unfolded in Europe after the Middle Ages.]

[FROM CHAPTER I]

The importation of gold and silver is not the principal, much less the sole benefit which a nation derives from its foreign trade. Between whatever places foreign trade is carried on, they all of them derive two distinct benefits from it. It carries out that surplus part of the produce of their land and labour for which there is no demand among them, and brings back in return for it something else for which there is a demand. It gives a value to their superfluities, by exchanging them for something else, which may satisfy a part of their wants, and increase their enjoyments. By means of it, the narrowness of the home market does not hinder the division of labour in any particular branch of art or manufacture from being carried to the highest perfection. By opening a more extensive market for whatever part of the produce of their labour may exceed the home consumption, it encourages them to improve its productive powers, and to augment its annual produce to the utmost, and thereby to increase the real revenue and wealth of the society. These great and important services foreign trade is continually occupied in performing, to all the different countries between which it is carried on. They all derive great benefit from it, though that in which the merchant resides generally derives the greatest, as he is generally more employed in supplying the wants, and carrying out the superfluities of his own, than of any other particular country. To import the gold and silver which may be wanted, into the countries which have no mines, is, no doubt, a part of the business of foreign commerce. It is, however, a most insignificant part of it. A country which carried on foreign trade merely upon this account, could scarce have occasion to freight a ship in a century.

It is not by the importation of gold and silver, that the discovery of America has enriched Europe. By the abundance of the American mines, those metals have become cheaper. A service of plate can now be purchased for about a third part of the corn, or a third part of the labour, which it would have cost in the fifteenth century. With the same annual expence of labour and commodities, Europe can annually purchase about three times the quantity of plate which it could have purchased at that time. But when a commodity comes to be sold for a third part of what had been its usual price, not only those who purchased it before can purchase three times their former quantity, but it is brought down to the level of a much greater number of purchasers, perhaps to more than ten, perhaps to more than twenty times the former number. So that there may be in Europe at present not only more than three times, but more than twenty or thirty times the quantity of plate which would have been in it, even in its present state of improvement, had the discovery of the American mines never been made. So far Europe has, no doubt, gained a real conveniency, though surely a very trifling one. The cheapness of gold and silver renders those metals rather less fit for the purposes of money than they were before. In order to make the same purchases, we must load ourselves with a greater quantity of them, and carry about a shilling in our pocket where a groat would have done before. It is difficult to say which is most trifling, this inconveniency, or the opposite conveniency. Neither the one nor the other could have made any very essential change in the state of Europe. The discovery of America, however, certainly made a most essential one. By opening a new and inexhaustible market to all the commodities of Europe, it gave occasion to new divisions of labour and improvements of art, which, in the narrow circle of the ancient commerce, could never have taken place for want of a market to take off the greater part of their produce. The productive powers of labour were improved, and its produce increased in all the different countries of Europe, and together with it the real revenue and wealth of the inhabitants. The commodities of Europe were almost all new to America, and many of those of America were new to Europe. A new set of exchanges, therefore, began to take place which had never been thought of before, and which should naturally have proved as advantageous to the new, as it certainly did to the old continent. The savage injustice of the Europeans rendered an event, which ought to have been beneficial to all, ruinous and destructive to several of those unfortunate countries.

The discovery of a passage to the East Indies, by the Cape of Good Hope, which happened much about the same time, opened, perhaps, a still more extensive range to foreign commerce than even that of America, notwithstanding the greater distance. There were but two nations in America, in any respect superior to savages, and these were destroyed almost as soon as discovered. The rest were mere savages. But the empires of China, Indostan, Japan, as well as several others in the East Indies, without having richer mines of gold or silver, were in every other respect much richer, better cultivated, and more advanced in all arts and manufactures than either Mexico or Peru, even though we should credit, what plainly deserves no credit, the exaggerated accounts of the Spanish writers, concerning the ancient state of those empires. But rich and civilized nations can always exchange to a much greater value with one another, than with savages and barbarians. Europe, however, has hitherto derived much less advantage from its commerce with the East Indies, than from that with America. The Portuguese monopolized the East India trade to themselves for about a century, and it was only indirectly and through them, that the other nations of Europe could either send out or receive any goods from that country. When the Dutch, in the beginning of the last century, began to encroach upon them, they vested their whole East India commerce in an exclusive company. The English, French, Swedes, and Danes, have all followed their example, so that no great nation in Europe has ever yet had the benefit of a free commerce to the East Indies. No other reason need be assigned why it has never been so advantageous as the trade to America, which, between almost every nation of Europe and its own colonies, is free to all its subjects. The exclusive privileges of those East India companies, their great riches, the great favour and protection which these have procured them from their respective governments, have excited much envy against them. This envy has frequently represented their trade as altogether pernicious, on account of the great quantities of silver, which it every year exports from the countries from which it is carried on. The parties concerned have replied, that their trade, by this continual exportation of silver, might, indeed, tend to impoverish Europe in general, but not the particular country from which it was carried on; because, by the exportation of a part of the returns to other European countries, it annually brought home a much greater quantity of that metal than it carried out. Both the objection and the reply are founded in the popular notion which I have been just now examining. It is, therefore, unnecessary to say any thing further about either. By the annual exportation of silver to the East Indies, plate is probably somewhat dearer in Europe than it otherwise might have been; and coined silver probably purchases a larger quantity both of labour and commodities. The former of these two effects is a very small loss, the latter a very small advantage; both too insignificant to deserve any part of the public attention. The trade to the East Indies, by opening a market to the commodities of Europe, or, what comes nearly to the same thing, to the gold and silver which is purchased with those commodities, must necessarily tend to increase the annual production of European commodities, and consequently the real wealth and revenue of Europe. That it has hitherto increased them so little, is probably owing to the restraints which it every-where labours under.

I thought it necessary, though at the hazard of being tedious, to examine at full length this popular notion that wealth consists in money, or in gold and silver. Money in common language, as I have already observed, frequently signifies wealth; and this ambiguity of expression has rendered this popular notion so familiar to us, that even they, who are convinced of its absurdity, are very apt to forget their own principles, and in the course of their reasonings to take it for granted as a certain and undeniable truth. Some of the best English writers upon commerce set out with observing, that the wealth of a country consists, not in its gold and silver only, but in its lands, houses, and consumable goods of all different kinds. In the course of their reasonings, however, the lands, houses, and consumable goods seem to slip out of their memory, and the strain of their argument frequently supposes that all wealth consists in gold and silver, and that to multiply those metals is the great object of national industry and commerce.

The two principles being established, however, that wealth consisted in gold and silver, and that those metals could be brought into a country which had no mines only by the balance of trade, or by exporting to a greater value than it imported; it necessarily became the great object of political oeconomy to diminish as much as possible the importation of foreign goods for home consumption, and to increase as much as possible the exportation of the produce of domestic industry. Its two great engines for enriching the country, therefore, were restraints upon importation, and encouragements to exportation.

The restraints upon importation were of two kinds.

First, Restraints upon the importation of such foreign goods for home consumption as could be produced at home, from whatever country they were imported.

Secondly, Restraints upon the importation of goods of almost all kinds from those particular countries with which the balance of trade was supposed to be disadvantageous.

Those different restraints consisted sometimes in high duties, and sometimes in absolute prohibitions.

Exportation was encouraged sometimes by drawbacks, sometimes by bounties, sometimes by advantageous treaties of commerce with foreign states, and sometimes by the establishment of colonies in distant countries.

Drawbacks were given upon two different occasions. When the home-manufactures were subject to any duty or excise, either the whole or a part of it was frequently drawn back upon their exportation; and when foreign goods liable to a duty were imported in order to be exported again, either the whole or a part of this duty was sometimes given back upon such exportation.

Bounties were given for the encouragement either of some beginning manufactures, or of such sorts of industry of other kinds as were supposed to deserve particular favour.

By advantageous treaties of commerce, particular privileges were procured in some foreign state for the goods and merchants of the country, beyond what were granted to those of other countries.

By the establishment of colonies in distant countries, not only particular privileges, but a monopoly was frequently procured for the goods and merchants of the country which established them.

The two sorts of restraints upon importation above-mentioned, together with these four encouragements to exportation, constitute the six principal means by which the commercial system proposes to increase the quantity of gold and silver in any country by turning the balance of trade in its favour. I shall consider each of them in a particular chapter, and without taking much further notice of their supposed tendency to bring money into the country, I shall examine chiefly what are likely to be the effects of each of them upon the annual produce of its industry. According as they tend either to increase or diminish the value of this annual produce, they must evidently tend either to increase or diminish the real wealth and revenue of the country.

CHAPTER II

OF RESTRAINTS UPON THE IMPORTATION FROM FOREIGN COUNTRIES OF SUCH GOODS AS CAN BE PRODUCED AT HOME

By restraining, either by high duties, or by absolute prohibitions, the importation of such goods from foreign countries as can be produced at home, the monopoly of the home market is more or less secured to the domestic industry employed in producing them. Thus the prohibition of importing either live cattle or salt provisions from foreign countries secures to the graziers of Great Britain the monopoly of the home market for butcher's meat. The high duties upon the importation of corn, which in times of moderate plenty amount to a prohibition, give a like advantage to the growers of that commodity. The prohibition of the importation of foreign woollens is equally favourable to the woollen manufacturers. The silk manufacture, though altogether employed upon foreign materials, has lately obtained the same advantage. The linen manufacture has not yet obtained it, but is making great strides towards it. Many other sorts of manufacturers have, in the same manner, obtained in Great Britain, either altogether, or very nearly a monopoly against their countrymen. The variety of goods of which the importation into Great Britain is prohibited, either absolutely, or under certain circumstances, greatly exceeds what can easily be suspected by those who are not well acquainted with the laws of the customs.

That this monopoly of the home-market frequently gives great encouragement to that particular species of industry which enjoys it, and frequently turns towards that employment a greater share of both the labour and stock of the society than would otherwise have gone to it, cannot be doubted. But whether it tends either to increase the general industry of the society, or to give it the most advantageous direction, is not, perhaps, altogether so evident.

The general industry of the society never can exceed what the capital of the society can employ. As the number of workmen that can be kept in employment by any particular person must bear a certain proportion to his capital, so the number of those that can be continually employed by all the members of a great society, must bear a certain proportion to the whole capital of that society, and never can exceed that proportion.

No regulation of commerce can increase the quantity of industry in any society beyond what its capital can maintain. It can only divert a part of it into a direction into which it might not otherwise have gone; and it is by no means certain that this artificial direction is likely to be more advantageous to the society than that into which it would have gone of its own accord.

Every individual is continually exerting himself to find out the most advantageous employment for whatever capital he can command. It is his own advantage, indeed, and not that of the society, which he has in view. But the study of his own advantage naturally, or rather necessarily leads him to prefer that employment which is most advantageous to the society.

First, every individual endeavours to employ his capital as near home as he can, and consequently as much as he can in the support of domestic industry; provided always that he can thereby obtain the ordinary, or not a great deal less than the ordinary profits of stock.

Thus, upon equal or nearly equal profits, every wholesale merchant naturally prefers the home-trade to the foreign trade of consumption, and the foreign trade of consumption to the carrying trade. In the home-trade his capital is never so long out of his sight as it frequently is in the foreign trade of consumption. He can know better the character and situation of the persons whom he trusts, and if he should happen to be deceived, he knows better the laws of the country from which he must seek redress. In the carrying trade, the capital of the merchant is, as it were, divided between two foreign countries, and no part of it is ever necessarily brought home, or placed under his own immediate view and command. The capital which an Amsterdam merchant employs in carrying corn from Konnigsberg to Lisbon, and fruit and wine from Lisbon to Konnigsberg, must generally be the one-half of it at Konnigsberg and the other half at Lisbon. No part of it need ever come to Amsterdam. The natural residence of such a merchant should either be at Konnigsberg or Lisbon, and it can only be some very particular circumstances which can make him prefer the residence of Amsterdam. The uneasiness, however, which he feels at being separated so far from his capital, generally determines him to bring part both of the Konnigsberg goods which he destines for the market of Lisbon, and of the Lisbon goods which he destines for that of Konnigsberg, to Amsterdam: and though this necessarily subjects him to a double charge of loading and unloading, as well as to the payment of some duties and customs, yet for the sake of having some part of his capital always under his own view and command, he willingly submits to this extraordinary charge; and it is in this manner that every country which has any considerable share of the carrying trade, becomes always the emporium, or general market, for the goods of all the different countries whose trade it carries on. The merchant, in order to save a second loading and unloading, endeavours always to sell in the home-market as much of the goods of all those different countries as he can, and thus, so far as he can, to convert his carrying trade into a foreign trade of consumption. A merchant, in the same manner, who is engaged in the foreign trade of consumption, when he collects goods for foreign markets, will always be glad, upon equal or nearly equal profits, to sell as great a part of them at home as he can. He saves himself the risk and trouble of exportation, when, so far as he can, he thus converts his foreign trade of consumption into a home-trade. Home is in this manner the center, if I may say so, round which the capitals of the inhabitants of every country are continually circulating, and towards which they are always tending, though by particular causes they may sometimes be driven off and repelled from it towards more distant employments. But a capital employed in the home-trade, it has already been shown, necessarily puts into motion a greater quantity of domestic industry, and gives revenue and employment to a greater number of the inhabitants of the country, than an equal capital employed in the foreign trade of consumption: and one employed in the foreign trade of consumption has the same advantage over an equal capital employed in the carrying trade. Upon equal, or only nearly equal profits, therefore, every individual naturally inclines to employ his capital in the manner in which it is likely to afford the greatest support to domestic industry, and to give revenue and employment to the greatest number of people of his own country.

Secondly, every individual who employs his capital in the support of domestic industry, necessarily endeavours so to direct that industry, that its produce may be of the greatest possible value.

The produce of industry is what it adds to the subject or materials upon which it is employed. In proportion as the value of this produce is great or small, so will likewise be the profits of the employer. But it is only for the sake of profit that any man employs a capital in the support of industry; and he will always, therefore, endeavour to employ it in the support of that industry of which the produce is likely to be of the greatest value, or to exchange for the greatest quantity either of money or of other goods.

But the annual revenue of every society is always precisely equal to the exchangeable value of the whole annual produce of its industry, or rather is precisely the same thing with that exchangeable value. As every individual, therefore, endeavours as much as he can both to employ his capital in the support of domestic industry, and so to direct that industry that its produce may be of the greatest value; every individual necessarily labours to render the annual revenue of the society as great as he can. He generally, indeed, neither intends to promote the public interest, nor knows how much he is promoting it. By preferring the support of domestic to that of foreign industry, he intends only his own security; and by directing that industry in such a manner as its produce may be of the greatest value, he intends only his own gain, and he is in this, as in many other cases, led by an invisible hand to promote an end which was no part of his intention. Nor is it always the worse for the society that it was no part of it. By pursuing his own interest he frequently promotes that of the society more effectually than when he really intends to promote it. I have never known much good done by those who affected to trade for the public good. It is an affectation, indeed, not very common among merchants, and very few words need be employed in dissuading them from it.

What is the species of domestic industry which his capital can employ, and of which the produce is likely to be of the greatest value, every individual, it is evident, can, in his local situation, judge much better than any statesman or lawgiver can do for him. The statesman, who should attempt to direct private people in what manner they ought to employ their capitals, would not only load himself with a most unnecessary attention, but assume an authority which could safely be trusted, not only to no single person, but to no council or senate whatever, and which would nowhere be so dangerous as in the hands of a man who had folly and presumption enough to fancy himself fit to exercise it.

To give the monopoly of the home-market to the produce of domestic industry, in any particular art or manufacture, is in some measure to direct private people in what manner they ought to employ their capitals, and must, in almost all cases, be either a useless or a hurtful regulation. If the produce of domestic can be brought there as cheap as that of foreign industry, the regulation is evidently useless. If it cannot, it must generally be hurtful. It is the maxim of every prudent master of a family, never to attempt to make at home what it will cost him more to make than to buy. The taylor does not attempt to make his own shoes, but buys them of the shoemaker. The shoemaker does not attempt to make his own clothes, but employs a taylor. The farmer attempts to make neither the one nor the other, but employs those different artificers. All of them find it for their interest to employ their whole industry in a way in which they have some advantage over their neighbours, and to purchase with a part of its produce, or what is the same thing, with the price of a part of it, whatever else they have occasion for.

What is prudence in the conduct of every private family, can scarce be folly in that of a great kingdom. If a foreign country can supply us with a commodity cheaper than we ourselves can make it, better buy it of them with some part of the produce of our own industry, employed in a way in which we have some advantage. The general industry of the country, being always in proportion to the capital which employs it, will not thereby be diminished, no more than that of the above-mentioned artificers; but only left to find out the way in which it can be employed with the greatest advantage. It is certainly not employed to the greatest advantage, when it is thus directed towards an object which it can buy cheaper than it can make. The value of its annual produce is certainly more or less diminished, when it is thus turned away from producing commodities evidently of more value than the commodity which it is directed to produce. According to the supposition, that commodity could be purchased from foreign countries cheaper than it can be made at home. It could, therefore, have been purchased with a part only of the commodities, or, what is the same thing, with a part only of the price of the commodities, which the industry employed by an equal capital would have produced at home, had it been left to follow its natural course. The industry of the country, therefore, is thus turned away from a more, to a less advantageous employment, and the exchangeable value of its annual produce, instead of being increased, according to the intention of the lawgiver, must necessarily be diminished by every such regulation.

[FROM CHAPTER II]

As there are two cases in which it will generally be advantageous to lay some burden upon foreign, for the encouragement of domestic industry; so there are two others in which it may sometimes be a matter of deliberation; in the one, how far it is proper to continue the free importation of certain foreign goods; and in the other, how far, or in what manner, it may be proper to restore that free importation after it has been for some time interrupted.

The case in which it may sometimes be a matter of deliberation how far it is proper to continue the free importation of certain foreign goods, is, when some foreign nation restrains by high duties or prohibitions the importation of some of our manufactures into their country. Revenge in this case naturally dictates retaliation, and that we should impose the like duties and prohibitions upon the importation of some or all of their manufactures into ours. Nations accordingly seldom fail to retaliate in this manner. The French have been particularly forward to favour their own manufactures by restraining the importation of such foreign goods as could come into competition with them. In this consisted a great part of the policy of Mr. Colbert, who, notwithstanding his great abilities, seems in this case to have been imposed upon by the sophistry of merchants and manufacturers, who are always demanding a monopoly against their countrymen. It is at present the opinion of the most intelligent men in France that his operations of this kind have not been beneficial to his country. That minister, by the tariff of 1667, imposed very high duties upon a great number of foreign manufactures. Upon his refusing to moderate them in favour of the Dutch, they in 1671 prohibited the importation of the wines, brandies and manufactures of France. The war of 1672 seems to have been in part occasioned by this commercial dispute. The peace of Nimeguen put an end to it in 1678, by moderating some of those duties in favour of the Dutch, who in consequence took off their prohibition. It was about the same time that the French and English began mutually to oppress each other's industry, by the like duties and prohibitions, of which the French, however, seem to have set the first example. The spirit of hostility which has subsisted between the two nations ever since, has hitherto hindered them from being moderated on either side. In 1697 the English prohibited the importation of bonelace, the manufacture of Flanders. The government of that country, at that time under the dominion of Spain, prohibited in return the importation of English woollens. In 1700, the prohibition of importing bonelace into England, was taken off upon condition that the importation of English woollens into Flanders should be put on the same footing as before.

There may be good policy in retaliations of this kind, when there is a probability that they will procure the repeal of the high duties or prohibitions complained of. The recovery of a great foreign market will generally more than compensate the transitory inconveniency of paying dearer during a short time for some sorts of goods. To judge whether such retaliations are likely to produce such an effect, does not, perhaps, belong so much to the science of a legislator, whose deliberations ought to be governed by general principles which are always the same, as to the skill of that insidious and crafty animal, vulgarly called a statesman or politician, whose councils are directed by the momentary fluctuations of affairs. When there is no probability that any such repeal can be procured, it seems a bad method of compensating the injury done to certain classes of our people, to do another injury ourselves, not only to those classes, but to almost all the other classes of them. When our neighbours prohibit some manufacture of ours, we generally prohibit, not only the same, for that alone would seldom affect them considerably, but some other manufacture of theirs. This may no doubt give encouragement to some particular class of workmen among ourselves, and by excluding some of their rivals, may enable them to raise their price in the home-market. Those workmen, however, who suffered by our neighbours' prohibition will not be benefited by ours. On the contrary, they and almost all the other classes of our citizens will thereby be obliged to pay dearer than before for certain goods. Every such law, therefore, imposes a real tax upon the whole country, not in favour of that particular class of workmen who were injured by our neighbours' prohibition, but of some other class.

The case in which it may sometimes be a matter of deliberation, how far, or in what manner, it is proper to restore the free importation of foreign goods, after it has been for some time interrupted, is, when particular manufactures, by means of high duties or prohibitions upon all foreign goods which can come into competition with them, have been so far extended as to employ a great multitude of hands. Humanity may in this case require that the freedom of trade should be restored only by slow gradations, and with a good deal of reserve and circumspection. Were those high duties and prohibitions taken away all at once, cheaper foreign goods of the same kind might be poured so fast into the home market, as to deprive all at once many thousands of our people of their ordinary employment and means of subsistence. The disorder which this would occasion might no doubt be very considerable. It would in all probability, however, be much less than is commonly imagined, for the two following reasons:

First, all those manufactures, of which any part is commonly exported to other European countries without a bounty, could be very little affected by the freest importation of foreign goods. Such manufactures must be sold as cheap abroad as any other foreign goods of the same quality and kind, and consequently must be sold cheaper at home. They would still, therefore, keep possession of the home market, and though a capricious man of fashion might sometimes prefer foreign wares, merely because they were foreign, to cheaper and better goods of the same kind that were made at home, this folly could, from the nature of things, extend to so few, that it could make no sensible impression upon the general employment of the people. But a great part of all the different branches of our woollen manufacture, of our tanned leather, and of our hard-ware, are annually exported to other European countries without any bounty, and these are the manufactures which employ the greatest number of hands. The silk, perhaps, is the manufacture which would suffer the most by this freedom of trade, and after it the linen, though the latter much less than the former.

Secondly, though a great number of people should, by thus restoring the freedom of trade, be thrown all at once out of their ordinary employment and common method of subsistence, it would by no means follow that they would thereby be deprived either of employment or subsistence. By the reduction of the army and navy at the end of the late war, more than a hundred thousand soldiers and seamen, a number equal to what is employed in the greatest manufactures, were all at once thrown out of their ordinary employment; but, though they no doubt suffered some inconveniency, they were not thereby deprived of all employment and subsistence. The greater part of the seamen, it is probable, gradually betook themselves to the merchant-service as they could find occasion, and in the meantime both they and the soldiers were absorbed in the great mass of the people, and employed in a great variety of occupations. Not only no great convulsion, but no sensible disorder arose from so great a change in the situation of more than a hundred thousand men, all accustomed to the use of arms, and many of them to rapine and plunder. The number of vagrants was scarce any-where sensibly increased by it, even the wages of labour were not reduced by it in any occupation, so far as I have been able to learn, except in that of seamen in the merchant-service. But if we compare together the habits of a soldier and of any sort of manufacturer, we shall find that those of the latter do not tend so much to disqualify him from being employed in a new trade, as those of the former from being employed in any. The manufacturer has always been accustomed to look for his subsistence from his labour only: the soldier to expect it from his pay. Application and industry have been familiar to the one; idleness and dissipation to the other. But it is surely much easier to change the direction of industry from one sort of labour to another, than to turn idleness and dissipation to any. To the greater part of manufactures besides, it has already been observed, there are other collateral manufactures of so similar a nature, that a workman can easily transfer his industry from one of them to another. The greater part of such workmen too are occasionally employed in country labour. The stock which employed them in a particular manufacture before, will still remain in the country to employ an equal number of people in some other way. The capital of the country remaining the same, the demand for labour will likewise be the same, or very nearly the same, though it may be exerted in different places and for different occupations. Soldiers and seamen, indeed, when discharged from the king's service, are at liberty to exercise any trade, within any town or place of Great Britain or Ireland. Let the same natural liberty of exercising what species of industry they please, be restored to all his majesty's subjects, in the same manner as to soldiers and seamen; that is, break down the exclusive privileges of corporations, and repeal the statute of apprenticeship, both which are real encroachments upon natural liberty, and add to these the repeal of the law of settlements, so that a poor workman, when thrown out of employment either in one trade or in one place, may seek for it in another trade or in another place, without the fear either of a prosecution or of a removal, and neither the public nor the individuals will suffer much more from the occasional disbanding some particular classes of manufacturers, than from that of soldiers. Our manufacturers have no doubt great merit with their country, but they cannot have more than those who defend it with their blood, nor deserve to be treated with more delicacy.

To expect, indeed, that the freedom of trade should ever be entirely restored in Great Britain, is as absurd as to expect that an Oceana or Utopia should ever be established in it. Not only the prejudices of the public, but what is much more unconquerable, the private interests of many individuals, irresistibly oppose it. Were the officers of the army to oppose with the same zeal and unanimity any reduction in the number of forces, with which master manufacturers set themselves against every law that is likely to increase the number of their rivals in the home market; were the former to animate their soldiers, in the same manner as the latter enflame their workmen, to attack with violence and outrage the proposers of any such regulation; to attempt to reduce the army would be as dangerous as it has now become to attempt to diminish in any respect the monopoly which our manufacturers have obtained against us. This monopoly has so much increased the number of some particular tribes of them, that, like an overgrown standing army, they have become formidable to the government, and upon many occasions intimidate the legislature. The member of parliament who supports every proposal for strengthening this monopoly, is sure to acquire not only the reputation of understanding trade, but great popularity and influence with an order of men whose numbers and wealth render them of great importance. If he opposes them, on the contrary, and still more if he has authority enough to be able to thwart them, neither the most acknowledged probity, nor the highest rank, nor the greatest public services, can protect him from the most infamous abuse and detraction, from personal insults, nor sometimes from real danger, arising from the insolent outrage of furious and disappointed monopolists.

The undertaker of a great manufacture, who, by the home markets being suddenly laid open to the competition of foreigners, should be obliged to abandon his trade, would no doubt suffer very considerably. That part of his capital which had usually been employed in purchasing materials and in paying his workmen, might, without much difficulty, perhaps, find another employment. But that part of it which was fixed in workhouses, and in the instruments of trade, could scarce be disposed of without considerable loss. The equitable regard, therefore, to his interest requires that changes of this kind should never be introduced suddenly, but slowly, gradually, and after a very long warning. The legislature, were it possible that its deliberations could be always directed, not by the clamorous importunity of partial interests, but by an extensive view of the general good, ought upon this very account, perhaps, to be particularly careful neither to establish any new monopolies of this kind, nor to extend further those which are already established. Every such regulation introduces some degree of real disorder into the constitution of the state, which it will be difficult afterwards to cure without occasioning another disorder.

How far it may be proper to impose taxes upon the importation of foreign goods, in order, not to prevent their importation, but to raise a revenue for government, I shall consider hereafter when I come to treat of taxes. Taxes imposed with a view to prevent, or even to diminish importation, are evidently as destructive of the revenue of the customs as of the freedom of trade.

[FROM CHAPTER III]

PART II

Of the Unreasonableness of those extraordinary Restraints upon other Principles

In the foregoing Part of this Chapter I have endeavoured to shew, even upon the principles of the commercial system, how unnecessary it is to lay extraordinary restraints upon the importation of goods from those countries with which the balance of trade is supposed to be disadvantageous.

Nothing, however, can be more absurd than this whole doctrine of the balance of trade, upon which, not only these restraints, but almost all the other regulations of commerce are founded. When two places trade with one another, this doctrine supposes that, if the balance be even, neither of them either loses or gains; but if it leans in any degree to one side, that one of them loses, and the other gains in proportion to its declension from the exact equilibrium. Both suppositions are false. A trade which is forced by means of bounties and monopolies, may be, and commonly is disadvantageous to the country in whose favour it is meant to be established, as I shall endeavour to shew hereafter. But that trade which, without force or constraint, is naturally and regularly carried on between any two places, is always advantageous, though not always equally so, to both.

By advantage or gain, I understand, not the increase of the quantity of gold and silver, but that of the exchangeable value of the annual produce of the land and labour of the country, or the increase of the annual revenue of its inhabitants.

If the balance be even, and if the trade between the two places consist altogether in the exchange of their native commodities, they will, upon most occasions, not only both gain, but they will gain equally, or very near equally: each will in this case afford a market for a part of the surplus produce of the other: each will replace a capital which had been employed in raising and preparing for the market this part of the surplus produce of the other, and which had been distributed among, and given revenue and maintenance to a certain number of its inhabitants. Some part of the inhabitants of each, therefore, will indirectly derive their revenue and maintenance from the other. As the commodities exchanged too are supposed to be of equal value, so the two capitals employed in the trade will, upon most occasions, be equal, or very nearly equal; and both being employed in raising the native commodities of the two countries, the revenue and maintenance which their distribution will afford to the inhabitants of each will be equal, or very nearly equal. This revenue and maintenance, thus mutually afforded, will be greater or smaller in proportion to the extent of their dealings. If these should annually amount to an hundred thousand pounds, for example, or to a million on each side, each of them would afford an annual revenue in the one case of an hundred thousand pounds, in the other, of a million, to the inhabitants of the other.

If their trade should be of such a nature that one of them exported to the other nothing but native commodities, while the returns of that other consisted altogether in foreign goods; the balance, in this case, would still be supposed even, commodities being paid for with commodities. They would, in this case too, both gain, but they would not gain equally; and the inhabitants of the country which exported nothing but native commodities would derive the greatest revenue from the trade. If England, for example, should import from France nothing but the native commodities of that country, and, not having such commodities of its own as were in demand there, should annually repay them by sending thither a large quantity of foreign goods, tobacco, we shall suppose, and East India goods; this trade, though it would give some revenue to the inhabitants of both countries, would give more to those of France than to those of England. The whole French capital annually employed in it would annually be distributed among the people of France. But that part of the English capital only which was employed in producing the English commodities with which those foreign goods were purchased, would be annually distributed among the people of England. The greater part of it would replace the capitals which had been employed in Virginia, Indostan, and China, and which had given revenue and maintenance to the inhabitants of those distant countries. If the capitals were equal, or nearly equal, therefore, this employment of the French capital would augment much more the revenue of the people of France, than that of the English capital would the revenue of the people of England. France would in this case carry on a direct foreign trade of consumption with England; whereas England would carry on a round-about trade of the same kind with France. The different effects of a capital employed in the direct, and of one employed in the round-about foreign trade of consumption, have already been fully explained.

There is not, probably, between any two countries, a trade which consists altogether in the exchange either of native commodities on both sides, or of native commodities on one side and of foreign goods on the other. Almost all countries exchange with one another partly native and partly foreign goods. That country, however, in whose cargoes there is the greatest proportion of native, and the least of foreign goods, will always be the principal gainer.

If it was not with tobacco and East India goods, but with gold and silver, that England paid for the commodities annually imported from France, the balance, in this case, would be supposed uneven, commodities not being paid for with commodities, but with gold and silver. The trade, however, would, in this case, as in the foregoing, give some revenue to the inhabitants of both countries, but more to those of France than to those of England. It would give some revenue to those of England. The capital which had been employed in producing the English goods that purchased this gold and silver, the capital which had been distributed among, and given revenue to, certain inhabitants of England, would thereby be replaced, and enabled to continue that employment. The whole capital of England would no more be diminished by this exportation of gold and silver, than by the exportation of an equal value of any other goods. On the contrary, it would, in most cases, be augmented. No goods are sent abroad but those for which the demand is supposed to be greater abroad than at home, and of which the returns consequently, it is expected, will be of more value at home than the commodities exported. If the tobacco which, in England, is worth only a hundred thousand pounds, when sent to France will purchase wine which is, in England, worth a hundred and ten thousand pounds, the exchange will augment the capital of England by ten thousand pounds. If a hundred thousand pounds of English gold, in the same manner, purchase French wine, which, in England, is worth a hundred and ten thousand, this exchange will equally augment the capital of England by ten thousand pounds. As a merchant who has a hundred and ten thousand pounds worth of wine in his cellar, is a richer man than he who has only a hundred thousand pounds worth of tobacco in his warehouse, so is he likewise a richer man than he who has only a hundred thousand pounds worth of gold in his coffers. He can put into motion a greater quantity of industry, and give revenue, maintenance, and employment, to a greater number of people than either of the other two. But the capital of the country is equal to the capitals of all its different inhabitants, and the quantity of industry which can be annually maintained in it, is equal to what all those different capitals can maintain. Both the capital of the country, therefore, and the quantity of industry which can be annually maintained in it, must generally be augmented by this exchange. It would, indeed, be more advantageous for England that it could purchase the wines of France with its own hard-ware and broad-cloth, than with either the tobacco of Virginia, or the gold and silver of Brazil and Peru. A direct foreign trade of consumption is always more advantageous than a round-about one. But a round-about foreign trade of consumption, which is carried on with gold and silver, does not seem to be less advantageous than any other equally round-about one. Neither is a country which has no mines, more likely to be exhausted of gold and silver by this annual exportation of those metals, than one which does not grow tobacco by the like annual exportation of that plant. As a country which has wherewithal to buy tobacco will never be long in want of it, so neither will one be long in want of gold and silver which has wherewithal to purchase those metals.

It is a losing trade, it is said, which a workman carries on with the alehouse; and the trade which a manufacturing nation would naturally carry on with a wine country, may be considered as a trade of the same nature. I answer, that the trade with the alehouse is not necessarily a losing trade. In its own nature it is just as advantageous as any other, though, perhaps, somewhat more liable to be abused. The employment of a brewer, and even that of a retailer of fermented liquors, are as necessary divisions of labour as any other. It will generally be more advantageous for a workman to buy of the brewer the quantity he has occasion for, than to brew it himself, and if he is a poor workman, it will generally be more advantageous for him to buy it, by little and little, of the retailer, than a large quantity of the brewer. He may no doubt buy too much of either, as he may of any other dealers in his neighbourhood, of the butcher, if he is a glutton, or of the draper, if he affects to be a beau among his companions. It is advantageous to the great body of workmen, notwithstanding, that all these trades should be free, though this freedom may be abused in all of them, and is more likely to be so, perhaps, in some than in others. Though individuals, besides, may sometimes ruin their fortunes by an excessive consumption of fermented liquors, there seems to be no risk that a nation should do so. Though in every country there are many people who spend upon such liquors more than they can afford, there are always many more who spend less. It deserves to be remarked too, that, if we consult experience, the cheapness of wine seems to be a cause, not of drunkenness, but of sobriety. The inhabitants of the wine countries are in general the soberest people in Europe; witness the Spaniards, the Italians, and the inhabitants of the southern provinces of France. People are seldom guilty of excess in what is their daily fare. Nobody affects the character of liberality and good fellowship, by being profuse of a liquor which is as cheap as small beer. On the contrary, in the countries which, either from excessive heat or cold, produce no grapes, and where wine consequently is dear and a rarity, drunkenness is a common vice, as among the northern nations, and all those who live between the tropics, the negroes, for example, on the coast of Guinea. When a French regiment comes from some of the northern provinces of France, where wine is somewhat dear, to be quartered in the southern, where it is very cheap, the soldiers, I have frequently heard it observed, are at first debauched by the cheapness and novelty of good wine; but after a few months residence, the greater part of them become as sober as the rest of the inhabitants. Were the duties upon foreign wines, and the excises upon malt, beer, and ale, to be taken away all at once, it might, in the same manner, occasion in Great Britain a pretty general and temporary drunkenness among the middling and inferior ranks of people, which would probably be soon followed by a permanent and almost universal sobriety. At present drunkenness is by no means the vice of people of fashion, or of those who can easily afford the most expensive liquors. A gentleman drunk with ale, has scarce ever been seen among us. The restraints upon the wine trade in Great Britain, besides, do not so much seem calculated to hinder the people from going, if I may say so, to the alehouse, as from going where they can buy the best and cheapest liquor. They favour the wine trade of Portugal, and discourage that of France. The Portuguese, it is said, indeed, are better customers for our manufactures than the French, and should therefore be encouraged in preference to them. As they give us their custom, it is pretended, we should give them ours. The sneaking arts of underling tradesmen are thus erected into political maxims for the conduct of a great empire; for it is the most underling tradesmen only who make it a rule to employ chiefly their own customers. A great trader purchases his goods always where they are cheapest and best, without regard to any little interest of this kind.

By such maxims as these, however, nations have been taught that their interest consisted in beggaring all their neighbours. Each nation has been made to look with an invidious eye upon the prosperity of all the nations with which it trades, and to consider their gain as its own loss. Commerce, which ought naturally to be, among nations, as among individuals, a bond of union and friendship, has become the most fertile source of discord and animosity. The capricious ambition of kings and ministers has not, during the present and the preceding century, been more fatal to the repose of Europe, than the impertinent jealousy of merchants and manufacturers. The violence and injustice of the rulers of mankind is an ancient evil, for which, I am afraid, the nature of human affairs can scarce admit of a remedy. But the mean rapacity, the monopolizing spirit of merchants and manufacturers, who neither are, nor ought to be, the rulers of mankind, though it cannot perhaps be corrected, may very easily be prevented from disturbing the tranquillity of any body but themselves.

That it was the spirit of monopoly which originally both invented and propagated this doctrine, cannot be doubted; and they who first taught it were by no means such fools as they who believed it. In every country it always is and must be the interest of the great body of the people to buy whatever they want of those who sell it cheapest. The proposition is so very manifest, that it seems ridiculous to take any pains to prove it; nor could it ever have been called in question, had not the interested sophistry of merchants and manufacturers confounded the common sense of mankind. Their interest is, in this respect, directly opposite to that of the great body of the people. As it is the interest of the freemen of a corporation to hinder the rest of the inhabitants from employing any workmen but themselves, so it is the interest of the merchants and manufacturers of every country to secure to themselves the monopoly of the home market. Hence in Great Britain, and in most other European countries, the extraordinary duties upon almost all goods imported by alien merchants. Hence the high duties and prohibitions upon all those foreign manufactures which can come into competition with our own. Hence too the extraordinary restraints upon the importation of almost all sorts of goods from those countries with which the balance of trade is supposed to be disadvantageous; that is, from those against whom national animosity happens to be most violently inflamed.

The wealth of a neighbouring nation, however, though dangerous in war and politics, is certainly advantageous in trade. In a state of hostility it may enable our enemies to maintain fleets and armies superior to our own; but in a state of peace and commerce it must likewise enable them to exchange with us to a greater value, and to afford a better market, either for the immediate produce of our own industry, or for whatever is purchased with that produce. As a rich man is likely to be a better customer to the industrious people in his neighbourhood, than a poor, so is likewise a rich nation. A rich man, indeed, who is himself a manufacturer, is a very dangerous neighbour to all those who deal in the same way. All the rest of the neighbourhood, however, by far the greatest number, profit by the good market which his expence affords them. They even profit by his underselling the poorer workmen who deal in the same way with him. The manufacturers of a rich nation, in the same manner, may no doubt be very dangerous rivals to those of their neighbours. This very competition, however, is advantageous to the great body of the people, who profit greatly besides by the good market which the great expence of such a nation affords them in every other way. Private people who want to make a fortune, never think of retiring to the remote and poor provinces of the country, but resort either to the capital, or to some of the great commercial towns. They know, that, where little wealth circulates, there is little to be got, but that where a great deal is in motion, some share of it may fall to them. The same maxims which would in this manner direct the common sense of one, or ten, or twenty individuals, should regulate the judgment of one, or ten, or twenty millions, and should make a whole nation regard the riches of its neighbours, as a probable cause and occasion for itself to acquire riches. A nation that would enrich itself by foreign trade, is certainly most likely to do so when its neighbours are all rich, industrious, and commercial nations. A great nation surrounded on all sides by wandering savages and poor barbarians might, no doubt, acquire riches by the cultivation of its own lands, and by its own interior commerce, but not by foreign trade. It seems to have been in this manner that the ancient Egyptians and the modern Chinese acquired their great wealth. The ancient Egyptians, it is said, neglected foreign commerce, and the modern Chinese, it is known, hold it in the utmost contempt, and scarce deign to afford it the decent protection of the laws. The modern maxims of foreign commerce, by aiming at the impoverishment of all our neighbours, so far as they are capable of producing their intended effect, tend to render that very commerce insignificant and contemptible.

It is in consequence of these maxims that the commerce between France and England has in both countries been subjected to so many discouragements and restraints. If those two countries, however, were to consider their real interest, without either mercantile jealousy or national animosity, the commerce of France might be more advantageous to Great Britain than that of any other country, and for the same reason that of Great Britain to France. France is the nearest neighbour to Great Britain. In the trade between the southern coast of England and the northern and north-western coasts of France, the returns might be expected, in the same manner as in the inland trade, four, five, or six times in the year. The capital, therefore, employed in this trade, could in each of the two countries keep in motion four, five, or six times the quantity of industry, and afford employment and subsistence to four, five, or six times the number of people, which an equal capital could do in the greater part of the other branches of foreign trade. Between the parts of France and Great Britain most remote from one another, the returns might be expected, at least, once in the year, and even this trade would so far be at least equally advantageous as the greater part of the other branches of our foreign European trade. It would be, at least, three times more advantageous, than the boasted trade with our North American colonies, in which the returns were seldom made in less than three years, frequently not in less than four or five years. France, besides, is supposed to contain twenty-four millions of inhabitants. Our North American colonies were never supposed to contain more than three millions: And France is a much richer country than North America; though, on account of the more unequal distribution of riches, there is much more poverty and beggary in the one country, than in the other. France therefore could afford a market at least eight times more extensive, and, on account of the superior frequency of the returns, four and twenty times more advantageous, than that which our North American colonies ever afforded. The trade of Great Britain would be just as advantageous to France, and, in proportion to the wealth, population and proximity of the respective countries, would have the same superiority over that which France carries on with her own colonies. Such is the very great difference between that trade which the wisdom of both nations has thought proper to discourage, and that which it has favoured the most.

But the very same circumstances which would have rendered an open and free commerce between the two countries so advantageous to both, have occasioned the principal obstructions to that commerce. Being neighbours, they are necessarily enemies, and the wealth and power of each becomes, upon that account, more formidable to the other; and what would increase the advantage of national friendship, serves only to inflame the violence of national animosity. They are both rich and industrious nations; and the merchants and manufacturers of each, dread the competition of the skill and activity of those of the other. Mercantile jealousy is excited, and both inflames, and is itself inflamed, by the violence of national animosity: And the traders of both countries have announced, with all the passionate confidence of interested falsehood, the certain ruin of each, in consequence of that unfavourable balance of trade, which, they pretend, would be the infallible effect of an unrestrained commerce with the other.

There is no commercial country in Europe of which the approaching ruin has not frequently been foretold by the pretended doctors of this system, from an unfavourable balance of trade. After all the anxiety, however, which they have excited about this, after all the vain attempts of almost all trading nations to turn that balance in their own favour and against their neighbours, it does not appear that any one nation in Europe has been in any respect impoverished by this cause. Every town and country, on the contrary, in proportion as they have opened their ports to all nations, instead of being ruined by this free trade, as the principles of the commercial system would lead us to expect, have been enriched by it. Though there are in Europe, indeed, a few towns which in some respects deserve the name of free ports, there is no country which does so. Holland, perhaps, approaches the nearest to this character of any, though still very remote from it; and Holland, it is acknowledged, not only derives its whole wealth, but a great part of its necessary subsistence, from foreign trade.

There is another balance, indeed, which has already been explained, very different from the balance of trade, and which, according as it happens to be either favourable or unfavourable, necessarily occasions the prosperity or decay of every nation. This is the balance of the annual produce and consumption. If the exchangeable value of the annual produce, it has already been observed, exceeds that of the annual consumption, the capital of the society must annually increase in proportion to this excess. The society in this case lives within its revenue, and what is annually saved out of its revenue, is naturally added to its capital, and employed so as to increase still further the annual produce. If the exchangeable value of the annual produce, on the contrary, fall short of the annual consumption, the capital of the society must annually decay in proportion to this deficiency. The expence of the society in this case exceeds its revenue, and necessarily encroaches upon its capital. Its capital, therefore, must necessarily decay, and, together with it, the exchangeable value of the annual produce of its industry.

This balance of produce and consumption is entirely different from, what is called, the balance of trade. It might take place in a nation which had no foreign trade, but which was entirely separated from all the world. It may take place in the whole globe of the earth, of which the wealth, population, and improvement may be either gradually increasing or gradually decaying.

The balance of produce and consumption may be constantly in favour of a nation, though what is called the balance of trade be generally against it. A nation may import to a greater value than it exports for half a century, perhaps, together; the gold and silver which comes into it during all this time may be all immediately sent out of it; its circulating coin may gradually decay, different sorts of paper money being substituted in its place, and even the debts too which it contracts in the principal nations with whom it deals, may be gradually increasing; and yet its real wealth, the exchangeable value of the annual produce of its lands and labour, may, during the same period, have been increasing in a much greater proportion. The state of our North American colonies, and of the trade which they carried on with Great Britain, before the commencement of the present disturbances, may serve as a proof that this is by no means an impossible supposition.

[FROM CHAPTER VII, PART THIRD]

The monopoly of the colony trade, therefore, like all the other mean and malignant expedients of the mercantile system, depresses the industry of all other countries, but chiefly that of the colonies, without in the least increasing, but on the contrary diminishing, that of the country in whose favour it is established.

The monopoly hinders the capital of that country, whatever may at any particular time be the extent of that capital, from maintaining so great a quantity of productive labour as it would otherwise maintain, and from affording so great a revenue to the industrious inhabitants as it would otherwise afford. But as capital can be increased only by savings from revenue, the monopoly, by hindering it from affording so great a revenue as it would otherwise afford, necessarily hinders it from increasing so fast as it would otherwise increase, and consequently from maintaining a still greater quantity of productive labour, and affording a still greater revenue to the industrious inhabitants of that country. One great original source of revenue, therefore, the wages of labour, the monopoly must necessarily have rendered at all times less abundant than it otherwise would have been.

By raising the rate of mercantile profit, the monopoly discourages the improvement of land. The profit of improvement depends upon the difference between what the land actually produces, and what, by the application of a certain capital, it can be made to produce. If this difference affords a greater profit than what can be drawn from an equal capital in any mercantile employment, the improvement of land will draw capital from all mercantile employments. If the profit is less, mercantile employments will draw capital from the improvement of land. Whatever therefore raises the rate of mercantile profit, either lessens the superiority or increases the inferiority of the profit of improvement; and in the one case hinders capital from going to improvement, and in the other draws capital from it. But by discouraging improvement, the monopoly necessarily retards the natural increase of another great original source of revenue, the rent of land. By raising the rate of profit too, the monopoly necessarily keeps up the market rate of interest higher than it otherwise would be. But the price of land in proportion to the rent which it affords, the number of years purchase which is commonly paid for it, necessarily falls as the rate of interest rises, and rises as the rate of interest falls. The monopoly,

therefore, hurts the interest of the landlord two different ways, by re-
tarding the natural increase, first, of his rent, and secondly, of the price
which he would get for his land in proportion to the rent which it affords.

The monopoly, indeed, raises the rate of mercantile profit, and thereby
augments somewhat the gain of our merchants. But as it obstructs the
natural increase of capital, it tends rather to diminish than to increase the
sum total of the revenue which the inhabitants of the country derive from
the profits of stock; a small profit upon a great capital generally affording
a greater revenue than a great profit upon a small one. The monopoly
raises the rate of profit, but it hinders the sum of profit from rising so
high as it otherwise would do.

All the original sources of revenue, the wages of labour, the rent of
land, and the profits of stock, the monopoly renders much less abundant
than they otherwise would be. To promote the little interest of one little
order of men in one country, it hurts the interest of all other orders of
men in that country, and of all men in all other countries.

It is solely by raising the ordinary rate of profit that the monopoly
either has proved or could prove advantageous to any one particular order
of men. But besides all the bad effects to the country in general, which
have already been mentioned as necessarily resulting from a high rate of
profit; there is one more fatal, perhaps, than all these put together, but
which, if we may judge from experience, is inseparably connected with
it. The high rate of profit seems every where to destroy that parsimony
which in other circumstances is natural to the character of the merchant.
When profits are high, that sober virtue seems to be superfluous, and
expensive luxury to suit better the affluence of his situation. But the
owners of the great mercantile capitals are necessarily the leaders and
conductors of the whole industry of every nation, and their example has
a much greater influence upon the manners of the whole industrious part
of it than that of any other order of men. If his employer is attentive and
parsimonious, the workman is very likely to be so too; but if the master
is dissolute and disorderly, the servant who shapes his work according to
the pattern which his master prescribes to him, will shape his life too
according to the example which he sets him. Accumulation is thus prevented in the hands of all those who are naturally the most disposed to
accumulate; and the funds destined for the maintenance of productive
labour receive no augmentation from the revenue of those who ought
naturally to augment them the most. The capital of the country, instead
of increasing, gradually dwindles away, and the quantity of productive
labour maintained in it grows every day less and less. Have the exorbitant
profits of the merchants of Cadiz and Lisbon augmented the capital of
Spain and Portugal? Have they alleviated the poverty, have they promoted

the industry of those two beggarly countries? Such has been the tone of mercantile expence in those two trading cities, that those exorbitant profits, far from augmenting the general capital of the country, seem scarce to have been sufficient to keep up the capitals upon which they were made. Foreign capitals are every day intruding themselves, if I may say so, more and more into the trade of Cadiz and Lisbon. It is to expel those foreign capitals from a trade which their own grows every day more and more insufficient for carrying on, that the Spaniards and Portuguese endeavour every day to straiten more and more the galling bands of their absurd monopoly. Compare the mercantile manners of Cadiz and Lisbon with those of Amsterdam, and you will be sensible how differently the conduct and character of merchants are affected by the high and by the low profits of stock. The merchants of London, indeed, have not yet generally become such magnificent lords as those of Cadiz and Lisbon; but neither are they in general such attentive and parsimonious burghers as those of Amsterdam. They are supposed, however, many of them, to be a good deal richer than the greater part of the former, and not quite so rich as many of the latter. But the rate of their profit is commonly much lower than that of the former, and a good deal higher than that of the latter. Light come light go, says the proverb; and the ordinary tone of expence seems every where to be regulated, not so much according to the real ability of spending as to the supposed facility of getting money to spend.

It is thus that the single advantage which the monopoly procures to a single order of men, is in many different ways hurtful to the general interest of the country. . . .

The discovery of America, and that of a passage to the East Indies by the Cape of Good Hope, are the two greatest and most important events recorded in the history of mankind. Their consequences have already been very great: but, in the short period of between two and three centuries which has elapsed since these discoveries were made, it is impossible that the whole extent of their consequences can have been seen. What benefits, or what misfortunes to mankind may hereafter result from those great events, no human wisdom can foresee. By uniting, in some measure, the most distant parts of the world, by enabling them to relieve one another's wants, to increase one another's enjoyments, and to encourage one another's industry, their general tendency would seem to be beneficial. To the natives, however, both of the East and West Indies, all the commercial benefits which can have resulted from those events have been sunk and lost in the dreadful misfortunes which they have occasioned. These misfortunes, however, seem to have arisen rather from accident than from any thing in the nature of those events themselves. At the particular time when these discoveries were made, the superiority of force happened to be so great on the side of the Europeans, that they were enabled to commit with impunity every sort of injustice in those remote countries. Hereafter, perhaps, the natives of those countries may grow stronger, or those of Europe may grow weaker, and the inhabitants of all the different quarters of the world may arrive at that equality of courage and force which, by inspiring mutual fear, can alone overawe the injustice of independent nations into some sort of respect for the rights of one another. But nothing seems more likely to establish this equality of force than that mutual communication of knowledge and of all sorts of improvements which an extensive commerce from all countries to all countries naturally, or rather necessarily, carries along with it.

In the mean time one of the principal effects of those discoveries has been to raise the mercantile system to a degree of splendour and glory which it could never otherwise have attained to. It is the object of that system to enrich a great nation rather by trade and manufactures than by the improvement and cultivation of land, rather by the industry of the towns than by that of the country. But, in consequence of those discoveries, the commercial towns of Europe, instead of being the manufacturers and carriers for but a very small part of the world (that part of Europe which is washed by the Atlantic ocean, and the countries which lie round the Baltic and Mediterranean seas), have now become the manufacturers for the numerous and thriving cultivators of America, and the carriers, and in some respects the manufacturers too, for almost all the different nations of Asia, Africa, and America. Two new worlds have been opened to their industry, each of them much greater and more extensive than the old one, and the market of one of them growing still greater and greater every day.

The countries which possess the colonies of America, and which trade directly to the East Indies, enjoy, indeed, the whole shew and splendour of this great commerce. Other countries, however, notwithstanding all the invidious restraints by which it is meant to exclude them, frequently enjoy a greater share of the real benefit of it. The colonies of Spain and Portugal, for example, give more real encouragement to the industry of other countries that to that of Spain and Portugal. In the single article of linen alone the consumption of those colonies amounts, it is said, but I do not pretend to warrant the quantity, to more than three millions sterling a year. But this great consumption is almost entirely supplied by France, Flanders, Holland, and Germany. Spain and Portugal furnish but a small part of it. The capital which supplies the colonies with this great quantity of linen is annually distributed among, and furnishes a revenue to the inhabitants of those other countries. The profits of it only are spent in Spain and Portugal, where they help to support the sumptuous profusion of the merchants of Cadiz and Lisbon.

Even the regulations by which each nation endeavours to secure to itself the exclusive trade of its own colonies, are frequently more hurtful to the countries in favour of which they are established than to those against which they are established. The unjust oppression of the industry of other countries falls back, if I may say so, upon the heads of the oppressors, and crushes their industry more than it does that of those other countries. By those regulations, for example, the merchant of Hamburgh must send the linen which he destines for the American market to London, and he must bring back from thence the tobacco which he destines for the German market; because he can neither send the one directly to America, nor bring back the other directly from thence. By this restraint he is probably obliged to sell the one somewhat cheaper, and to buy the other somewhat dearer than he otherwise might have done; and his profits are probably somewhat abridged by means of it. In this trade, however, between Hamburgh and London, he certainly receives the returns of his capital much more quickly than he could possibly have done in the direct trade to America, even though we should suppose, what is by no means the case, that the payments of America were as punctual as those of London. In the trade, therefore, to which those regulations confine the merchant of Hamburgh, his capital can keep in constant employment a much greater quantity of German industry than it possibly could have done in the trade from which he is excluded. Though the one employment, therefore, may to him perhaps be less profitable than the other, it cannot be less advantageous to his country. It is quite otherwise with the employment into which the monopoly naturally attracts, if I may say so, the capital of the London merchant. That employment may, perhaps, be more profitable to him than the greater part of other employments, but, on account of the slowness of the returns, it cannot be more advantageous to his country.

After all the unjust attempts, therefore, of every country in Europe to engross to itself the whole advantage of the trade of its own colonies, no country has yet been able to engross to itself any thing but the expence of supporting in time of peace and of defending in time of war the oppressive authority which it assumes over them. The inconveniencies resulting from the possession of its colonies, every country has engrossed to itself completely. The advantages resulting from their trade it has been obliged to share with many other countries.

At first sight, no doubt, the monopoly of the great commerce of America, naturally seems to be an acquisition of the highest value. To the undiscerning eye of giddy ambition, it naturally presents itself amidst the confused scramble of politics and war, as a very dazzling object to fight for. The dazzling splendour of the object, however, the immense greatness of the commerce, is the very quality which renders the monopoly of it hurtful, or which makes one employment, in its own nature necessarily less advantageous to the country than the greater part of other employments, absorb a much greater proportion of the capital of the country than what would otherwise have gone to it.

The mercantile stock of every country, it has been shewn in the second book, naturally seeks, if one may say so, the employment most advantageous to that country. If it is employed in the carrying trade, the country to which it belongs becomes the emporium of the goods of all the countries whose trade that stock carries on. But the owner of that stock necessarily wishes to dispose of as great a part of those goods as he can at home. He thereby saves himself the trouble, risk, and expence of exportation, and he will upon that account be glad to sell them at home, not only for a much smaller price, but with somewhat a smaller profit than he might expect to make by sending them abroad. He naturally, therefore, endeavours as much as he can to turn his carrying trade into a foreign trade of consumption. If his stock again is employed in a foreign trade of consumption, he will, for the same reason, be glad to dispose of at home as great a part as he can of the home goods, which he collects in order to export to some foreign market, and he will thus endeavour, as much as he can, to turn his foreign trade of consumption into a home trade. The mercantile stock of every country naturally courts in this manner the near, and shuns the distant employment; naturally courts the employment in which the returns are frequent, and shuns that in which they are distant and slow; naturally courts the employment in which it can maintain the greatest quantity of productive labour in the country to which it belongs, or in which its owner resides, and shuns that in which it can maintain there the smallest quantity. It naturally courts the employment which in ordinary cases is most advantageous, and shuns that which in ordinary cases is least advantageous to that country.

But if in any of those distant employments, which in ordinary cases are less advantageous to the country, the profit should happen to rise somewhat higher than what is sufficient to balance the natural preference which is given to nearer employments, this superiority of profit will draw stock from those nearer employments, till the profits of all return to their proper level. This superiority of profit, however, is a proof that, in the actual circumstances of the society, those distant employments are somewhat under-stocked in proportion to other employments, and that the stock of the society is not distributed in the properest manner among all the different employments carried on in it. It is a proof that something is either bought cheaper or sold dearer than it ought to be, and that some particular class of citizens is more or less oppressed either by paying more or by getting less than what is suitable to that equality, which ought to take place, and which naturally does take place among all the different classes of them. Though the same capital never will maintain the same quantity of productive labour in a distant as in a near employment, yet a distant employment may be as necessary for the welfare of the society as a near one; the goods which the distant employment deals in being necessary, perhaps, for carrying on many of the nearer employments. But if the profits of those who deal in such goods are above their proper level, those goods will be sold dearer than they ought to be, or somewhat above their natural price, and all those engaged in the nearer employments will be more or less oppressed by this high price. Their interest, therefore, in this case requires that some stock should be withdrawn from those nearer employments, and turned towards that distant one, in order to reduce its profits to their proper level, and the price of the goods which it deals in to their natural price. In this extraordinary case, the public interest requires that some stock should be withdrawn from those employments which in ordinary cases are more advantageous, and turned towards one which in ordinary cases is less advantageous to the public: and in this extraordinary case, the natural interests and inclinations of men coincide as exactly with the public interest as in all other ordinary cases, and lead them to withdraw stock from the near, and to turn it towards the distant employment.

It is thus that the private interests and passions of individuals naturally dispose them to turn their stock towards the employments which in ordinary cases are most advantageous to the society. But if from this natural preference they should turn too much of it towards those employments, the fall of profit in them and the rise of it in all others immediately dispose them to alter this faulty distribution. Without any intervention of law, therefore, the private interests and passions of men naturally lead them to divide and distribute the stock of every society, among all the different employments carried on in it, as nearly as possible in the proportion which is most agreeable to the interest of the whole society.

All the different regulations of the mercantile system, necessarily derange more or less this natural and most advantageous distribution of stock. But those which concern the trade to America and the East Indies derange it perhaps more than any other; because the trade to those two great continents absorbs a greater quantity of stock than any two other branches of trade. The regulations, however, by which this derangement is effected in those two different branches of trade are not altogether the same. Monopoly is the great engine of both; but it is a different sort of monopoly. Monopoly of one kind or another, indeed, seems to be the sole engine of the mercantile system.

[Throughout Books II, III, and IV there is much evidence that Smith availed himself of the economic writings of the physiocrats (e.g., Quesnay, Mirabeau, and Turgot) to conceptualize some of the argument of the *WN* (See Appendices I–III for this). In Chapter IX, Book IV, Smith discusses the physiocrats in not very generous terms. This is somewhat surprising insofar as Smith once planned to dedicate the *WN* to Quesnay. Given Smith's own agrarian bias, his strictures about the lack of balance in physiocratic writings are puzzling.]

CHAPTER IX

OF THE AGRICULTURAL SYSTEMS, OR OF THOSE SYSTEMS OF POLITICAL OECONOMY, WHICH REPRESENT THE PRODUCE OF LAND AS EITHER THE SOLE OR THE PRINCIPAL SOURCE OF THE REVENUE AND WEALTH OF EVERY COUNTRY

The agricultural systems of political oeconomy will not require so long an explanation as that which I have thought it necessary to bestow upon the mercantile or commercial system.

That system which represents the produce of land as the sole source of the revenue and wealth of every country has, so far as I know, never been adopted by any nation, and it at present exists only in the speculations of a few men of great learning and ingenuity in France. It would not, surely, be worth while to examine at great length the errors of a system which never has done, and probably never will do any harm in any part of the world. I shall endeavour to explain, however, as distinctly as I can, the great outlines of this very ingenious system.

Mr. Colbert, the famous minister of Lewis XIV. was a man of probity, of great industry and knowledge of detail; of great experience and acuteness in the examination of public accounts, and of abilities, in short, every way fitted for introducing method and good order into the collection and expenditure of the public revenue. That minister had unfortunately embraced all the prejudices of the mercantile system, in its nature and essence a system of restraint and regulation, and such as could scarce fail to be agreeable to a laborious and plodding man of business, who had been accustomed to regulate the different departments of public offices, and to establish the necessary checks and controuls for confining each to its proper sphere. The industry and commerce of a great country he endeavoured to regulate upon the same model as the departments of a public office; and instead of allowing every man to pursue his own interest his own way, upon the liberal plan of equality, liberty and justice, he bestowed upon certain branches of industry extraordinary privileges, while he laid others under as extraordinary restraints. He was not only disposed, like other European ministers, to encourage more the industry of the towns than that of the country; but, in order to support the industry of the towns, he was willing even to depress and keep down that of the country. In order to render provisions cheap to the inhabitants of the towns, and thereby to encourage manufactures and foreign commerce, he prohibited altogether the exportation of corn, and thus excluded the inhabitants of the country from every foreign market for by far the most important part of the produce of their industry. This prohibition, joined to the restraints imposed by the ancient provincial laws of France upon the transportation of corn from one province to another, and to the arbitrary and degrading taxes which are levied upon the cultivators in almost all the provinces, discouraged and kept down the agriculture of that country very much below the state to which it would naturally have risen in so very fertile a soil and so very happy a climate. This state of discouragement and depression was felt more or less in every different part of the country, and many different inquiries were set on foot concerning the causes of it. One of those causes appeared to be the preference given, by the institutions of Mr. Colbert, to the industry of the towns above that of the country.

If the rod be bent too much one way, says the proverb, in order to make it straight you must bend it as much the other. The French philosophers, who have proposed the system which represents agriculture as the sole source of the revenue and wealth of every country, seem to have adopted this proverbial maxim; and as in the plan of Mr. Colbert the industry of the towns was certainly over-valued in comparison with that of the country; so in their system it seems to be as certainly under-valued.

The different orders of people who have ever been supposed to contribute in any respect towards the annual produce of the land and labour of the country, they divide into three classes. The first is the class of the proprietors of land. The second is the class of the cultivators, of farmers and country labourers, whom they honour with the peculiar appellation of the productive class. The third is the class of artificers, manufacturers and merchants, whom they endeavour to degrade by the humiliating appellation of the barren or unproductive class. . . .

Some speculative physicians seem to have imagined that the health of the human body could be preserved only by a certain precise regimen of diet and exercise, of which every, the smallest, violation necessarily occasioned some degree of disease or disorder proportioned to the degree of the violation. Experience, however, would seem to show, that the human body frequently preserves, to all appearance at least, the most perfect state of health under a vast variety of different regimens; even under some which are generally believed to be very far from being perfectly wholesome. But the healthful state of the human body, it would seem, contains in itself some unknown principle of preservation, capable either of preventing or of correcting, in many respects, the bad effects even of a very faulty regimen. Mr. Quesnai, who was himself a physician, and a very speculative physician, seems to have entertained a notion of the same kind concerning the political body, and to have imagined that it would thrive and prosper only under a certain precise regimen, the exact regimen of perfect liberty and perfect justice. He seems not to have considered that in the political body, the natural effort which every man is continually making to better his own condition, is a principle of preservation capable of preventing and correcting, in many respects, the bad effects of a political oeconomy, in some degree both partial and oppressive. Such a political oeconomy, though it no doubt retards more or less, is not always capable of stopping altogether the natural progress of a nation towards wealth and prosperity, and still less of making it go backwards. If a nation could not prosper without the enjoyment of perfect liberty and perfect justice, there is not in the world a nation which could ever have prospered. In the political body, however, the wisdom of nature has fortunately made ample provision for remedying many of the bad effects of the folly and injustice of man; in the same manner as it has done in the natural body, for remedying those of his sloth and intemperance.

The capital error of this system, however, seems to lie in its representing the class of artificers, manufacturers and merchants, as altogether barren and unproductive. The following observations may serve to show the impropriety of this representation.

First, this class, it is acknowledged, reproduces annually the value of its own annual consumption, and continues, at least, the existence of the stock or capital which maintains and employs it. But upon this account alone the denomination of barren or unproductive should seem to be very improperly applied to it. We should not call a marriage barren or unproductive, though it produced only a son and a daughter, to replace the father and mother, and though it did not increase the number of the human species, but only continued it as it was before. Farmers and country labourers, indeed, over and above the stock which maintains and employs them, reproduce annually a neat produce, a free rent to the landlord. As a marriage which affords three children is certainly more productive than one which affords only two; so the labour of farmers and country labourers is certainly more productive than that of merchants, artificers and manufacturers. The superior produce of the one class, however, does not render the other barren or unproductive.

Secondly, it seems, upon this account, altogether improper to consider artificers, manufacturers and merchants, in the same light as menial servants. The labour of menial servants does not continue the existence of the fund which maintains and employs them. Their maintenance and employment is altogether at the expence of their masters, and the work which they perform is not of a nature to repay that expence. That work consists in services which perish generally in the very instant of their performance, and does not fix or realize itself in any vendible commodity which can replace the value of their wages and maintenance. The labour, on the contrary, of artificers, manufacturers and merchants, naturally does fix and realize itself in some such vendible commodity. It is upon this account that, in the chapter in which I treat of productive and unproductive labour, I have classed artificers, manufacturers and merchants, among the productive labourers, and menial servants among the barren or unproductive.

Thirdly, it seems, upon every supposition, improper to say, that the labour of artificers, manufacturers and merchants, does not increase the real revenue of the society. Though we should suppose, for example, as it seems to be supposed in this system, that the value of the daily, monthly, and yearly consumption of this class was exactly equal to that of its daily, monthly, and yearly production; yet it would not from thence follow that its labour added nothing to the real revenue, to the real value of the annual produce of the land and labour of the society. An artificer, for example, who, in the first six months after harvest, executes ten pounds worth of work, though he should in the same time consume ten pounds worth of corn and other necessaries, yet really adds the value of ten pounds to the annual produce of the land and labour of the society. While he has been consuming a half yearly revenue of ten pounds worth of corn and other necessaries, he has produced an equal value of work capable of purchasing, either to himself or to some other person, an equal half yearly revenue. The value, therefore, of what has been consumed and produced during these six months is equal, not to ten, but to twenty pounds. It is possible, indeed, that no more than ten pounds worth of this value, may ever have existed at any one moment of time. But if the ten pounds worth of corn and other necessaries, which were consumed by the artificer, had been consumed by a soldier or by a menial servant, the value of that part of the annual produce which existed at the end of the six months, would have been ten pounds less than it actually is in consequence of the labour of the artificer. Though the value of what the artificer produces, therefore, should not at any one moment of time be supposed greater than the value he consumes, yet at every moment of time the actually existing value of goods in the market is, in consequence of what he produces, greater than it otherwise would be.

When the patrons of this system assert, that the consumption of artificers, manufacturers and merchants, is equal to the value of what they produce, they probably mean no more than that their revenue, or the fund destined for their consumption, is equal to it. But if they had expressed themselves more accurately, and only asserted, that the revenue of this class was equal to the value of what they produced, it might readily have occurred to the reader, that what would naturally be saved out of this revenue, must necessarily increase more or less the real wealth of the society. In order, therefore, to make out something like an argument, it was necessary that they should express themselves as they have done; and this argument, even supposing things actually were as it seems to presume them to be, turns out to be a very inconclusive one.

Fourthly, farmers and country labourers can no more augment, without parsimony, the real revenue, the annual produce of the land and labour of their society, than artificers, manufacturers and merchants. The annual produce of the land and labour of any society can be augmented only in two ways; either, first, by some improvement in the productive powers of the useful labour actually maintained within it; or, secondly, by some increase in the quantity of that labour.

The improvement in the productive powers of useful labour depends, first, upon the improvement in the ability of the workman; and, secondly, upon that of the machinery with which he works. But the labour of artificers and manufacturers, as it is capable of being more subdivided, and the labour of each workman reduced to a greater simplicity of operation, than that of farmers and country labourers, so it is likewise capable of both these sorts of improvement in a much higher degree. In this respect, therefore, the class of cultivators can have no sort of advantage over that of artificers and manufacturers.

The increase in the quantity of useful labour actually employed within any society, must depend altogether upon the increase of the capital which employs it; and the increase of that capital again must be exactly equal to the amount of the savings from the revenue, either of the particular persons who manage and direct the employment of that capital, or of some other persons who lend it to them. If merchants, artificers and manufacturers are, as this system seems to suppose, naturally more inclined to parsimony and saving than proprietors and cultivators, they are, so far, more likely to augment the quantity of useful labour employed within their society, and consequently to increase its real revenue, the annual produce of its land and labour.

Fifthly and lastly, though the revenue of the inhabitants of every country was supposed to consist altogether, as this system seems to suppose, in the quantity of subsistence which their industry could procure to them; yet even upon this supposition, the revenue of a trading and manufacturing country must, other things being equal, always be much greater than that of one without trade or manufactures. By means of trade and manufactures, a greater quantity of subsistence can be annually imported into a particular country than what its own lands, in the actual state of their cultivation, could afford. The inhabitants of a town, though they frequently possess no lands of their own, yet draw to themselves by their industry such a quantity of the rude produce of the lands of other people as supplies them, not only with the materials of their work, but with the fund of their subsistence. What a town always is with regard to the country in its neighbourhood, one independent state or country may frequently be with regard to other independent states or countries. It is thus that Holland draws a great part of its subsistence from other countries; live cattle from Holstein and Jutland, and corn from almost all the different countries of Europe. A small quantity of manufactured produce purchases a great quantity of rude produce. A trading and manufacturing country, therefore, naturally purchases with a small part of its manufactured produce a great part of the rude produce of other countries; while, on the contrary, a country without trade and manufactures is generally obliged to purchase, at the expence of a great part of its rude produce, a very small part of the manufactured produce of other countries. The one exports what can subsist and accommodate but a very few, and imports the subsistence and accommodation of a great number. The other exports the accommodation and subsistence of a great number, and imports that of a very few only. The inhabitants of the one must always enjoy a much greater quantity of subsistence than what their own lands, in the actual state of their cultivation, could afford. The inhabitants of the other must always enjoy a much smaller quantity.

This system, however, with all its imperfections, is, perhaps, the nearest approximation to the truth that has yet been published upon the subject of political oeconomy, and is upon that account well worth the consideration of every man who wishes to examine with attention the principles of that very important science. Though in representing the labour which is employed upon land as the only productive labour, the notions which it inculcates are perhaps too narrow and confined; yet in representing the wealth of nations as consisting, not in the unconsumable riches of money, but in the consumable goods annually reproduced by the labour of the society; and in representing perfect liberty as the only effectual expedient for rendering this annual reproduction the greatest possible, its doctrine seems to be in every respect as just as it is generous and liberal. Its followers are very numerous; and as men are fond of paradoxes, and of appearing to understand what surpasses the comprehension of ordinary people, the paradox which it maintains, concerning the unproductive nature of manufacturing labour, has not perhaps contributed a little to increase the number of its admirers. They have for some years past made a pretty considerable sect, distinguished in the French republic of letters by the name of, The Oeconomists. Their works have certainly been of some service to their country; not only by bringing into general discussion, many subjects which had never been well examined before, but by influencing in some measure the public administration in favour of agriculture. It has been in consequence of their representations, accordingly, that the agriculture of France has been delivered from several of the oppressions which it before laboured under. The term during which such a lease can be granted, as will be valid against every future purchaser or proprietor of the land, has been prolonged from nine to twenty-seven years. The ancient provincial restraints upon the transportation of corn from one province of the kingdom to another, have been entirely taken away, and the liberty of exporting it to all foreign countries, has been established as the common law of the kingdom in all ordinary cases. This sect, in their works, which are very numerous, and which treat not only of what is properly called Political Oeconomy, or of the nature and causes of the wealth of nations, but of every other branch of the system of civil government, all follow implicitly, and without any sensible variation, the doctrine of Mr. Quesnai. There is upon this account little variety in the greater part of their works. The most distinct and best connected account of this doctrine is to be found in a little book written by Mr. Mercier de la Riviere, sometime Intendant of Martinico, intitled, The natural and essential Order of Political Societies. The admiration of this whole sect for their master, who was himself a man of the greatest modesty and simplicity, is not inferior to that of any of the ancient philosophers for the founders of their respective systems. "There have been, since the world began," says a very diligent and respectable author, the Marquis de Mirabeau, "three great inventions which have principally given stability to political societies, independent of many other inventions which have enriched and adorned them. The first, is the invention of writing, which alone gives human nature the power of transmitting, without alteration, its laws, its contracts, its annals, and its discoveries. The second, is the invention of money, which binds together all the relations between civilized societies. The third, is the Oeconomical Table, the result of the other two, which completes them both by perfecting their object; the great discovery of our age, but of which our posterity will reap the benefit."

As the political oeconomy of the nations of modern Europe, has been more favourable to manufactures and foreign trade, the industry of the towns, than to agriculture, the industry of the country; so that of other nations has followed a different plan, and has been more favourable to agriculture than to manufactures and foreign trade.

The policy of China favours agriculture more than all other employments. In China, the condition of a labourer is said to be as much superior to that of an artificer; as in most parts of Europe, that of an artificer is to that of a labourer. In China, the great ambition of every man is to get possession of some little bit of land, either in property or in lease; and leases are there said to be granted upon very moderate terms, and to be sufficiently secured to the lessees. The Chinese have little respect for foreign trade. Your beggarly commerce! was the language in which the Mandarins of Pekin used to talk to Mr. de Lange, the Russian envoy, concerning it. Except with Japan, the Chinese carry on, themselves, and in their own bottoms, little or no foreign trade; and it is only into one or two ports of their kingdom that they even admit the ships of foreign nations. Foreign trade, therefore, is, in China, every way confined within a much narrower circle than that to which it would naturally extend itself, if more freedom was allowed to it, either in their own ships, or in those of foreign nations.

Manufactures, as in a small bulk they frequently contain a great value, and can upon that account be transported at less expence from one country to another than most parts of rude produce, are, in almost all countries, the principal support of foreign trade. In countries, besides, less extensive and less favourably circumstanced for interior commerce than China, they generally require the support of foreign trade. Without an extensive foreign market, they could not well flourish, either in countries so moderately extensive as to afford but a narrow home market; or in countries where the communication between one province and another was so difficult, as to render it impossible for the goods of any particular place to enjoy the whole of that home market which the country could afford. The perfection of manufacturing industry, it must be remembered, depends altogether upon the division of labour; and the degree to which the division of labour can be introduced into any manufacture, is necessarily regulated, it has already been shown, by the extent of the market. But the great extent of the empire of China, the vast multitude of its inhabitants, the variety of climate, and consequently of productions in its different provinces, and the easy communication by means of water carriage between the greater part of them, render the home market of that country of so great extent, as to be alone sufficient to support very great manufactures, and to admit of very considerable subdivisions of labour. The home market of China is, perhaps, in extent, not much inferior to the market of all the different countries of Europe put together. A more extensive foreign trade, however, which to this great home market added the foreign market of all the rest of the world; especially if any considerable part of this trade was carried on in Chinese ships; could scarce fail to increase very much the manufactures of China, and to improve very much the productive powers of its manufacturing industry. By a more extensive navigation, the Chinese would naturally learn the art of using and constructing themselves all the different machines made use of in other countries, as well as the other improvements of art and industry which are practised in all the different parts of the world. Upon their present plan they have little opportunity of improving themselves by the example of any other nation; except that of the Japanese.

The policy of ancient Egypt too, and that of the Gentoo government of Indostan, seem to have favoured agriculture more than all other employments.

Both in ancient Egypt and Indostan, the whole body of the people was divided into different casts or tribes, each of which was confined, from father to son, to a particular employment or class of employments. The son of a priest was necessarily a priest; the son of a soldier, a soldier; the son of a labourer, a labourer; the son of a weaver, a weaver; the son of a taylor, a taylor; &c. In both countries, the cast of the priests held the highest rank, and that of the soldiers the next; and in both countries, the cast of the farmers and labourers was superior to the casts of merchants and manufacturers.

The government of both countries was particularly attentive to the interest of agriculture. The works constructed by the ancient sovereigns of Egypt for the proper distribution of the waters of the Nile were famous in antiquity; and the ruined remains of some of them are still the admiration of travellers. Those of the same kind which were constructed by the ancient sovereigns of Indostan, for the proper distribution of the waters of the Ganges as well as of many other rivers, though they have been less celebrated, seem to have been equally great. Both countries, accordingly, though subject occasionally to dearths, have been famous for their great fertility. Though both were extremely populous, yet, in years of moderate plenty, they were both able to export great quantities of grain to their neighbours.

The ancient Egyptians had a superstitious aversion to the sea; and as the Gentoo religion does not permit its followers to light a fire, nor consequently to dress any victuals upon the water, it in effect prohibits them from all distant sea voyages. Both the Egyptians and Indians must have depended almost altogether upon the navigation of other nations for the exportation of their surplus produce; and this dependency, as it must have confined the market, so it must have discouraged the increase of this surplus produce. It must have discouraged too the increase of the manufactured produce more than that of the rude produce. Manufactures require a much more extensive market than the most important parts of the rude produce of the land. A single shoemaker will make more than three hundred pairs of shoes in the year; and his own family will not perhaps wear out six pairs. Unless therefore he has the custom of at least fifty such families as his own, he cannot dispose of the whole produce of his own labour. The most numerous class of artificers will seldom, in a large country, make more than one in fifty or one in a hundred of the whole number of families contained in it. But in such large countries as France and England, the number of people employed in agriculture has by some authors been computed at a half, by others at a third, and by no author that I know of, at less than a fifth of the whole inhabitants of the country. But as the produce of the agriculture of both France and England is, the far greater part of it, consumed at home, each person employed in it must, according to these computations, require little more than the custom of one, two, or, at most, of four such families as his own, in order to dispose of the whole produce of his own labour. Agriculture, therefore, can support itself under the discouragement of a confined market, much better than manufactures. In both ancient Egypt and Indostan, indeed, the confinement of the foreign market was in some measure compensated by the conveniency of many inland navigations, which opened, in the most advantageous manner, the whole extent of the home market to every part of the produce of every different district of those countries. The great extent of Indostan too rendered the home market of that country very great, and sufficient to support a great variety of manufactures. But the small extent of ancient Egypt, which was never equal to England, must at all times have rendered the home market of that country too narrow for supporting any great variety of manufactures. Bengal, accordingly, the province of Indostan which commonly exports the greatest quantity of rice, has always been more remarkable for the exportation of a great variety of manufactures, than for that of its grain. Ancient Egypt, on the contrary, though it exported some manufactures, fine linen in particular, as well as some other goods, was always most distinguished for its great exportation of grain. It was long the granary of the Roman empire.

The sovereigns of China, of ancient Egypt, and of the different kingdoms into which Indostan has at different times been divided, have always derived the whole, or by far the most considerable part, of their revenue from some sort of land-tax or land-rent. This land-tax or land-rent, like the tithe in Europe, consisted in a certain proportion, a fifth, it is said, of the produce of the land, which was either delivered in kind, or paid in money, according to a certain valuation, and which therefore varied from year to year according to all the variations of the produce. It was natural therefore, that the sovereigns of those countries should be particularly attentive to the interests of agriculture, upon the prosperity or declension of which immediately depended the yearly increase or diminution of their own revenue.

The policy of the ancient republics of Greece, and that of Rome, though it honoured agriculture more than manufactures or foreign trade, yet seems rather to have discouraged the latter employments, than to have given any direct or intentional encouragement to the former. In several of the ancient states of Greece, foreign trade was prohibited altogether; and in several others the employments of artificers and manufacturers were considered as hurtful to the strength and agility of the human body, as rendering it incapable of those habits which their military and gymnastic exercises endeavoured to form in it, and as thereby disqualifying it more or less for undergoing the fatigues and encountering the dangers of war. Such occupations were considered as fit only for slaves, and the free citizens of the state were prohibited from exercising them. Even in those states where no such prohibition took place, as in Rome and Athens, the great body of the people were in effect excluded from all the trades which are now commonly exercised by the lower sort of the inhabitants of towns. Such trades were, at Athens and Rome, all occupied by the slaves of the rich, who exercised them for the benefit of their masters, whose wealth, power, and protection, made it almost impossible for a poor freeman to find a market for his work, when it came into competition with that of the slaves of the rich. Slaves, however, are very seldom inventive; and all the most important improvements, either in machinery, or in the arrangement and distribution of work, which facilitate and abridge labour, have been the discoveries of freemen. Should a slave propose any improvement of this kind, his master would be very apt to consider the proposal as the suggestion of laziness, and of a desire to save his own labour at the master's expence. The poor slave, instead of reward, would probably meet with much abuse, perhaps with some punishment. In the manufactures carried on by slaves, therefore, more labour must generally have been employed to execute the same quantity of work, than in those carried on by freemen. The work of the former must, upon that account, generally have been dearer than that of the latter. The Hungarian mines, it is remarked by Mr. Montesquieu, though not richer, have always been wrought with less expence, and therefore with more profit, than the Turkish mines in their neighbourhood. The Turkish mines are wrought by slaves; and the arms of those slaves are the only machines which the Turks have ever thought of employing. The Hungarian mines are wrought by freemen, who employ a great deal of machinery, by which they facilitate and abridge their own labour. From the very little that is known about the price of manufactures in the times of the Greeks and Romans, it would appear that those of the finer sort were excessively dear. Silk sold for its weight in gold. It was not, indeed, in those times a European manufacture; and as it was all brought from the East Indies, the distance of the carriage may in some measure account for the greatness of the price. The price, however, which a lady, it is said, would sometimes pay for a piece of very fine linen, seems to have been equally extravagant; and as linen was always either a European, or, at farthest, an Egyptian manufacture, this high price can be accounted for only by the great expence of the labour which must have been employed about it, and the expence of this labour again could arise from nothing but the awkwardness of the machinery which it made use of. The price of fine woollens too, though not quite so extravagant, seems however to have been much above that of the present times. Some cloths, we are told by Pliny, dyed in a particular manner, cost a hundred denarii, or three pounds six shillings and eight pence the pound weight. Others dyed in another manner cost a thousand denarii the pound weight, or thirty-three pounds six shillings and eight pence. The Roman pound, it must be remembered, contained only twelve of our avoirdupois ounces. This high price, indeed, seems to have been principally owing to the dye. But had not the cloths themselves been much dearer than any which are made in the present times, so very expensive a dye would not probably have been bestowed upon them. The disproportion would have been too great between the value of the accessory and that of the principal. The price mentioned by the same author of some Triclinaria, a sort of woollen pillows or cushions made use of to lean upon as they reclined upon their couches at table, passes all credibility; some of them being said to have cost more than thirty thousand, others more than three hundred thousand pounds. This high price too is not said to have arisen from the dye. In the dress of the people of fashion of both sexes, there seems to have been much less variety, it is observed by Dr. Arbuthnot, in ancient than in modern times; and the very little variety which we find in that of the ancient statues confirms his observation. He infers from this, that their dress must upon the whole have been cheaper than ours: but the conclusion does not seem to follow. When the expence of fashionable dress is very great, the variety must be very small. But when, by the improvements in the productive powers of manufacturing art and industry, the expence of any one dress comes to be very moderate, the variety will naturally be very great. The rich not being able to distinguish themselves by the expence of any one dress, will naturally endeavour to do so by the multitude and variety of their dresses.

The greatest and most important branch of the commerce of every nation, it has already been observed, is that which is carried on between the inhabitants of the town and those of the country. The inhabitants of the town draw from the country the rude produce which constitutes both the materials of their work and the fund of their subsistence; and they pay for this rude produce by sending back to the country a certain portion of it manufactured and prepared for immediate use. The trade which is carried on between those two different sets of people, consists ultimately in a certain quantity of rude produce exchanged for a certain quantity of manufactured produce. The dearer the latter, therefore, the cheaper the former; and whatever tends in any country to raise the price of manufactured produce, tends to lower that of the rude produce of the land, and thereby to discourage agriculture. The smaller the quantity of manufactured produce which any given quantity of rude produce, or, which comes to the same thing, which the price of any given quantity of rude produce is capable of purchasing, the smaller the exchangeable value of that given quantity of rude produce; the smaller the encouragement which either the landlord has to increase its quantity by improving, or the farmer by cultivating the land. Whatever, besides, tends to diminish in any country the number of artificers and manufacturers, tends to diminish the home market, the most important of all markets for the rude produce of the land, and thereby still further to discourage agriculture.

Those systems, therefore, which preferring agriculture to all other employments, in order to promote it, impose restraints upon manufactures and foreign trade, act contrary to the very end which they propose, and indirectly discourage that very species of industry which they mean to promote. They are so far, perhaps, more inconsistent than even the mercantile system. That system, by encouraging manufactures and foreign trade more than agriculture, turns a certain portion of the capital of the society from supporting a more advantageous, to support a less advantageous species of industry. But still it really and in the end encourages that species of industry which it means to promote. Those agricultural systems, on the contrary, really and in the end discourage their own favourite species of industry.

It is thus that every system which endeavours, either, by extraordinary encouragements, to draw towards a particular species of industry a greater share of the capital of the society than what would naturally go to it; or, by extraordinary restraints, to force from a particular species of industry some share of the capital which would otherwise be employed in it; is in reality subversive of the great purpose which it means to promote. It retards, instead of accelerating, the progress of the society towards real wealth and greatness; and diminishes, instead of increasing, the real value of the annual produce of its land and labour.

All systems either of preference or of restraint, therefore, being thus completely taken away, the obvious and simple system of natural liberty establishes itself of its own accord. Every man, as long as he does not violate the laws of justice, is left perfectly free to pursue his own interest his own way, and to bring both his industry and capital into competition with those of any other man, or order of men. The sovereign is completely discharged from a duty, in the attempting to perform which he must always be exposed to innumerable delusions, and for the proper performance of which no human wisdom or knowledge could ever be sufficient; the duty of superintending the industry of private people, and of directing it towards the employments most suitable to the interest of the society. According to the system of natural liberty, the sovereign has only three duties to attend to; three duties of great importance, indeed, but plain and intelligible to common understandings: first, the duty of protecting the society from the violence and invasion of other independent societies; secondly, the duty of protecting, as far as possible, every member of the society from the injustice or oppression of every other member of it, or the duty of establishing an exact administration of justice; and, thirdly, the duty of erecting and maintaining certain public works and certain public institutions, which it can never be for the interest of any individual, or small number of individuals, to erect and maintain; because the profit could never repay the expence to any individual or small number of individuals, though it may frequently do much more than repay it to a great society.

The proper performance of those several duties of the sovereign necessarily supposes a certain expence; and this expence again necessarily requires a certain revenue to support it. In the following book, therefore, I shall endeavour to explain; first, what are the necessary expences of the sovereign or commonwealth; and which of those expences ought to be defrayed by the general contribution of the whole society; and which of them, by that of some particular part only, or of some particular members of the society: secondly, what are the different methods in which the whole society may be made to contribute towards defraying the expences incumbent on the whole society, and what are the principal advantages and inconveniences of each of those methods: and, thirdly, what are the reasons and causes which have induced almost all modern governments to mortgage some part of this revenue, or to contract debts, and what have been the effects of those debts upon the real wealth, the annual produce of the land and labour of the society. The following book, therefore, will naturally be divided into three chapters.

BOOK V

Of the Revenue of the Sovereign or Commonwealth

[Book V is famous for the interventions Smith allows the government to make in the affairs of society and in the economy. As I try to show in Appendix IV, though, there are other ways to interpret the argument of Book V. On that score, the major issues are: (1) how to account for what Smith says about "justice" in his discussion of the relations between rich and poor in commercial societies; and (2) how to evaluate what "civil governments" are suppose to achieve—collective moral up-lift in the name of social justice or social control of a potentially revolutionary group of distressed citizens—by taking charge of society's educational institutions the way Smith would have them do. Before Smith gets into these themes, however, he focuses on matters of military security—especially with regard to the militia versus standing army options for national defence. This is an old and contentious argument with many ramifications for Smith's theory of commercial society. The entire issue has been ably discussed by J. Robertson (1983).]

CHAPTER I

OF THE EXPENCES OF THE SOVEREIGN OR COMMONWEALTH

PART I

Of the Expence of Defence

The first duty of the sovereign, that of protecting the society from the violence and invasion of other independent societies, can be performed only by means of a military force. But the expence both of preparing this military force in time of peace, and of employing it in time of war, is very different in the different states of society, in the different periods of improvement.

Among nations of hunters, the lowest and rudest state of society, such as we find it among the native tribes of North America, every man is a warrior as well as a hunter. When he goes to war, either to defend his society, or to revenge the injuries which have been done to it by other societies, he maintains himself by his own labour, in the same manner as when he lives at home. His society, for in this state of things there is properly neither sovereign nor commonwealth, is at no sort of expence, either to prepare him for the field, or to maintain him while he is in it.

Among nations of shepherds, a more advanced state of society, such as we find it among the Tartars and Arabs, every man is, in the same manner, a warrior. Such nations have commonly no fixed habitation, but live, either in tents, or in a sort of covered waggons which are easily transported from place to place. The whole tribe or nation changes its situation according to the different seasons of the year, as well as according to other accidents. When its herds and flocks have consumed the forage of one part of the country, it removes to another, and from that to a third. In the dry season, it comes down to the banks of the rivers; in the wet season it retires to the upper country. When such a nation goes to war, the warriors will not trust their herds and flocks to the feeble defence of their old men, their women and children, and their old men, their women and children, will not be left behind without defence and without subsistence. The whole nation, besides, being accustomed to a wandering life, even in time of peace, easily takes the field in time of war. Whether it marches as an army, or moves about as a company of herdsmen, the way of life is nearly the same, though the object proposed by it be very different. They all go to war together, therefore, and every one does as well as he can. Among the Tartars, even the women have been frequently known to engage in battle. If they conquer, whatever belongs to the hostile tribe is the recompence of the victory. But if they are vanquished, all is lost, and not only their herds and flocks, but their women and children, become the booty of the conqueror. Even the greater part of those who survive the action are obliged to submit to him for the sake of immediate subsistence. The rest are commonly dissipated and dispersed in the desart.

The ordinary life, the ordinary exercises of a Tartar or Arab, prepare him sufficiently for war. Running, wrestling, cudgel-playing, throwing the javelin, drawing the bow, &c. are the common pastimes of those who live in the open air, and are all of them the images of war. When a Tartar or Arab actually goes to war, he is maintained, by his own herds and flocks which he carries with him, in the same manner as in peace. His chief or sovereign, for those nations have all chiefs or sovereigns, is at no sort of expence in preparing him for the field; and when he is in it, the chance of plunder is the only pay which he either expects or requires.

An army of hunters can seldom exceed two or three hundred men. The precarious subsistence which the chace affords could seldom allow a greater number to keep together for any considerable time. An army of shepherds, on the contrary, may sometimes amount to two or three hundred thousand. As long as nothing stops their progress, as long as they can go on from one district, of which they have consumed the forage, to another which is yet entire; there seems to be scarce any limit to the number who can march on together. A nation of hunters can never be formidable to the civilized nations in their neighbourhood. A nation of shepherds may. Nothing can be more contemptible than an Indian war in North America. Nothing, on the contrary, can be more dreadful than a Tartar invasion has frequently been in Asia. The judgment of Thucydides, that both Europe and Asia could not resist the Scythians united, has been verified by the experience of all ages. The inhabitants of the extensive, but defenceless plains of Scythia or Tartary, have been frequently united under the dominion of the chief of some conquering horde or clan; and the havoc and devastation of Asia have always signalized their union. The inhabitants of the inhospitable desarts of Arabia, the other great nation of shepherds, have never been united but once; under Mahomet and his immediate successors. Their union, which was more the effect of religious enthusiasm than of conquest, was signalized in the same manner. If the hunting nations of America should ever become shepherds, their neighbourhood would be much more dangerous to the European colonies than it is at present.

In a yet more advanced state of society, among those nations of husbandmen who have little foreign commerce, and no other manufactures but those coarse and household ones which almost every private family prepares for its own use; every man, in the same manner, either is a warrior, or easily becomes such. They who live by agriculture generally pass the whole day in the open air, exposed to all the inclemencies of the seasons. The hardiness of their ordinary life prepares them for the fatigues of war, to some of which their necessary occupations bear a great analogy. The necessary occupation of a ditcher prepares him to work in the trenches, and to fortify a camp as well as to enclose a field. The ordinary pastimes of such husbandmen are the same as those of shepherds, and are in the same manner the images of war. But as husbandmen have less leisure than shepherds, they are not so frequently employed in those pastimes. They are soldiers, but soldiers not quite so much masters of their exercise. Such as they are, however, it seldom costs the sovereign or commonwealth any expence to prepare them for the field.

Agriculture, even in its rudest and lowest state, supposes a settlement; some sort of fixed habitation which cannot be abandoned without great loss. When a nation of mere husbandmen, therefore, goes to war, the whole people cannot take the field together. The old men, the women and children, at least, must remain at home to take care of the habitation. All the men of the military age, however, may take the field, and, in small nations of this kind, have frequently done so. In every nation the men of the military age are supposed to amount to about a fourth or a fifth part of the whole body of the people. If the campaign too should begin after seed-time, and end before harvest, both the husbandman and his principal labourers can be spared from the farm without much loss. He trusts that the work which must be done in the mean time can be well enough executed by the old men, the women and the children. He is not unwilling, therefore, to serve without pay during a short campaign, and it frequently costs the sovereign or commonwealth as little to maintain him in the field as to prepare him for it. The citizens of all the different states of ancient Greece seem to have served in this manner till after the second Persian war; and the people of Peloponesus till after the Peloponesian war. The Peloponesians, Thucydides observes, generally left the field in the summer, and returned home to reap the harvest. The Roman people under their kings, and during the first ages of the republic, served in the same manner. It was not till the siege of Veii, that they, who staid at home, began to contribute something towards maintaining those who went to war. In the European monarchies, which were founded upon the ruins of the Roman empire, both before and for some time after the establishment of what is properly called the feudal law, the great lords, with all their immediate dependents, used to serve the crown at their own expence. In the field, in the same manner as at home, they maintained themselves by their own revenue, and not by any stipend or pay which they received from the king upon that particular occasion.

In a more advanced state of society, two different causes contribute to render it altogether impossible that they, who take the field, should maintain themselves at their own expence. Those two causes are, the progress of manufactures, and the improvement in the art of war.

Though a husbandman should be employed in an expedition, provided it begins after seed-time and ends before harvest, the interruption of his business will not always occasion any considerable diminution of his revenue. Without the intervention of his labour, nature does herself the greater part of the work which remains to be done. But the moment that an artificer, a smith, a carpenter, or a weaver, for example, quits his workhouse, the sole source of his revenue is completely dried up. Nature does nothing for him, he does all for himself. When he takes the field, therefore, in defence of the public, as he has no revenue to maintain himself, he must necessarily be maintained by the public. But in a country of which a greater part of the inhabitants are artificers and manufacturers, a great part of the people who go to war must be drawn from those classes, and must therefore be maintained by the public as long as they are employed in its service.

When the art of war too has gradually grown up to be a very intricate and complicated science, when the event of war ceases to be determined, as in the first ages of society, by a single irregular skirmish or battle, but when the contest is generally spun out through several different campaigns, each of which lasts during the greater part of the year; it becomes universally necessary that the public should maintain those who serve the public in war, at least while they are employed in that service. Whatever in time of peace might be the ordinary occupation of those who go to war, so very tedious and expensive a service would otherwise be by far too heavy a burden upon them. After the second Persian war, accordingly, the armies of Athens seem to have been generally composed of mercenary troops; consisting, indeed, partly of citizens, but partly too of foreigners; and all of them equally hired and paid at the expence of the state. From the time of the siege of Veii, the armies of Rome received pay for their service during the time which they remained in the field. Under the feudal governments the military service both of the great lords and of their immediate dependents was, after a certain period, universally exchanged for a payment in money, which was employed to maintain those who served in their stead.

The number of those who can go to war, in proportion to the whole number of the people, is necessarily much smaller in a civilized, than in a rude state of society. In a civilized society, as the soldiers are maintained altogether by the labour of those who are not soldiers, the number of the former can never exceed what the latter can maintain, over and above maintaining, in a manner suitable to their respective stations, both themselves and the other officers of government, and law, whom they are obliged to maintain. In the little agrarian states of ancient Greece, a fourth or a fifth part of the whole body of the people considered themselves as soldiers, and would sometimes, it is said, take the field. Among the civilized nations of modern Europe, it is commonly computed, that not more than one hundredth part of the inhabitants of any country can be employed as soldiers, without ruin to the country which pays the expence of their service.

The expence of preparing the army for the field seems not to have become considerable in any nation, till long after that of maintaining it in the field had devolved entirely upon the sovereign or commonwealth. In all the different republics of ancient Greece, to learn his military exercises, was a necessary part of education imposed by the state upon every free citizen. In every city there seems to have been a public field, in which, under the protection of the public magistrate, the young people were taught their different exercises by different masters. In this very simple institution, consisted the whole expence which any Grecian state seems ever to have been at, in preparing its citizens for war. In ancient Rome the exercises of the Campus Martius answered the same purpose with those of the Gymnasium in ancient Greece. Under the feudal governments, the many public ordinances that the citizens of every district should practise archery as well as several other military exercises, were intended for promoting the same purpose, but do not seem to have promoted it so well. Either from want of interest in the officers entrusted with the execution of those ordinances, or from some other cause, they appear to have been universally neglected; and in the progress of all those governments, military exercises seem to have gone gradually into disuse among the great body of the people.

In the republics of ancient Greece and Rome, during the whole period of their existence, and under the feudal governments for a considerable time after their first establishment, the trade of a soldier was not a separate, distinct trade, which constituted the sole or principal occupation of a particular class of citizens. Every subject of the state, whatever might be the ordinary trade or occupation by which he gained his livelihood, considered himself, upon all ordinary occasions, as fit likewise to exercise the trade of a soldier, and upon many extraordinary occasions as bound to exercise it.

The art of war, however, as it is certainly the noblest of all arts, so in the progress of improvement it necessarily becomes one of the most complicated among them. The state of the mechanical, as well as of some other arts, with which it is necessarily connected, determines the degree of perfection to which it is capable of being carried at any particular time. But in order to carry it to this degree of perfection, it is necessary that it should become the sole or principal occupation of a particular class of citizens, and the division of labour is as necessary for the improvement of this, as of every other art. Into other arts the division of labour is naturally introduced by the prudence of individuals, who find that they promote their private interest better by confining themselves to a particular trade, than by exercising a great number. But it is the wisdom of the state only which can render the trade of a soldier a particular trade separate and distinct from all others. A private citizen who, in time of profound peace, and without any particular encouragement from the public, should spend the greater part of his time in military exercises, might, no doubt, both improve himself very much in them, and amuse himself very well; but he certainly would not promote his own interest.

It is the wisdom of the state only which can render it for his interest to give up the greater part of his time to this peculiar occupation: and states have not always had this wisdom, even when their circumstances had become such, that the preservation of their existence required that they should have it.

A shepherd has a great deal of leisure; a husbandman, in the rude state of husbandry, has some; an artificer or manufacturer has none at all. The first may, without any loss, employ a great deal of his time in martial exercises; the second may employ some part of it; but the last cannot employ a single hour in them without some loss, and his attention to his own interest naturally leads him to neglect them altogether. Those improvements in husbandry too, which the progress of arts and manufactures necessarily introduces, leave the husbandman as little leisure as the artificer. Military exercises come to be as much neglected by the inhabitants of the country as by those of the town, and the great body of the people becomes altogether unwarlike. That wealth, at the same time, which always follows the improvements of agriculture and manufactures, and which in reality is no more than the accumulated produce of those improvements, provokes the invasion of all their neighbours. An industrious, and upon that account a wealthy nation, is of all nations the most likely to be attacked; and unless the state takes some new measures for the public defence, the natural habits of the people render them altogether incapable of defending themselves.

In these circumstances, there seem to be but two methods, by which the state can make any tolerable provision for the public defence.

It may either, first, by means of a very rigorous police, and in spite of the whole bent of the interest, genius and inclinations of the people, enforce the practice of military exercises, and oblige either all the citizens of the military age, or a certain number of them, to join in some measure the trade of a soldier to whatever other trade or profession they may happen to carry on.

Or secondly, by maintaining and employing a certain number of citizens in the constant practice of military exercises, it may render the trade of a soldier a particular trade, separate and distinct from all others.

If the state has recourse to the first of those two expedients, its military force is said to consist in a militia; if to the second, it is said to consist in a standing army. The practice of military exercises is the sole or principal occupation of the soldiers of a standing army, and the maintenance or pay which the state affords them is the principal and ordinary fund of their subsistence. The practice of military exercises is only the occasional occupation of the soldiers of a militia, and they derive the principal and ordinary fund of their subsistence from some other occupation. In a militia, the character of the labourer, artificer, or tradesman, predominates over that of the soldier: in a standing army, that of the soldier predominates over every other character; and in this distinction seems to consist the essential difference between those two different species of military force.

Militias have been of several different kinds. In some countries the citizens destined for defending the state, seem to have been exercised only, without being, if I may say so, regimented; that is, without being divided into separate and distinct bodies of troops, each of which performed its exercises under its own proper and permanent officers. In the republics of ancient Greece and Rome, each citizen, as long as he remained at home, seems to have practised his exercises either separately and independently, or with such of his equals as he liked best; and not to have been attached to any particular body of troops till he was actually called upon to take the field. In other countries, the militia has not only been exercised, but regimented. In England, in Switzerland, and, I believe, in every other country of modern Europe, where any imperfect military force of this kind has been established, every militia-man is, even in time of peace, attached to a particular body of troops, which performs its exercises under its own proper and permanent officers.

Before the invention of fire-arms, that army was superior in which the soldiers had, each individually, the greatest skill and dexterity in the use of their arms. Strength and agility of body were of the highest consequence, and commonly determined the fate of battles. But this skill and dexterity in the use of their arms, could be acquired only, in the same manner as fencing is at present, by practising, not in great bodies, but each man separately, in a particular school, under a particular master, or with his own particular equals and companions. Since the invention of fire-arms, strength and agility of body, or even extraordinary dexterity and skill in the use of arms, though they are far from being of no consequence, are, however, of less consequence. The nature of the weapon, though it by no means puts the awkward upon a level with the skilful, puts him more nearly so than he ever was before. All the dexterity and skill, it is supposed, which are necessary for using it, can be well enough acquired by practising in great bodies.

Regularity, order, and prompt obedience to command, are qualities which, in modern armies, are of more importance towards determining the fate of battles, than the dexterity and skill of the soldiers in the use of their arms. But the noise of fire-arms, the smoke, and the invisible death to which every man feels himself every moment exposed, as soon as he comes within cannon-shot, and frequently a long time before the battle can be well said to be engaged, must render it very difficult to maintain any considerable degree of this regularity, order, and prompt obedience, even in the beginning of a modern battle. In an ancient battle there was no noise but what arose from the human voice; there was no smoke, there was no invisible cause of wounds or death. Every man, till some mortal weapon actually did approach him, saw clearly that no such weapon was near him. In these circumstances, and among troops who had some confidence in their own skill and dexterity in the use of their arms, it must have been a good deal less difficult to preserve some degree of regularity and order, not only in the beginning, but through the whole progress of an ancient battle, and till one of the two armies was fairly defeated. But the habits of regularity, order, and prompt obedience to command, can be acquired only by troops which are exercised in great bodies.

A militia, however, in whatever manner it may be either disciplined or exercised, must always be much inferior to a well-disciplined and well-exercised standing army. . . .

When a civilized nation depends for its defence upon a militia, it is at all times exposed to be conquered by any barbarous nation which happens to be in its neighbourhood. The frequent conquests of all the civilized countries in Asia by the Tartars, sufficiently demonstrates the natural superiority, which the militia of a barbarous, has over that of a civilized nation. A well-regulated standing army is superior to every militia. Such an army, as it can best be maintained by an opulent and civilized nation, so it can alone defend such a nation against the invasion of a poor and barbarous neighbour. It is only by means of a standing army, therefore, that the civilization of any country can be perpetuated, or even preserved for any considerable time.

As it is only by means of a well-regulated standing army that a civilized country can be defended; so it is only by means of it, that a barbarous country can be suddenly and tolerably civilized. A standing army establishes, with an irresistible force, the law of the sovereign through the remotest provinces of the empire, and maintains some degree of regular government in countries which could not otherwise admit of any. Whoever examines, with attention, the improvements which Peter the Great introduced into the Russian empire, will find that they almost all resolve themselves into the establishment of a well-regulated standing army. It is the instrument which executes and maintains all his other regulations. That degree of order and internal peace, which that empire has ever since enjoyed, is altogether owing to the influence of that army.

Men of republican principles have been jealous of a standing army as dangerous to liberty. It certainly is so, wherever the interest of the general and that of the principal officers are not necessarily connected with the support of the constitution of the state. The standing army of Cæsar destroyed the Roman republic. The standing army of Cromwel turned the long parliament out of doors. But where the sovereign is himself the general, and the principal nobility and gentry of the country the chief officers of the army; where the military force is placed under the command of those who have the greatest interest in the support of the civil authority, because they have themselves the greatest share of that authority, a standing army can never be dangerous to liberty. On the contrary, it may in some cases be favourable to liberty. The security which it gives to the sovereign renders unnecessary that troublesome jealousy, which, in some modern republics, seems to watch over the minutest actions, and to be at all times ready to disturb the peace of every citizen. Where the security of the magistrate, though supported by the principal people of the country, is endangered by every popular discontent; where a small tumult is capable of bringing about in a few hours a great revolution, the whole authority of government must be employed to suppress and punish every murmur and complaint against it. To a sovereign, on the contrary, who feels himself supported, not only by the natural aristocracy of the country, but by a well-regulated standing army, the rudest, the most groundless, and the most licentious remonstrances can give little disturbance. He can safely pardon or neglect them, and his consciousness of his own superiority naturally disposes him to do so. That degree of liberty which approaches to licentiousness can be tolerated only in countries where the sovereign is secured by a well-regulated standing army. It is in such countries only, that the public safety does not require, that the sovereign should be trusted with any discretionary power, for suppressing even the impertinent wantonness of this licentious liberty.

The first duty of the sovereign, therefore, that of defending the society from the violence and injustice of other independent societies, grows gradually more and more expensive, as the society advances in civilization. The military force of the society, which originally cost the sovereign no expence either in time of peace or in time of war, must, in the progress of improvement, first be maintained by him in time of war, and afterwards even in time of peace.

The great change introduced into the art of war by the invention of fire-arms, has enhanced still further both the expence of exercising and disciplining any particular number of soldiers in time of peace, and that of employing them in time of war. Both their arms and their ammunition are become more expensive. A musquet is a more expensive machine than a javelin or a bow and arrows; a cannon or a mortar than a balista or a catapulta. The powder, which is spent in a modern review, is lost irrecoverably, and occasions a very considerable expence. The javelins and arrows which were thrown or shot in an ancient one, could easily be picked up again, and were besides of very little value. The cannon and the mortar are, not only much dearer, but much heavier machines than the balista or catapulta, and require a greater expence, not only to prepare them for the field, but to carry them to it. As the superiority of the modern artillery too, over that of the ancients is very great; it has become much more difficult, and consequently much more expensive, to fortify a town so as to resist even for a few weeks the attack of that superior artillery. In modern times many different causes contribute to render the defence of the society more expensive. The unavoidable effects of the natural progress of improvement have, in this respect, been a good deal enhanced by a great revolution in the art of war, to which a mere accident, the invention of gunpowder, seems to have given occasion.

In modern war the great expence of fire-arms gives an evident advantage to the nation which can best afford that expence; and consequently, to an opulent and civilized, over a poor and barbarous nation. In ancient times the opulent and civilized found it difficult to defend themselves against the poor and barbarous nations. In modern times the poor and barbarous find it difficult to defend themselves against the opulent and civilized. The invention of firearms, an invention which at first sight appears to be so pernicious, is certainly favourable both to the permanency and to the extension of civilization.

PART II

Of the Expence of Justice

The second duty of the sovereign, that of protecting, as far as possible, every member of the society from the injustice or oppression of every other member of it, or the duty of establishing an exact administration of justice requires two very different degrees of expence in the different periods of society.

Among nations of hunters, as there is scarce any property, or at least none that exceeds the value of two or three days labour; so there is seldom any established magistrate or any regular administration of justice. Men who have no property can injure one another only in their persons or reputations. But when one man kills, wounds, beats, or defames another, though he to whom the injury is done suffers, he who does it receives no benefit. It is otherwise with the injuries to property. The benefit of the person who does the injury is often equal to the loss of him who suffers it. Envy, malice, or resentment, are the only passions which can prompt one man to injure another in his person or reputation. But the greater part of men are not very frequently under the influence of those passions;

and the very worst men are so only occasionally. As their gratification too, how agreeable soever it may be to certain characters, is not attended with any real or permanent advantage, it is in the greater part of men commonly restrained by prudential considerations. Men may live together in society with some tolerable degree of security, though there is no civil magistrate to protect them from the injustice of those passions. But avarice and ambition in the rich, in the poor the hatred of labour and the love of present ease and enjoyment, are the passions which prompt to invade property, passions much more steady in their operation, and much more universal in their influence. Wherever there is great property, there is great inequality. For one very rich man, there must be at least five hundred poor, and the affluence of the few supposes the indigence of the many. The affluence of the rich excites the indignation of the poor, who are often both driven by want, and prompted by envy, to invade his possessions. It is only under the shelter of the civil magistrate that the owner of that valuable property, which is acquired by the labour of many years, or perhaps of many successive generations, can sleep a single night in security. He is at all times surrounded by unknown enemies, whom, though he never provoked, he can never appease, and from whose injustice he can be protected only by the powerful arm of the civil magistrate continually held up to chastise it. The acquisition of valuable and extensive property, therefore, necessarily requires the establishment of civil government. Where there is no property, or at least none that exceeds the value of two or three days labour, civil government is not so necessary.

Civil government supposed a certain subordination. But as the necessity of civil government gradually grows up with the acquisition of valuable property, so the principal causes which naturally introduce subordination gradually grow up with the growth of that valuable property.

The causes or circumstances which naturally introduce subordination, or which naturally, and antecedent to any civil institution, give some men some superiority over the greater part of their brethren, seem to be four in number.

The first of those causes or circumstances is the superiority of personal qualifications, of strength, beauty, and agility of body; of wisdom, and virtue, of prudence, justice, fortitude, and moderation of mind. The qualifications of the body, unless supported by those of the mind, can give little authority in any period of society. He is a very strong man, who, by mere strength of body, can force two weak ones to obey him. The qualifications of the mind can alone give very great authority. They are, however, invisible qualities; always disputable, and generally disputed. No society, whether barbarous or civilized, has ever found it convenient to settle the rules of precedency of rank and subordination, according to those invisible qualities; but according to something that is more plain and palpable.

The second of those causes or circumstances is the superiority of age. An old man, provided his age is not so far advanced as to give suspicion of dotage, is every where more respected than a young man of equal rank, fortune, and abilities. Among nations of hunters, such as the native tribes of North America, age is the sole foundation of rank and precedency. Among them, father is the appellation of a superior; brother, of an equal; and son, of an inferior. In the most opulent and civilized nations, age regulates rank among those who are in every other respect equal, and among whom, therefore, there is nothing else to regulate it. Among brothers and among sisters, the eldest always take place; and in the succession of the paternal estate every thing which cannot be divided, but must go entire to one person, such as a title of honour, is in most cases given to the eldest. Age is a plain and palpable quality which admits of no dispute.

The third of those causes or circumstances is the superiority of fortune. The authority of riches, however, though great in every age of society, is perhaps greatest in the rudest age of society which admits of any considerable inequality of fortune. A Tartar chief, the increase of whose herds and flocks is sufficient to maintain a thousand men, cannot well employ that increase in any other way than in maintaining a thousand men. The rude state of his society does not afford him any manufactured produce, any trinkets or baubles of any kind, for which he can exchange that part of his rude produce which is over and above his own consumption. The thousand men whom he thus maintains, depending entirely upon him for their subsistence, must both obey his orders in war, and submit to his jurisdiction in peace. He is necessarily both their general and their judge, and his chieftainship is the necessary effect of the superiority of his fortune. In an opulent and civilized society a man may possess a much greater fortune, and yet not be able to command a dozen of people. Though the produce of his estate may be sufficient to maintain, and may perhaps actually maintain, more than a thousand people, yet as those people pay for every thing which they get from him, as he gives scarce any thing to any body but in exchange for an equivalent, there is scarce any body who considers himself as entirely dependent upon him, and his authority extends only over a few menial servants. The authority of fortune, however, is very great even in an opulent and civilized society. That it is much greater than that, either of age, or of personal qualities, has been the constant complaint of every period of society which admitted of any considerable inequality of fortune. The first period of society, that of hunters, admits of no such inequality. Universal poverty establishes there universal equality, and the superiority, either of age, or of personal qualities, are the feeble, but the sole foundations of authority and subordination. There is therefore little or no authority or subordination in this period of society. The second period of society, that of shepherds, admits of very great inequalities of fortune, and there is no period in which the superiority of fortune gives so great authority to those who possess it. There is no period accordingly in which authority and subordination are more perfectly established. The authority of an Arabian scherif is very great; that of a Tartar khan altogether despotical.

The fourth of those causes or circumstances is the superiority of birth. Superiority of birth supposes an ancient superiority of fortune in the family of the person who claims it. All families are equally ancient; and the ancestors of the prince, though they may be better known, cannot well be more numerous than those of the beggar. Antiquity of family means every where the antiquity either of wealth, or of that greatness which is commonly either founded upon wealth, or accompanied with it. Upstart greatness is every where less respected than ancient greatness. The hatred of usurpers, the love of the family of an ancient monarch, are, in a great measure, founded upon the contempt which men naturally have for the former, and upon their veneration for the latter. As a military officer submits without reluctance to the authority of a superior by whom he has always been commanded, but cannot bear that his inferior should be set over his head; so men easily submit to a family to whom they and their ancestors have always submitted; but are fired with indignation when another family, in whom they had never acknowledged any such superiority, assumes a dominion over them.

The distinction of birth, being subsequent to the inequality of fortune, can have no place in nations of hunters, among whom all men, being equal in fortune, must likewise be very nearly equal in birth. The son of a wise and brave man may, indeed, even among them, be somewhat more respected than a man of equal merit who has the misfortune to be the son of a fool or a coward. The difference, however, will not be very great; and there never was, I believe, a great family in the world whose illustration was entirely derived from the inheritance of wisdom and virtue.

The distinction of birth not only may, but always does take place among nations of shepherds. Such nations are always strangers to every sort of luxury, and great wealth can scarce ever be dissipated among them by improvident profusion. There are no nations accordingly who abound more in families revered and honoured on account of their descent from a long race of great and illustrious ancestors; because there are no nations among whom wealth is likely to continue longer in the same families.

Birth and fortune are evidently the two circumstances which principally set one man above another. They are the two great sources of personal distinction, and are therefore the principal causes which naturally establish authority and subordination among men. Among nations of shepherds both those causes operate with their full force. The great shepherd or herdsman, respected on account of his great wealth, and of the great number of those who depend upon him for subsistence, and revered on account of the nobleness of his birth, and of the immemorial antiquity of his illustrious family, has a natural authority over all the inferior shepherds or herdsmen of his horde or clan. He can command the united force of a greater number of people than any of them. His military power is greater than that of any of them. In time of war they are all of them naturally disposed to muster themselves under his banner, rather than under that of any other person, and his birth and fortune thus naturally procure to him some sort of executive power. By commanding too the united force of a greater number of people than any of them, he is best able to compel any one of them who may have injured another to compensate the wrong. He is the person, therefore, to whom all those who are too weak to defend themselves naturally look up for protection. It is to him that they naturally complain of the injuries which they imagine have been done to them, and his interposition in such cases is more easily submitted to, even by the person complained of, than that of any other person would be. His birth and fortune thus naturally procure him some sort of judicial authority.

It is in the age of shepherds, in the second period of society, that the inequality of fortune first begins to take place, and introduces among men a degree of authority and subordination which could not possibly exist before. It thereby introduces some degree of that civil government which is indispensably necessary for its own preservation: and it seems to do this naturally, and even independent of the consideration of that necessity. The consideration of that necessity comes no doubt afterwards to contribute very much to maintain and secure that authority and subordination. The rich, in particular, are necessarily interested to support that order of things, which can alone secure them in the possession of their own advantages. Men of inferior wealth combine to defend those of superior wealth in the possession of their property, in order that men of superior wealth may combine to defend them in the possession of theirs. All the inferior shepherds and herdsmen feel that the security of their own herds and flocks depends upon the security of those of the great shepherd or herdsman; that the maintenance of their lesser authority depends upon that of his greater authority, and that upon their subordination to him depends his power of keeping their inferiors in subordination to them. They constitute a sort of little nobility, who feel themselves interested to defend the property and to support the authority of their own little sovereign, in order that he may be able to defend their property and to support their authority. Civil government, so far as it is instituted for the security of property, is in reality instituted for the defence of the rich against the poor, or of those who have some property against those who have none at all.

PART III

Of the Expence of public Works and public Institutions

ARTICLE II

Of the Expence of the Institutions for the Education of Youth

But though the public schools and universities of Europe were originally intended only for the education of a particular profession, that of churchmen; and though they were not always very diligent in instructing their pupils even in the sciences which were supposed necessary for that profession, yet they gradually drew to themselves the education of almost all other people, particularly of almost all gentlemen and men of fortune. No better method, it seems, could be fallen upon of spending, with any advantage, the long interval between infancy and that period of life at which men begin to apply in good earnest to the real business of the world, the business which is to employ them during the remainder of their days. The greater part of what is taught in schools and universities, however, does not seem to be the most proper preparation for that business.

In England, it becomes every day more and more the custom to send young people to travel in foreign countries immediately upon their leaving school, and without sending them to any university. Our young people, it is said, generally return home much improved by their travels. A young man who goes abroad at seventeen or eighteen, and returns home at one and twenty, returns three or four years older than he was when he went abroad; and at that age it is very difficult not to improve a good deal in three or four years. In the course of his travels, he generally acquires some knowledge of one or two foreign languages; a knowledge, however, which is seldom sufficient to enable him either to speak or write them with propriety. In other respects, he commonly returns home more conceited, more unprincipled, more dissipated, and more incapable of any serious application either to study or to business, than he could well have become in so short a time, had he lived at home. By travelling so very young, by spending in the most frivolous dissipation the most precious years of his life, at a distance from the inspection and controul of his parents and relations, every useful habit, which the earlier parts of his education might have had some tendency to form in him, instead of being rivetted and confirmed, is almost necessarily either weakened or effaced. Nothing but the discredit into which the universities are allowing themselves to fall, could ever have brought into repute so very absurd a practice as that of travelling at this early period of life. By sending his son abroad, a father delivers himself, at least for some time, from so disagreeable an object as that of a son unemployed, neglected, and going to ruin before his eyes.

Such have been the effects of some of the modern institutions for education.

Different plans and different institutions for education seem to have taken place in other ages and nations.

In the republics of ancient Greece, every free citizen was instructed, under the direction of the public magistrate, in gymnastic exercises and in music. By gymnastic exercises it was intended to harden his body, to sharpen his courage, and to prepare him for the fatigues and dangers of war; and as the Greek militia was, by all accounts, one of the best that ever was in the world, this part of their public education must have answered completely the purpose for which it was intended. By the other part, music, it was proposed, at least by the philosophers and historians who have given us an account of those institutions, to humanize the mind, to soften the temper, and to dispose it for performing all the social and moral duties both of public and private life.

In ancient Rome the exercises of the Campus Martius answered the same purpose as those of the Gymnazium in ancient Greece, and they seem to have answered it equally well. But among the Romans there was nothing which corresponded to the musical education of the Greeks. The morals of the Romans, however, both in private and public life, seem to have been, not only equal, but, upon the whole, a good deal superior to those of the Greeks. That they were superior in private life, we have the express testimony of Polybius and of Dionysius of Halicarnassus, two authors well acquainted with both nations; and the whole tenor of the Greek and Roman history bears witness to the superiority of the public morals of the Romans. The good temper and moderation of contending factions seems to be the most essential circumstance in the public morals of a free people. But the factions of the Greeks were almost always violent and sanguinary; whereas, till the time of the Gracchi, no blood had ever been shed in any Roman faction; and from the time of the Gracchi the Roman republic may be considered as in reality dissolved. Notwithstanding, therefore, the very respectable authority of Plato, Aristotle, and Polybius, and notwithstanding the very ingenious reasons by which Mr. Montesquieu endeavours to support that authority, it seems probable that the musical education of the Greeks had no great effect in mending their morals, since, without any such education, those of the Romans were upon the whole superior. The respect of those ancient sages for the institutions of their ancestors, had probably disposed them to find much political wisdom in what was, perhaps, merely an ancient custom, contin-ued, without interruption, from the earliest period of those societies, to the times in which they had arrived at a considerable degree of refinement. Music and dancing are the great amusements of almost all barbarous nations, and the great accomplishments which are supposed to fit any man for entertaining his society. It is so at this day among the negroes on the coast of Africa. It was so among the ancient Celtes, among the ancient Scandinavians, and, as we may learn from Homer, among the ancient Greeks in the times preceding the Trojan war. When the Greek tribes had formed themselves into little republics, it was natural that the study of those accomplishments should, for a long time, make a part of the public and common education of the people.

The masters who instructed the young people either in music or in military exercises, do not seem to have been paid, or even appointed by the state, either in Rome or even in Athens, the Greek republic of whose laws and customs we are the best informed. The state required that every free citizen should fit himself for defending it in war, and should, upon that account, learn his military exercises. But it left him to learn them of such masters as he could find, and it seems to have advanced nothing for this purpose, but a public field or place of exercise, in which he should practise and perform them.

In the early ages both of the Greek and Roman republics, the other parts of education seem to have consisted in learning to read, write, and account according to the arithmetic of the times. These accomplishments the richer citizens seem frequently to have acquired at home, by the assistance of some domestic pedagogue, who was generally, either a slave, or a freed-man; and the poorer citizens, in the schools of such masters as made a trade of teaching for hire. Such parts of education, however, were abandoned altogether to the care of the parents or guardians of each individual. It does not appear that the state ever assumed any inspection or direction of them. By a law of Solon, indeed, the children were acquit-ted from maintaining those parents in their old age, who had neglected to instruct them in some profitable trade or business.

In the progress of refinement, when philosophy and rhetoric came into fashion, the better sort of people used to send their children to the schools of philosophers and rhetoricians, in order to be instructed in these fashion-able sciences. But those schools were not supported by the public. They were for a long time barely tolerated by it. The demand for philosophy and rhetoric was for a long time so small, that the first professed teachers of either could not find constant employment in any one city, but were obliged to travel about from place to place. In this manner lived Zeno of Elea, Protagoras, Gorgias, Hippias, and many others. As the demand increased, the schools both of philosophy and rhetoric became stationary; first in Athens, and afterwards in several other cities. The state, however, seems never to have encouraged them further than by assigning to some of them a particular place to teach in, which was sometimes done too by private donors. The state seems to have assigned the Academy to Plato, the Lyceum to Aristotle, and the Portico to Zeno of Citta, the founder of the Stoics. But Epicurus bequeathed his gardens to his own school. Till about the time of Marcus Antoninus, however, no teacher appears to have had any salary from the public, or to have had any other emoluments, but what arose from the honoraries or fees of his scholars. The bounty which that philosophical emperor, as we learn from Lucian, bestowed upon one of the teachers of philosophy, probably lasted no longer than his own life. There was nothing equivalent to the privileges of graduation, and to have attended any of those schools was not necessary, in order to be permitted to practise any particular trade or profession. If the opinion of their own utility could not draw scholars to them, the law neither forced any body to go to them, nor rewarded any body for having gone to them. The teachers had no jurisdiction over their pupils, nor any other authority besides that natural authority, which superior virtue and abilities never fail to procure from young people towards those who are entrusted with any part of their education.

At Rome, the study of the civil law made a part of the education, not of the greater part of the citizens, but of some particular families. The young people, however, who wished to acquire knowledge in the law, had no public school to go to, and had no other method of studying it, than by frequenting the company of such of their relations and friends, as were supposed to understand it. It is perhaps worth while to remark, that though the laws of the twelve tables were, many of them, copied from those of some ancient Greek republics, yet law never seems to have grown up to be a science in any republic of ancient Greece. In Rome it became a science very early, and gave a considerable degree of illustration to those citizens who had the reputation of understanding it. In the republics of ancient Greece, particularly in Athens, the ordinary courts of justice consisted of numerous, and therefore disorderly, bodies of people, who frequently decided almost at random, or as clamour, faction and party spirit happened to determine. The ignominy of an unjust decision, when it was to be divided among five hundred, a thousand, or fifteen hundred people (for some of their courts were so very numerous), could not fall very heavy upon any individual. At Rome, on the contrary, the principal courts of justice consisted either of a single judge, or of a small number of judges, whose characters, especially as they deliberated always in public, could not fail to be very much affected by any rash or unjust decision. In doubtful cases, such courts, from their anxiety to avoid blame, would naturally endeavour to shelter themselves under the example, or precedent, of the judges who had sat before them, either in the same, or in some other court. This attention to practice and precedent, necessarily formed the Roman law into that regular and orderly system in which it has been delivered down to us; and the like attention has had the like effects upon the laws of every other country where such attention has taken place. The superiority of character in the Romans over that of the Greeks, so much remarked by Polybius and Dionysius of Halicarnassus, was probably more owing to the better constitution of their courts of justice, than to any of the circumstances to which those authors ascribe it. The Romans are said to have been particularly distinguished for their superior respect to an oath. But the people who were accustomed to make oath only before some diligent and well-informed court of justice, would naturally be much more attentive to what they swore, than they who were accustomed to do the same thing before mobbish and disorderly assemblies.

The abilities, both civil and military, of the Greeks and Romans, will readily be allowed to have been, at least, equal to those of any modern nation. Our prejudice is perhaps rather to overrate them. But except in what related to military exercises, the state seems to have been at no pains to form those great abilities: for I cannot be induced to believe, that the musical education of the Greeks could be of much consequence in forming them. Masters, however, had been found, it seems, for instructing the better sort of people among those nations in every art and science in which the circumstances of their society rendered it necessary or convenient for them to be instructed. The demand for such instruction produced, what it always produces, the talent for giving it; and the emulation which an unrestrained competition never fails to excite, appears to have brought that talent to a very high degree of perfection. In the attention which the ancient philosophers excited, in the empire which they acquired over the opinions and principles of their auditors, in the faculty which they possessed of giving a certain tone and character to the conduct and conversation of those auditors; they appear to have been much superior to any modern teachers. In modern times, the diligence of public teachers is more or less corrupted by the circumstances, which render them more or less independent of their success and reputation in their particular professions. Their salaries too put the private teacher, who would pretend to come into competition with them, in the same state with a merchant who attempts to trade without a bounty, in competition with those who trade with a considerable one. If he sells his goods at nearly the same price, he cannot have the same profit, and poverty and beggary at least, if not bankruptcy and ruin will infallibly be his lot. If he attempts to sell them much dearer, he is likely to have so few customers that his circumstances will not be much mended. The privileges of graduation, besides, are in many countries necessary, or at least extremely convenient to most men of learned professions; that is, to the far greater part of those who have occasion for a learned education. But those privileges can be obtained only by attending the lectures of the public teachers. The most careful attendance upon the ablest instructions of any private teacher, cannot always give any title to demand them. It is from these different causes that the private teacher of any of the sciences which are commonly taught in universities, is in modern times generally considered as in the very lowest order of men of letters. A man of real abilities can scarce find out a more humiliating or a more unprofitable employment to turn them to. The endowments of schools and colleges have, in this manner, not only corrupted the diligence of public teachers, but have rendered it almost impossible to have any good private ones.

Were there no public institutions for education, no system, no science would be taught for which there was not some demand; or which the circumstances of the times did not render it either necessary, or convenient, or at least fashionable, to learn. A private teacher could never find his account in teaching, either an exploded and antiquated system of a science acknowledged to be useful, or a science universally believed to be a mere useless and pedantic heap of sophistry and nonsense. Such systems, such sciences, can subsist no where, but in those incorporated societies for education whose prosperity and revenue are in a great measure independent of their reputation, and altogether independent of their industry. Were there no public institutions for education, a gentleman, after going through, with application and abilities, the most complete course of education which the circumstances of the times were supposed to afford, could not come into the world completely ignorant of every thing which is the common subject of conversation among gentlemen and men of the world.

There are no public institutions for the education of women, and there is accordingly nothing useless, absurd, or fantastical in the common course of their education. They are taught what their parents or guardians judge it necessary or useful for them to learn; and they are taught nothing else. Every part of their education tends evidently to some useful purpose; either to improve the natural attractions of their person, or to form their mind to reserve, to modesty, to chastity, and to oeconomy; to render them both likely to become the mistresses of a family, and to behave properly when they have become such. In every part of her life a woman feels some conveniency or advantage from every part of her education. It seldom happens that a man, in any part of his life, derives any conveniency or advantage from some of the most laborious and troublesome parts of his education.

Ought the public, therefore, to give no attention, it may be asked, to the education of the people? Or if it ought to give any, what are the different parts of education which it ought to attend to in the different orders of the people? and in what manner ought it to attend to them?

In some cases the state of the society necessarily places the greater part of individuals in such situations as naturally form in them, without any attention of government, almost all the abilities and virtues which that state requires, or perhaps can admit of. In other cases the state of the society does not place the greater part of individuals in such situations, and some attention of government is necessary in order to prevent the almost entire corruption and degeneracy of the great body of the people.

In the progress of the division of labour, the employment of the far greater part of those who live by labour, that is, of the great body of the people, comes to be confined to a few very simple operations, frequently to one or two. But the understandings of the greater part of men are necessarily formed by their ordinary employments. The man whose whole life is spent in performing a few simple operations, of which the effects too are, perhaps, always the same, or very nearly the same, has no occasion to exert his understanding, or to exercise his invention in finding out expedients for removing difficulties which never occur. He naturally loses, therefore, the habit of such exertion, and generally becomes as stupid and ignorant as it is possible for a human creature to become. The torpor of his mind renders him, not only incapable of relishing or bearing a part in any rational conversation, but of conceiving any generous, noble, or tender sentiment, and consequently of forming any just judgment concerning many even of the ordinary duties of private life. Of the great and extensive interests of his country he is altogether incapable of judging; and unless very particular pains have been taken to render him otherwise, he is equally incapable of defending his country in war. The uniformity of his stationary life naturally corrupts the courage of his mind, and makes him regard with abhorrence the irregular, uncertain, and adventurous life of a soldier. It corrupts even the activity of his body, and renders him incapable of exerting his strength with vigour and perseverance, in any other employment than that to which he has been bred. His dexterity at his own particular trade seems, in this manner, to be acquired at the expence of his intellectual, social, and martial virtues. But in every improved and civilized society this is the state into which the labouring poor, that is, the great body of the people, must necessarily fall, unless government takes some pains to prevent it.

It is otherwise in the barbarous societies, as they are commonly called, of hunters, of shepherds, and even of husbandmen in that rude state of husbandry which precedes the improvement of manufactures, and the extension of foreign commerce. In such societies the varied occupations of every man oblige every man to exert his capacity, and to invent expedients for removing difficulties which are continually occurring. Invention is kept alive, and the mind is not suffered to fall into that drowsy stupidity, which, in a civilized society, seems to benumb the understanding of almost all the inferior ranks of people. In those barbarous societies, as they are called, every man, it has already been observed, is a warrior. Every man too is in some measure a statesman, and can form a tolerable judgment concerning the interest of the society, and the conduct of those who govern it. How far their chiefs are good judges in peace, or good leaders in war, is obvious to the observation of almost every single man among them. In such a society indeed, no man can well acquire that improved and refined understanding, which a few men sometimes possess in a more civilized state. Though in a rude society there is a good deal of variety in the occupations of every individual, there is not a great deal in those of the whole society. Every man does, or is capable of doing, almost every thing which any other man does, or is capable of doing. Every man has a considerable degree of knowledge, ingenuity, and invention; but scarce any man has a great degree. The degree, however, which is commonly possessed, is generally sufficient for conducting the whole simple business of the society. In a civilized state, on the contrary, though there is little variety in the occupations of the greater part of individuals, there is an almost infinite variety in those of the whole society. These varied occupations present an almost infinite variety of objects to the contemplation of those few, who, being attached to no particular occupation themselves, have leisure and inclination to examine the occupations of other people. The contemplation of so great a variety of objects necessarily exercises their minds in endless comparisons and combinations, and renders their understandings, in an extraordinary degree, both acute and comprehensive. Unless those few, however, happen to be placed in some very particular situations, their great abilities, though honourable to themselves, may contribute very little to the good government or happiness of their society. Notwithstanding the great abilities of those few, all the nobler parts of the human character may be, in a great measure, obliterated and extinguished in the great body of the people.

The education of the common people requires, perhaps, in a civilized and commercial society, the attention of the public more than that of people of some rank and fortune. People of some rank and fortune are generally eighteen or nineteen years of age before they enter upon that particular business, profession, or trade, by which they propose to distinguish themselves in the world. They have before that full time to acquire, or at least to fit themselves for afterwards acquiring, every accomplishment which can recommend them to the public esteem, or render them worthy of it. Their parents or guardians are generally sufficiently anxious that they should be so accomplished, and are, in most cases, willing enough to lay out the expence which is necessary for that purpose. If they are not always properly educated, it is seldom from the want of expence laid out upon their education; but from the improper application of that expence. It is seldom from the want of masters; but from the negligence and incapacity of the masters who are to be had, and from the difficulty, or rather from the impossibility which there is, in the present state of things, of finding any better. The employments too in which people of some rank or fortune spend the greater part of their lives, are not, like those of the common people, simple and uniform. They are almost all of them extremely complicated, and such as exercise the head more than the hands. The understandings of those who are engaged in such employments can seldom grow torpid for want of exercise. The employments of people of some rank and fortune, besides, are seldom such as harass them from morning to night. They generally have a good deal of leisure, during which they may perfect themselves in every branch either of useful or ornamental knowledge of which they may have laid the foundation, or for which they may have acquired some taste in the earlier part of life.

It is otherwise with the common people. They have little time to spare for education. Their parents can scarce afford to maintain them even in infancy. As soon as they are able to work, they must apply to some trade by which they can earn their subsistence. That trade too is generally so simple and uniform as to give little exercise to the understanding; while, at the same time, their labour is both so constant and so severe, that it leaves them little leisure and less inclination to apply to, or even to think of any thing else.

But though the common people cannot, in any civilized society, be so well instructed as people of some rank and fortune, the most essential parts of education, however, to read, write, and account, can be acquired at so early a period of life, that the greater part even of those who are to be bred to the lowest occupations, have time to acquire them before they can be employed in those occupations. For a very small expence the public can facilitate, can encourage, and can even impose upon almost the whole body of the people, the necessity of acquiring those most essential parts of education.

The public can facilitate this acquisition by establishing in every parish or district a little school, where children may be taught for a reward so moderate, that even a common labourer may afford it; the master being partly, but not wholly paid by the public; because, if he was wholly, or even principally paid by it, he would soon learn to neglect his business. In Scotland the establishment of such parish schools has taught almost the whole common people to read, and a very great proportion of them to write and account. In England the establishment of charity schools has had an effect of the same kind, though not so universally, because the establishment is not so universal. If in those little schools the books, by which the children are taught to read, were a little more instructive than they commonly are; and if, instead of a little smattering of Latin, which the children of the common people are sometimes taught there, and which can scarce ever be of any use to them; they were instructed in the elementary parts of geometry and mechanics, the literary education of this rank of people would perhaps be as complete as it can be. There is scarce a common trade which does not afford some opportunities of applying to it the principles of geometry and mechanics, and which would not therefore gradually exercise and improve the common people in those principles, the necessary introduction to the most sublime as well as to the most useful sciences.

The public can encourage the acquisition of those most essential parts of education by giving small premiums, and little badges of distinction, to the children of the common people who excel in them.

The public can impose upon almost the whole body of the people the necessity of acquiring those most essential parts of education, by obliging every man to undergo an examination or probation in them before he can obtain the freedom in any corporation, or be allowed to set up any trade either in a village or town corporate.

It was in this manner, by facilitating the acquisition of their military and gymnastic exercises, by encouraging it, and even by imposing upon the whole body of the people the necessity of learning those exercises, that the Greek and Roman republics maintained the martial spirit of their respective citizens. They facilitated the acquisition of those exercises by appointing a certain place for learning and practising them, and by granting to certain masters the privilege of teaching in that place. Those masters do not appear to have had either salaries or exclusive privileges of any kind. Their reward consisted altogether in what they got from their scholars; and a citizen who had learnt his exercises in the public Gymnasia, had no sort of legal advantage over one who had learnt them privately, provided the latter had learnt them equally well. Those republics encouraged the acquisition of those exercises, by bestowing little premiums and badges of distinction upon those who excelled in them. To have gained a prize in the Olympic, Isthmian or Nemæan games gave illustration, not only to the person who gained it, but to his whole family and kindred. The obligation which every citizen was under to serve a certain number of years, if called upon, in the armies of the republic, sufficiently imposed the necessity of learning those exercises without which he could not be fit for that service.

That in the progress of improvement the practice of military exercises, unless government takes proper pains to support it, goes gradually to decay, and, together with it, the martial spirit of the great body of the people, the example of modern Europe sufficiently demonstrates. But the security of every society must always depend, more or less, upon the martial spirit of the great body of the people. In the present times, indeed, that martial spirit alone, and unsupported by a well-disciplined standing army, would not, perhaps, be sufficient for the defence and security of any society. But where every citizen had the spirit of a soldier, a smaller standing army would surely be requisite. That spirit, besides, would necessarily diminish very much the dangers to liberty, whether real or imaginary, which are commonly apprehended from a standing army. As it would very much facilitate the operations of that army against a foreign invader, so it would obstruct them as much if unfortunately they should ever be directed against the constitution of the state.

The ancient institutions of Greece and Rome seem to have been much more effectual, for maintaining the martial spirit of the great body of the people, than the establishment of what are called the militias of modern times. They were much more simple. When they were once established, they executed themselves, and it required little or no attention from government to maintain them in the most perfect vigour. Whereas to maintain, even in tolerable execution, the complex regulations of any modern militia, requires the continual and painful attention of government, without which they are constantly falling into total neglect and disuse. The influence, besides, of the ancient institutions was much more universal. By means of them the whole body of the people was completely instructed in the use of arms. Whereas it is but a very small part of them who can ever be so instructed by the regulations of any modern militia; except, perhaps, that of Switzerland. But a coward, a man incapable either of defending or of revenging himself, evidently wants one of the most essential parts of the character of a man. He is as much mutilated and deformed in his mind as another is in his body, who is either deprived of some of its most essential members, or has lost the use of them. He is evidently the more wretched and miserable of the two; because happiness and misery, which reside altogether in the mind, must necessarily depend more upon the healthful or unhealthful, the mutilated or entire state of the mind, than upon that of the body. Even though the martial spirit of the people were of no use towards the defence of the society, yet to prevent that sort of mental mutilation, deformity, and wretchedness, which cowardice necessarily involves in it, from spreading themselves through the great body of the people, would still deserve the most serious attention of government; in the same manner as it would deserve its most serious attention to prevent a leprosy or any other loathsome and offensive disease, though neither mortal nor dangerous, from spreading itself among them; though, perhaps, no other public good might result from such attention besides the prevention of so great a public evil.

The same thing may be said of the gross ignorance and stupidity which, in a civilized society, seem so frequently to benumb the understandings of all the inferior ranks of people. A man without the proper use of the intellectual faculties of a man, is, if possible, more contemptible than even a coward, and seems to be mutilated and deformed in a still more essential part of the character of human nature. Though the state was to derive no advantage from the instruction of the inferior ranks of people, it would still deserve its attention that they should not be altogether uninstructed. The state, however, derives no inconsiderable advantage from their instruction. The more they are instructed, the less liable they are to the delusions of enthusiasm and superstition, which, among ignorant nations, frequently occasion the most dreadful disorders. An instructed and intelligent people besides, are always more decent and orderly than an ignorant and stupid one. They feel themselves, each individually more respectable, and more likely to obtain the respect of their lawful superiors, and they are therefore more disposed to respect those superiors. They are more disposed to examine, and more capable of seeing through, the interested complaints of faction and sedition, and they are, upon that account, less apt to be misled into any wanton or unnecessary opposition to the measures of government. In free countries, where the safety of government depends very much upon the favourable judgment which the people may form of its conduct, it must surely be of the highest importance that they should not be disposed to judge rashly or capriciously concerning it.

ARTICLE III

Of the Expence of the Institutions for the Instruction of People of all Ages

In every civilized society, in every society where the distinction of ranks has once been completely established, there have been always two different schemes or systems of morality current at the same time; of which the one may be called the strict or austere; the other the liberal, or, if you will, the loose system. The former is generally admired and revered by the common people: the latter is commonly more esteemed and adopted by what are called people of fashion. The degree of disapprobation with which we ought to mark the vices of levity, the vices which are apt to arise from great prosperity, and from the excess of gaiety and good humour, seems to constitute the principal distinction between those two opposite schemes or systems. In the liberal or loose system, luxury, wanton and even disorderly mirth, the pursuit of pleasure to some degree of intemperance, the breach of chastity, at least in one of the two sexes, &c. provided they are not accompanied with gross indecency, and do not lead to falsehood or injustice, are generally treated with a good deal of indulgence, and are easily either excused or pardoned altogether. In the austere system, on the contrary, those excesses are regarded with the utmost abhorrence and detestation. The vices of levity are always ruinous to the common people, and a single week's thoughtlessness and dissipation is often sufficient to undo a poor workman for ever, and to drive him through despair upon committing the most enormous crimes. The wiser and better sort of the common people, therefore, have always the utmost abhorrence and detestation of such excesses, which their experience tells them are so immediately fatal to people of their condition. The disorder and extravagance of several years, on the contrary, will not always ruin a man of fashion, and people of that rank are very apt to consider the power of indulging in some degree of excess as one of the advantages of their fortune, and the liberty of doing so without censure or reproach, as one of the privileges which belong to their station. In people of their own station, therefore, they regard such excesses with but a small degree of disapprobation, and censure them either very slightly or not at all.

Almost all religious sects have begun among the common people, from whom they have generally drawn their earliest, as well as their most numerous proselytes. The austere system of morality has, accordingly, been adopted by those sects almost constantly, or with very few exceptions; for there have been some. It was the system by which they could best recommend themselves to that order of people to whom they first proposed their plan of reformation upon what had been before established. Many of them, perhaps the greater part of them, have even endeavoured to gain credit by refining upon this austere system, and by carrying it to some degree of folly and extravagance; and this excessive rigour has frequently recommended them more than any thing else to the respect and veneration of the common people.

A man of rank and fortune is by his station the distinguished member of a great society, who attend to every part of his conduct, and who thereby oblige him to attend to every part of it himself. His authority and consideration depend very much upon the respect which this society bears to him. He dare not do any thing which would disgrace or discredit him in it, and he is obliged to a very strict observation of that species of morals, whether liberal or austere, which the general consent of this society prescribes to persons of his rank and fortune. A man of low condition, on the contrary, is far from being a distinguished member of any great society. While he remains in a country village his conduct may be attended to, and he may be obliged to attend to it himself. In this situation, and in this situation only, he may have what is called a character to lose. But as soon as he comes into a great city, he is sunk in obscurity and darkness. His conduct is observed and attended to by nobody, and he is therefore very likely to neglect it himself, and to abandon himself to every sort of low profligacy and vice. He never emerges so effectually from this obscurity, his conduct never excites so much the attention of any respectable society, as by his becoming the member of a small religious sect. He from that moment acquires a degree of consideration which he never had before. All his brother sectaries are, for the credit of the sect, interested to observe his conduct, and if he gives occasion to any scandal, if he deviates very much from those austere morals which they almost always require of one another, to punish him by what is always a very severe punishment, even where no civil effects attend it, expulsion or excommunication from the sect. In little religious sects, accordingly, the morals of the common people have been almost always remarkably regular and orderly; generally much more so than in the established church. The morals of those little sects, indeed, have frequently been rather disagreeably rigorous and unsocial.

There are two very easy and effectual remedies, however, by whose joint operation the state might, without violence, correct whatever was unsocial or disagreeably rigorous in the morals of all the little sects into which the country was divided.

The first of those remedies is the study of science and philosophy, which the state might render almost universal among all people of middling or more than middling rank and fortune; not by giving salaries to teachers in order to make them negligent and idle, but by instituting some sort of probation, even in the higher and more difficult sciences, to be undergone by every person before he was permitted to exercise any liberal profession, or before he could be received as a candidate for any honourable office of trust or profit. If the state imposed upon this order of men the necessity of learning, it would have no occasion to give itself any trouble about providing them with proper teachers. They would soon find better teachers for themselves than any whom the state could provide for them. Science is the great antidote to the poison of enthusiasm and superstition; and where all the superior ranks of people were secured from it, the inferior ranks could not be much exposed to it.

The second of those remedies is the frequency and gaiety of public diversions. The state, by encouraging, that is by giving entire liberty to all those who for their own interest would attempt, without scandal or indecency, to amuse and divert the people by painting, poetry, music, dancing; by all sorts of dramatic representations and exhibitions, would easily dissipate, in the greater part of them, that melancholy and gloomy humour which is almost always the nurse of popular superstition and enthusiasm. Public diversions have always been the objects of dread and hatred, to all the fanatical promoters of those popular frenzies. The gaiety and good humour which those diversions inspire were altogether inconsistent with that temper of mind, which was fittest for their purpose, or which they could best work upon. Dramatic representations besides, frequently exposing their artifices to public ridicule, and sometimes even to public execration, were upon that account, more than all other diversions, the objects of their peculiar abhorrence.

In a country where the law favoured the teachers of no one religion more than those of another, it would not be necessary that any of them should have any particular or immediate dependency upon the sovereign or executive power; or that he should have any thing to do, either in appointing, or in dismissing them from their offices. In such a situation he would have no occasion to give himself any concern about them, further than to keep the peace among them, in the same manner as among the rest of his subjects; that is, to hinder them from persecuting, abusing, or oppressing one another. But it is quite otherwise in countries where there is an established or governing religion. The sovereign can in this case never be secure, unless he has the means of influencing in a considerable degree the greater part of the teachers of that religion. . . .

The gradual improvements of arts, manufactures, and commerce, the same causes which destroyed the power of the great barons, destroyed in the same manner, through the greater part of Europe, the whole temporal power of the clergy. In the produce of arts, manufactures, and commerce, the clergy, like the great barons, found something for which they could exchange their rude produce, and thereby discovered the means of spending their whole revenues upon their own persons, without giving any considerable share of them to other people. Their charity became gradually less extensive, their hospitality less liberal or less profuse. Their retainers became consequently less numerous, and by degrees dwindled away altogether. The clergy too, like the great barons, wished to get a better rent from their landed estates, in order to spend it, in the same manner, upon the gratification of their own private vanity and folly.

But this increase of rent could be got only by granting leases to their tenants, who thereby became in a great measure independent of them. The ties of interest, which bound the inferior ranks of people to the clergy, were in this manner gradually broken and dissolved. They were even broken and dissolved sooner than those which bound the same ranks of people to the great barons: because the benefices of the church being, the greater part of them, much smaller than the estates of the great barons, the possessor of each benefice was much sooner able to spend the whole of its revenue upon his own person. During the greater part of the fourteenth and fifteenth centuries the power of the great barons was, through the greater part of Europe, in full vigour. But the temporal power of the clergy, the absolute command which they had once had over the great body of the people, was very much decayed. The power of the church was by that time very nearly reduced through the greater part of Europe to what arose from her spiritual authority; and even that spiritual authority was much weakened when it ceased to be supported by the charity and hospitality of the clergy. The inferior ranks of people no longer looked upon that order, as they had done before, as the comforters of their distress, and the relievers of their indigence. On the contrary, they were provoked and disgusted by the vanity, luxury, and expence of the richer clergy, who appeared to spend upon their own pleasures what had always before been regarded as the patrimony of the poor.

In this situation of things, the sovereigns in the different states of Europe endeavoured to recover the influence which they had once had in the disposal of the great benefices of the church, by procuring to the deans and chapters of each diocese the restoration of their ancient right of electing the bishop, and to the monks of each abbacy that of electing the abbot. The re-establishing of this ancient order was the object of several statutes enacted in England during the course of the fourteenth century, particularly of what is called the statute of provisors; and of the pragmatic sanction established in France in the fifteenth century. In order to render the election valid, it was necessary that the sovereign should both consent to it before-hand, and afterwards approve of the person elected; and though the election was still supposed to be free, he had, however, all the indirect means which his situation necessarily afforded him, of influencing the clergy in his own dominions. Other regulations of a similar tendency were established in other parts of Europe. But the power of the pope in the collation of the great benefices of the church seems, before the reformation, to have been nowhere so effectually and so universally restrained as in France and England. The Concordat afterwards, in the sixteenth century, gave to the kings of France the absolute right of presenting to all the great, or what are called the consistorial benefices of the Gallican church.

Since the establishment of the Pragmatic sanction and of the Concordat, the clergy of France have in general shown less respect to the decrees of the papal court than the clergy of any other catholic country. In all the disputes which their sovereign has had with the pope, they have almost constantly taken party with the former. This independency of the clergy of France upon the court of Rome, seems to be principally founded upon the Pragmatic sanction and the Concordat. In the earlier periods of the monarchy, the clergy of France appear to have been as much devoted to the pope as those of any other country. When Robert, the second prince of the Capetian race, was most unjustly excommunicated by the court of Rome, his own servants, it is said, threw the victuals which came from his table to the dogs, and refused to taste any thing themselves which had been polluted by the contact of a person in his situation. They were taught to do so, it may very safely be presumed, by the clergy of his own dominions.

The claim of collating to the great benefices of the church, a claim in defence of which the court of Rome had frequently shaken, and sometimes overturned the thrones of some of the greatest sovereigns in Christendom, was in this manner either restrained or modified, or given up altogether, in many different parts of Europe, even before the time of the reformation. As the clergy had now less influence over the people, so the state had more influence over the clergy. The clergy therefore had both less power and less inclination to disturb the state.

The authority of the church of Rome was in this state of declension, when the disputes which gave birth to the reformation, began in Germany, and soon spread themselves through every part of Europe. The new doctrines were every where received with a high degree of popular favour. They were propagated with all that enthusiastic zeal which commonly animates the spirit of party, when it attacks established authority. The teachers of those doctrines, though perhaps in other respects not more learned than many of the divines who defended the established church, seem in general to have been better acquainted with ecclesiastical history, and with the origin and progress of that system of opinions upon which the authority of the church was established, and they had thereby some advantage in almost every dispute. The austerity of their manners gave them authority with the common people, who contrasted the strict regularity of their conduct with the disorderly lives of the greater part of their own clergy. They possessed too in a much higher degree than their adversaries, all the arts of popularity and of gaining proselytes, arts which the lofty and dignified sons of the church had long neglected, as being to them in a great measure useless. The reason of the new doctrines recommended them to some, their novelty to many; the hatred and contempt of the established clergy to a still greater number; but the zealous, passionate, and fanatical, though frequently coarse and rustic, eloquence with which they were almost every where inculcated, recommended them to by far the greatest number.

The success of the new doctrines was almost every where so great, that the princes who at that time happened to be on bad terms with the court of Rome, were by means of them easily enabled, in their own dominions, to overturn the church, which, having lost the respect and veneration of the inferior ranks of people, could make scarce any resistance. The court of Rome had disobliged some of the smaller princes in the northern parts of Germany, whom it had probably considered as too insignificant to be worth the managing. They universally, therefore, established the reformation in their own dominions. The tyranny of Christiern II. and of Troll, archbishop of Upsal, enabled Gustavus Vasa to expel them both from Sweden. The pope favoured the tyrant and the archbishop, and Gustavus Vasa found no difficulty in establishing the reformation in Sweden. Christiern II. was afterwards deposed from the throne of Denmark, where his conduct had rendered him as odious as in Sweden. The pope, however, was still disposed to favour him, and Frederic of Holstein, who had mounted the throne in his stead, revenged himself by following the example of Gustavus Vasa. The magistrates of Berne and Zurich, who had no particular quarrel with the pope, established with great ease the reformation in their respective cantons, where just before some of the clergy had, by an imposture somewhat grosser than ordinary, rendered the whole order both odious and contemptible.

In this critical situation of its affairs, the papal court was at sufficient pains to cultivate the friendship of the powerful sovereigns of France and Spain, of whom the latter was at that time emperor of Germany. With their assistance it was enabled, though not without great difficulty and much bloodshed, either to suppress altogether, or to obstruct very much the progress of the reformation in their dominions. It was well enough inclined too to be complaisant to the king of England. But from the circumstances of the times, it could not be so without giving offence to a still greater sovereign, Charles V. king of Spain and emperor of Germany. Henry VIII. accordingly, though he did not embrace himself the greater part of the doctrines of the reformation, was yet enabled, by their general prevalence, to suppress all the monasteries, and to abolish the authority of the church of Rome in his dominions. That he should go so far, though he went no further, gave some satisfaction to the patrons of the reformation, who having got possession of the government in the reign of his son and successor, completed without any difficulty the work which Henry VIII. had begun.

In some countries, as in Scotland, where the government was weak, unpopular, and not very firmly established, the reformation was strong enough to overturn, not only the church, but the state likewise for attempting to support the church.

Among the followers of the reformation, dispersed in all the different countries of Europe, there was no general tribunal, which, like that of the court of Rome, or an oecumenical council, could settle all disputes among them, and with irresistible authority prescribe to all of them the precise limits of orthodoxy. When the followers of the reformation in one country, therefore, happened to differ from their brethren in another, as they had no common judge to appeal to, the dispute could never be decided; and many such disputes arose among them. Those concerning the government of the church, and the right of conferring ecclesiastical benefices, were perhaps the most interesting to the peace and welfare of civil society. They gave birth accordingly to the two principal parties or sects among the followers of the reformation, the Lutheran and Calvinistic sects, the only sects among them, of which the doctrine and discipline have ever yet been established by law in any part of Europe.

The followers of Luther, together with what is called the church of England, preserved more or less of the episcopal government, established subordination among the clergy, gave the sovereign the disposal of all the bishoprics, and other consistorial benefices within his dominions, and thereby rendered him the real head of the church; and without depriving the bishop of the right of collating to the smaller benefices within his diocese, they, even to those benefices, not only admitted, but favoured the right of presentation both in the sovereign and in all other lay patrons. This system of church government was from the beginning favourable to peace and good order, and to submission to the civil sovereign. It has never, accordingly, been the occasion of any tumult or civil commotion in any country in which it has once been established. The church of England in particular has always valued herself, with great reason, upon the unexceptionable loyalty of her principles. Under such a government the clergy naturally endeavour to recommend themselves to the sovereign, to the court, and to the nobility and gentry of the country, by whose influence they chiefly expect to obtain preferment. They pay court to those patrons, sometimes, no doubt, by the vilest flattery and assentation, but frequently too by cultivating all those arts which best deserve, and which are therefore most likely to gain them the esteem of people of rank and fortune; by their knowledge in all the different branches of useful and ornamental learning, by the decent liberality of their manners, by the social good humour of their conversation, and by their avowed contempt of those absurd and hypocritical austerities which fanatics inculcate and pretend to practise, in order to draw upon themselves the veneration, and upon the greater part of men of rank and fortune, who avow that they do not practise them, the abhorrence of the common people. Such a clergy, however, while they pay their court in this manner to the higher ranks of life, are very apt to neglect altogether the means of maintaining their influence and authority with the lower. They are listened to, esteemed and respected by their superiors; but before their inferiors they are frequently incapable of defending, effectually and to the conviction of such hearers, their own sober and moderate doctrines against the most ignorant enthusiast who chuses to attack them.

The followers of Zuinglius, or more properly those of Calvin, on the contrary, bestowed upon the people of each parish, whenever the church became vacant, the right of electing their own pastor; and established at the same time the most perfect equality among the clergy. The former part of this institution, as long as it remained in vigour, seems to have been productive of nothing but disorder and confusion, and to have tended equally to corrupt the morals both of the clergy and of the people. The latter part seems never to have had any effects but what were perfectly agreeable.

As long as the people of each parish preserved the right of electing their own pastors, they acted almost always under the influence of the clergy, and generally of the most factious and fanatical of the order. The clergy, in order to preserve their influence in those popular elections, became, or affected to become, many of them, fanatics themselves, encouraged fanaticism among the people, and gave the preference almost always to the most fanatical candidate. So small a matter as the appointment of a parish priest occasioned almost always a violent contest, not only in one parish, but in all the neighbouring parishes, who seldom failed to take part in the quarrel. When the parish happened to be situated in a great city, it divided all the inhabitants into two parties; and when that city happened either to constitute itself a little republic, or to be the head and capital of a little republic, as is the case with many of the considerable cities in Switzerland and Holland, every paltry dispute of this kind, over and above exasperating the animosity of all their other factions, threatened to leave behind it both a new schism in the church, and a new faction in the state. In those small republics, therefore, the magistrate very soon found it necessary, for the sake of preserving the public peace, to assume to himself the right of presenting to all vacant benefices. In Scotland, the most extensive country in which this presbyterian form of church government has ever been established, the rights of patronage were in effect abolished by the act which established presbytery in the beginning of the reign of William III. That act at least put it in the power of certain classes of people in each parish, to purchase, for a very small price, the right of electing their own pastor. The constitution which this act established was allowed to subsist for about two and twenty years, but was abolished by the 10th of queen Anne, ch. 12. on account of the confusions and disorders which this more popular mode of election had almost every where occasioned. In so extensive a country as Scotland, however, a tumult in a remote parish was not so likely to give disturbance to government, as in a smaller state. The 10th of queen Anne restored the rights of patronage. But though in Scotland the law gives the benefice without any exception to the person presented by the patron; yet the church requires sometimes (for she has not in this respect been very uniform in her decisions) a certain concurrence of the people, before she will confer upon the presentee what is called the cure of souls, or the ecclesiastical jurisdiction in the parish. She sometimes at least, from an affected concern for the peace of the parish, delays the settlement till this concurrence can be procured. The private tampering of some of the neighbouring clergy, sometimes to procure, but more frequently to prevent this concurrence, and the popular arts which they cultivate in order to enable them upon such occasions to tamper more effectually, are perhaps the causes which principally keep up whatever remains of the old fanatical spirit, either in the clergy or in the people of Scotland.

The equality which the presbyterian form of church government establishes among the clergy, consists, first, in the equality of authority or ecclesiastical jurisdiction; and, secondly, in the equality of benefice. In all presbyterian churches the equality of authority is perfect: that of benefice is not so. The difference, however, between one benefice and another, is seldom so considerable as commonly to tempt the possessor even of the small one to pay court to his patron, by the vile arts of flattery and assentation, in order to get a better. In all the presbyterian churches, where the rights of patronage are thoroughly established, it is by nobler and better arts that the established clergy in general endeavour to gain the favour of their superiors; by their learning, by the irreproachable regularity of their life, and by the faithful and diligent discharge of their duty. Their patrons even frequently complain of the independency of their spirit, which they are apt to construe into ingratitude for past favours, but which at worst, perhaps, is seldom any more than that indifference which naturally arises from the consciousness that no further favours of the kind are ever to be expected. There is scarce perhaps to be found any where in Europe a more learned, decent, independent, and respectable set of men, than the greater part of the presbyterian clergy of Holland, Geneva, Switzerland, and Scotland.

Where the church benefices are all nearly equal, none of them can be very great, and this mediocrity of benefice, though it may no doubt be carried too far, has, however, some very agreeable effects. Nothing but the most exemplary morals can give dignity to a man of small fortune. The vices of levity and vanity necessarily render him ridiculous, and are, besides, almost as ruinous to him as they are to the common people. In his own conduct, therefore, he is obliged to follow that system of morals which the common people respect the most. He gains their esteem and affection by that plan of life which his own interest and situation would lead him to follow. The common people look upon him with that kindness with which we naturally regard one who approaches somewhat to our own condition, but who, we think, ought to be in a higher. Their kindness naturally provokes his kindness. He becomes careful to instruct them, and attentive to assist and relieve them. He does not even despise the prejudices of people who are disposed to be so favourable to him, and never treats them with those contemptuous and arrogant airs which we so often meet with in the proud dignitaries of opulent and well-endowed churches. The presbyterian clergy, accordingly, have more influence over the minds of the common people than perhaps the clergy of any other established church. It is accordingly in presbyterian countries only that we ever find the common people converted, without persecution, completely, and almost to a man, to the established church.

In countries where church benefices are the greater part of them very moderate, a chair in a university is generally a better establishment than a church benefice. The universities have, in this case, the picking and chusing of their members from all the churchmen of the country, who, in every country, constitute by far the most numerous class of men of letters. Where church benefices, on the contrary, are many of them very considerable, the church naturally draws from the universities the greater part of their eminent men of letters; who generally find some patron who does himself honour by procuring them church preferment. In the former situation we are likely to find the universities filled with the most eminent men of letters that are to be found in the country. In the latter we are likely to find few eminent men among them, and those few among the youngest members of the society, who are likely too to be drained away from it, before they can have acquired experience and knowledge enough to be of much use to it. It is observed by Mr. de Voltaire, that father Porrée, a jesuit of no great eminence in the republic of letters, was the only professor they had ever had in France whose works were worth the reading. In a country which has produced so many eminent men of letters, it must appear somewhat singular, that scarce one of them should have been a professor in a university. The famous Gassendi was, in the beginning of his life, a professor in the university of Aix. Upon the first dawning of his genius, it was represented to him, that by going into the church he could easily find a much more quiet and comfortable subsistence, as well as a better situation for pursuing his studies; and he immediately followed the advice. The observation of Mr. de Voltaire may be applied, I believe, not only to France, but to all other Roman catholic countries. We very rarely find, in any of them, an eminent man of letters who is a professor in a university, except, perhaps, in the professions of law and physic; professions from which the church is not so likely to draw them. After the church of Rome, that of England is by far the richest and best endowed church in Christendom. In England, accordingly, the church is continually draining the universities of all their best and ablest members; and an old college tutor who is known and distinguished in Europe as an eminent man of letters, is as rarely to be found there as in any Roman catholic country. In Geneva, on the contrary, in the protestant cantons of Switzerland, in the protestant countries of Germany, in Holland, in Scotland, in Sweden, and Denmark, the most eminent men of letters whom those countries have produced, have, not all indeed, but the far greater part of them, been professors in universities. In those countries the universities are continually draining the church of all its most eminent men of letters.

It may, perhaps, be worth while to remark, that, if we except the poets, a few orators, and a few historians, the far greater part of the other eminent men of letters, both of Greece and Rome, appear to have been either public or private teachers; generally either of philosophy or of rhetoric. This remark will be found to hold true from the days of Lysias and Isocrates, of Plato and Aristotle, down to those of Plutarch and Epictetus, of Suetonius and Quintilian. To impose upon any man the necessity of teaching, year after year, any particular branch of science, seems, in reality, to be the most effectual method of rendering him completely master of it himself. By being obliged to go every year over the same ground, if he is good for any thing, he necessarily becomes, in a few years, well acquainted with every part of it: and if upon any particular point he should form too hasty an opinion one year, when he comes in the course of his lectures to re-consider the same subject the year thereafter, he is very likely to correct it. As to be a teacher of science is certainly the natural employment of a mere man of letters; so is it likewise, perhaps, the education which is most likely to render him a man of solid learning and knowledge. The mediocrity of church benefices naturally tends to draw the greater part of men of letters, in the country where it takes place, to the employment in which they can be the most useful to the public, and, at the same time, to give them the best education, perhaps, they are capable of receiving. It tends to render their learning both as solid as possible, and as useful as possible.

The revenue of every established church, such parts of it excepted as may arise from particular lands or manors, is a branch, it ought to be observed, of the general revenue of the state, which is thus diverted to a purpose very different from the defence of the state. The tythe, for example, is a real land-tax, which puts it out of the power of the proprietors of land to contribute so largely towards the defence of the state as they otherwise might be able to do. The rent of land, however, is, according to some, the sole fund, and according to others, the principal fund, from which, in all great monarchies, the exigencies of the state must be ultimately supplied. The more of this fund that is given to the church, the less, it is evident, can be spared to the state. It may be laid down as a certain maxim, that, all other things being supposed equal, the richer the church, the poorer must necessarily be, either the sovereign on the one hand, or the people on the other; and, in all cases, the less able must the state be to defend itself. In several protestant countries, particularly in all the protestant cantons of Switzerland, the revenue which anciently belonged to the Roman catholic church, the tythes and church lands, has been found a fund sufficient, not only to afford competent salaries to the established clergy, but to defray, with little or no addition, all the other expences of the state. The magistrates of the powerful canton of Berne, in particular, have accumulated out of the savings from this fund a very large sum, supposed to amount to several millions, part of which is deposited in a public treasure, and part is placed at interest in what are called the public funds of the different indebted nations of Europe; chiefly in those of France and Great Britain. What may be the amount of the whole expence which the church, either of Berne, or of any other protestant canton, costs the state, I do not pretend to know. By a very exact account it appears, that, in 1755, the whole revenue of the clergy of the church of Scotland, including their glebe or church lands, and the rent of their manses or dwelling-houses, estimated according to a reasonable valuation, amounted only to 68,514*l*. 1*s*. 5*d*. 1/12. This very moderate revenue affords a decent subsistence to nine hundred and forty-four ministers. The whole expence of the church, including what is occasionally laid out for the building and reparation of churches, and of the manses of ministers, cannot well be supposed to exceed eighty or eighty-five thousand pounds a-year. The most opulent church in Christendom does not maintain better the uniformity of faith, the fervour of devotion, the spirit of order, regularity, and austere morals in the great body of the people, than this very poorly endowed church of Scotland. All the good effects, both civil and religious, which an established church can be supposed to produce, are produced by it as completely as by any other. The greater part of the protestant churches of Switzerland, which in general are not better endowed than the church of Scotland, produce those effects in a still higher degree. In the greater part of the protestant cantons, there is not a single person to be found who does not profess himself to be of the established church. If he professes himself to be of any other, indeed, the law obliges him to leave the canton. But so severe, or rather indeed so oppressive a law, could never have been executed in such free countries, had not the diligence of the clergy before-hand converted to the established church the whole body of the people, with the exception of, perhaps, a few individuals only. In some parts of Switzerland, accordingly, where, from the accidental union of a protestant and Roman catholic country, the conversion has not been so complete, both religions are not only tolerated but established by law.

The proper performance of every service seems to require that its pay or recompence should be, as exactly as possible, proportioned to the nature of the service. If any service is very much under-paid, it is very apt to suffer by the meanness and incapacity of the greater part of those who are employed in it. If it is very much over-paid, it is apt to suffer, perhaps, still more by their negligence and idleness. A man of a large revenue, whatever may be his profession, thinks he ought to live like other men of large revenues; and to spend a great part of his time in festivity, in vanity, and in dissipation. But in a clergyman this train of life not only consumes the time which ought to be employed in the duties of his function, but in the eyes of the common people destroys almost entirely that sanctity of character which can alone enable him to perform those duties with proper weight and authority.

CHAPTER III

OF PUBLIC DEBTS

[The *WN* ends on an abrupt note. There is, as it were, no grand summing up of the book's main themes. The opening pages here offer a decent summary of some of what has come before.]

In that rude state of society which precedes the extension of commerce and the improvement of manufactures, when those expensive luxuries which commerce and manufactures can alone introduce, are altogether unknown, the person who possesses a large revenue, I have endeavoured to show in the third book of this Inquiry, can spend or enjoy that revenue in no other way than by maintaining nearly as many people as it can maintain. A large revenue may at all times be said to consist in the command of a large quantity of the necessaries of life. In that rude state of things it is commonly paid in a large quantity of those necessaries, in the materials of plain food and coarse clothing, in corn and cattle, in wool and raw hides. When neither commerce nor manufactures furnish any thing for which the owner can exchange the greater part of those materials which are over and above his own consumption, he can do nothing with the surplus but feed and clothe nearly as many people as it will feed and clothe. A hospitality in which there is no luxury, and a liberality in which there is no ostentation, occasion, in this situation of things, the principal expences of the rich and the great. But these, I have likewise endeavoured to show in the same book, are expences by which people are not very apt to ruin themselves. There is not, perhaps, any selfish pleasure so frivolous, of which the pursuit has not sometimes ruined even sensible men. A passion for cock-fighting has ruined many. But the instances, I believe, are not very numerous of people who have been ruined by a hospitality or liberality of this kind; though the hospitality of luxury and the liberality of ostentation have ruined many. Among our feudal ancestors, the long time during which estates used to continue in the same family, sufficiently demonstrates the general disposition of people to live within their income. Though the rustic hospitality, constantly exercised by the great land-holders, may not, to us in the present times, seem consistent with that order, which we are apt to consider as inseparably connected with good oeconomy, yet we must certainly allow them to have been at least so far frugal as not commonly to have spent their whole income. A part of their wool and raw hides they had generally an opportunity of selling for money. Some part of this money, perhaps, they spent in purchasing the few objects of vanity and luxury, with which the circumstances of the times could furnish them; but some part of it they seem commonly to have hoarded. They could not well indeed do anything else but hoard whatever money they saved. To trade was disgraceful to a gentleman, and to lend money at interest, which at that time was considered as usury and prohibited by law, would have been still more so. In those times of violence and disorder, besides, it was convenient to have a hoard of money at hand, that in case they should be driven from their own home, they might have something of known value to carry with them to some place of safety. The same violence, which made it convenient to hoard, made it equally convenient to conceal the hoard. The frequency of treasure-trove, or of treasure found of which no owner was known, sufficiently demonstrates the frequency in those times both of hoarding and of concealing the hoard. Treasure-trove was then considered as an important branch of the revenue of the sovereign. All the treasure-trove of the kingdom would scarce perhaps in the present times make an important branch of the revenue of a private gentleman of a good estate.

The same disposition to save and to hoard prevailed in the sovereign, as well as in the subjects. Among nations to whom commerce and manufactures are little known, the sovereign, it has already been observed in the fourth book, is in a situation which naturally disposes him to the parsimony requisite for accumulation. In that situation the expence even of a sovereign cannot be directed by that vanity which delights in the gaudy finery of a court. The ignorance of the times affords but few of the trinkets in which that finery consists. Standing armies are not then necessary, so that the expence even of a sovereign, like that of any other great lord, can be employed in scarce any thing but bounty to his tenants, and hospitality to his retainers. But bounty and hospitality very seldom lead to extravagance; though vanity almost always does. All the ancient sovereigns of Europe accordingly, it has already been observed, had treasures. Every Tartar chief in the present times is said to have one.

In a commercial country abounding with every sort of expensive luxury, the sovereign, in the same manner as almost all the great proprietors in his dominions, naturally spends a great part of his revenue in purchasing those luxuries. His own and the neighbouring countries supply him abundantly with all the costly trinkets which compose the splendid, but insignificant pageantry of a court. For the sake of an inferior pageantry of the same kind, his nobles dismiss their retainers, make their tenants independent, and become gradually themselves as insignificant as the greater part of the wealthy burghers in his dominions. The same frivolous passions, which influence their conduct, influence his. How can it be supposed that he should be the only rich man in his dominions who is insensible to pleasures of this kind? If he does not, what he is very likely to do, spend upon those pleasures so great a part of his revenue as to debilitate very much the defensive power of the state, it cannot well be expected that he should not spend upon them all that part of it which is over and above what is necessary for supporting that defensive power. His ordinary expence becomes equal to his ordinary revenue, and it is well if it does not frequently exceed it. The amassing of treasure can no longer be expected, and when extraordinary exigencies require extraordinary expences, he must necessarily call upon his subjects for an extraordinary aid. The present and the late king of Prussia are the only great princes of Europe, who, since the death of Henry IV. of France in 1610, are supposed to have amassed any considerable treasure. The parsimony which leads to accumulation has become almost as rare in republican as in monarchical governments. The Italian republics, the United Provinces of the Netherlands, are all in debt. The canton of Berne is the single republic in Europe which has amassed any considerable treasure. The other Swiss republics have not. The taste for some sort of pageantry, for splendid buildings, at least, and other public ornaments, frequently prevails as much in the apparently sober senate-house of a little republic, as in the dissipated court of the greatest king.

The want of parsimony in time of peace, imposes the necessity of contracting debt in time of war. When war comes, there is no money in the treasury but what is necessary for carrying on the ordinary expence of the peace establishment. In war an establishment of three or four times that expence becomes necessary for the defence of the state, and consequently a revenue three or four times greater than the peace revenue. Supposing that the sovereign should have, what he scarce ever has, the immediate means of augmenting his revenue in proportion to the augmentation of his expence, yet still the produce of the taxes, from which this increase of revenue must be drawn, will not begin to come into the treasury till perhaps ten or twelve months after they are imposed. But the moment in which war begins, or rather the moment in which it appears likely to begin, the army must be augmented, the fleet must be fitted out, the garrisoned towns must be put into a posture of defence; that army, that fleet, those garrisoned towns must be furnished with arms, ammunition, and provisions. An immediate and great expence must be incurred in that moment of immediate danger, which will not wait for the gradual and slow returns of the new taxes. In this exigency government can have no other resource but in borrowing.

The same commercial state of society which, by the operation of moral causes, brings government in this manner into the necessity of borrowing, produces in the subjects both an ability and an inclination to lend. If it commonly brings along with it the necessity of borrowing, it likewise brings along with it the facility of doing so.

A country abounding with merchants and manufacturers, necessarily abounds with a set of people through whose hands not only their own capitals, but the capitals of all those who either lend them money, or trust them with goods, pass as frequently, or more frequently, than the revenue of a private man, who, without trade or business, lives upon his income, passes through his hands. The revenue of such a man can regularly pass through his hands only once in a year. But the whole amount of the capital and credit of a merchant, who deals in a trade of which the returns are very quick, may sometimes pass through his hands two, three, or four times in a year. A country abounding with merchants and manufacturers, therefore, necessarily abounds with a set of people who have it at all times in their power to advance, if they chuse to do so, a very large sum of money to government. Hence the ability in the subjects of a commercial state to lend.

Commerce and manufactures can seldom flourish long in any state which does not enjoy a regular administration of justice, in which the people do not feel themselves secure in the possession of their property, in which the faith of contracts is not supported by law, and in which the authority of the state is not supposed to be regularly employed in enforcing the payment of debts from all those who are able to pay. Commerce and manufactures, in short, can seldom flourish in any state in which there is not a certain degree of confidence in the justice of government. The same confidence which disposes great merchants and manufacturers, upon ordinary occasions, to trust their property to the protection of a particular government; disposes them, upon extraordinary occasions, to trust that government with the use of their property. By lending money to government, they do not even for a moment diminish their ability to carry on their trade and manufactures. On the contrary, they commonly augment it. The necessities of the state render government upon most occasions willing to borrow upon terms extremely advantageous to the lender. The security which it grants to the original creditor, is made transferable to any other creditor, and, from the universal confidence in the justice of the state, generally sells in the market for more than was originally paid for it. The merchant or monied man makes money by lending money to government, and instead of diminishing, increases his trading capital. He generally considers it as a favour, therefore, when the administration admits him to a share in the first subscription for a new loan. Hence the inclination or willingness in the subjects of a commercial state to lend.

The government of such a state is very apt to repose itself upon this ability and willingness of its subjects to lend it their money on extraordinary occasions. It foresees the facility of borrowing, and therefore dispenses itself from the duty of saving.

In a rude state of society there are no great mercantile or manufacturing capitals. The individuals, who hoard whatever money they can save, and who conceal their hoard, do so from a distrust of the justice of government, from a fear that if it was known that they had a hoard, and where that hoard was to be found, they would quickly be plundered. In such a state of things few people would be able, and no body would be willing, to lend their money to government on extraordinary exigencies. The sovereign feels that he must provide for such exigencies by saving, because he foresees the absolute impossibility of borrowing. This foresight increases still further his natural disposition to save.

The progress of the enormous debts which at present oppress, and will in the long-run probably ruin, all the great nations of Europe, has been pretty uniform. Nations, like private men, have generally begun to borrow upon what may be called personal credit, without assigning or mortgaging any particular fund for the payment of the debt; and when this resource has failed them, they have gone on to borrow upon assignments or mortgages of particular funds. . . .

APPENDICES

APPENDIX I. ON BOOK II:

Economics and Ethics in Smith's Theory of Capital Accumulation.

Long ago two informed and resourceful students of the history of economic thinking—E. Cannan and J. Schumpeter—drew attention to a peculiarity in the structure of the argument of the *WN*. What Cannan noticed was how Book II of the *WN*—the book in which Smith developed his famous theory of capital accumulation—could have been, in his words, "omitted" from the larger project without any serious loss to the arguments Smith advanced in Book I and III–V (1976, p. xxxv). For his part, Schumpeter regarded Book II as "a new wing added to an old structure" (1954, p. 191). By that he meant that, while much of the material in Books I and III–V date from the 1750s and early 1760s, much of the argument of Book II seems to have taken form in Smith's mind from the mid-1760s on. According to Schumpeter, insertion of this material into the *WN* played havoc with the structure of Smith's book, forcing him to resort to narrative techniques to smooth over some newly emergent rough spots in the argument. To that end, Smith tried to make it appear as if Book II followed logically from what was said in Book I, when that was in fact not the case at all. So, instead of presenting the transition from Book I to II in terms of a discontinuity in the mode of narrative continuity, Smith used narrative continuity to conceal a discontinuity in the structure and argument of the book.

The notion that Smith's theory of capital arose at a relatively "late stage" in his thinking (Schumpeter 1954, p. 193) has prompted Smith scholars to seek out the inspiration for this highly important development in his thought. In this connection, Schumpeter offered some intriguing comments on what he called the "Turgot-Smith theory of saving and investment" (1954, p. 324). Noting similarities between the theories of capital that Turgot and Smith developed in the 1760s and recalling that Smith had met Turgot (and Quesnay) in France during his travels there between early 1764 and late 1766, Schumpeter explored this connection without necessarily wishing to attribute "influence" to Turgot on Smith (Schumpeter 1954, pp. 191–93, 323f.). So, somewhat awkwardly, Schumpeter spoke of a "parallelism" between the two thinkers (1954, p. 192), and explained it as a consequence of each thinker's independent critique of Quesnay's views on capital. More recently, T. Hutchison, resurrecting key parts of Schumpeter's older argument about the Turgot-Smith link, has suggested that the argument of Book II—"of saving, investment, and capital, which was to become the central pillar of classical macro-economics"—was almost "entirely absent" from Smith's work before the mid-1760s (1988, pp. 353, 366ff.).

The great merit of Hutchison's work, however, lies less in its explanation of the Turgot-Smith parallel than in the claim that inserting Book II into the *WN* complicated and confused Smith's argument about economic growth. Since a major issue of how to read the *WN* arises here—as a result of our being sensitive to how the *WN* developed as a book over time—it is worth examining the matter in more detail.

By and large, Smith scholars have long agreed that the theoretical core of the *WN* is articulated in Books I and II (Letwin 1990, p. 29; Tribe 1977, pp. 319, 325, 335, 341n7; Coats 1962, p. 39). Those, of course, are the books twentieth-century economists single out as vital to the discipline of "scientific economics." And, as M. Blaug has rather jokingly reminded us, these two books are generally the only parts of the *WN* economists ever read (1968, p. 38).

Of the so-called "normative" principles Smith is supposed to have developed in these books, two are instrumental for economics in general and for strategies of economic growth in particular: namely, the division of labor, the central theme of Book I; and the theory of capital, the organizing principle for the discussion of Book II. Hutchison elucidates these two principles, which he prefers to identify as historico-economic "processes" rather than as normative economic principles, while discussing Smith's views on the "economic progress of society" (1988, p. 359). Summarizing Smith's position, Hutchison begins by pointing out that in Book I the division of labor sets industry in motion and, in the process, creates networks of socio-economic cooperation which, over time, form themselves into markets around which commercial societies gradually form. By the same token, and as Smith demonstrates in Book II, capital accumulation facilitates advances in the subdivision of labor as well as in the division of labor itself. Thus, as most conventional readings of Books I and II would have it, the division of labor and capital are seen as working together to improve "the productive power of labor" and increase the wealth of society, hence the importance of these two books for modern economic thinking.

While outlining Smith's views on economic growth, Hutchison offers some penetrating observations as to what he thinks Smith was really doing in Books I and II. He starts by carefully noting how, as the argument of Book II unfolds, another "force" for growth comes into play. That force, he quite rightly notes, is "frugality" (Hutchison 1988, p. 360). In Book II, therefore, a rather obvious connection emerges in Smith's thinking between frugality and capital accumulation, and, if we add to this the connection already posited between capital accumulation and advances in the division of labor, we see that the argument Smith develops in Books I and II hinges on an interplay between these three forces, not just the first two of them. In Hutchison's judgment, moreover, these forces constitute the core of what Smith referred to as his "system of natural liberty" (1988, pp. 358ff.).

The attention Hutchison gives to the emergence of frugality in Book II raises a pivotal point as to how to interpret the *WN*, for the meaning of Smith's argument changes significantly depending on how we view the relationship outlined in Books I and II between the division of labor, capital accumulation, and frugality. If, for example, we approach Books I and II with the idea—inculcated in generations of readers of the *WN* by economists—that Smith is developing the "normative" core of modern economics in these books, then Smith's "system" and its three main theoretical props will have tremendous coherence as a prescription for how to foster and sustain economic growth.

The inclination to read the *WN* this way is all the more compelling because the "Plan" Smith himself devised to guide readers through the *WN* presents the topics taken up in Books I and II in extremely matter-of-fact terms—as if the *sequence* of themes—the division of labor followed by discussions first of capital and then of frugality—was irrelevant to the *analytical structure* of the *WN*. Or, to put it another way, the "Plan" Smith attached to the front of the *WN* disposes us to interpret the trinity of themes as forming together one indivisible analytical whole—the theoretical core, as it were, of modern economics. Needless to say, if that is how one conceptualizes the argument of Books I and II, Smith's rather late insertion of the material of Book II into the larger project of the *WN* presents no interpretive problem at all.

Following Schumpeter and Hutchison, my own view is that we miss a lot of what Smith is doing in the *WN* by reading the book this way—as if the argument of the *WN* simply unfolded in accordance with the outline set down in the "Plan." More than any other scholar, Schumpeter glimpsed what was at issue here when he characterized Smith's attempt to link Books I and II as "weak" and "unconvincing" (1954, p. 191). Pushing Schumpeter's insight further, it would not be too much to say that the reason the transition between Books I to II fails to satisfy has less to do with the faulty narrative bridge Smith built to connect the two books than with the fundamental restructuring of the argument of the *WN* that Smith undertakes there. Indeed, the restructuring occurred precisely because, in the process of inserting the theory of capital accumulation into the *WN*, Smith began to privilege capital accumulation rather than the division of labor as the primary cause of economic growth.

The restructuring that Smith undertakes here begins in the "Introduction" to Book II and culminates in Chapters 2, 3, and 5 of that book. There, Smith succeeds in what I shall call "capitalizing the division of labor"—that is, he spells out in detail there why it is "in the nature of things" for capital accumulation to be "previous to the division of labor." As a consequence of this change in priorities, Smith subtly shifts the textual context for his discussion of economic growth from one in which the division of labor as a complex and impersonal socio-historical process is dominant to one in which capital accumulation fulfills that role.

In the *WN*, then, the transition from Book I to Book II involves a major shift in the principles governing Smith's argument. This is all the more important because of the great investment Smith had already made in Book I in identifying the division of labor as the motor of economic development (Schumpeter 1954, p. 187). But since the argument of Book II begins with a discussion of the division of labor, it is easy for readers to miss the change in priority between the two.

Now, this change would not be all that significant were Smith simply to have said—as Bentham would say in 1787 in the *Defence of Usury*—that the availability of capital (as well as the extent of the market) sets certain limits to the quantity of productive labor that a society can set in motion at any given time (Bentham 1952, p. 201; cf. 212, 233). Nor would the change be of such importance if all Smith did was to posit a relation between the savings generated by the division of labor and enhanced opportunities for capital investment by those entrepreneurs who had engaged in primitive accumulation. But the argument of Book II goes much further than that, for as it unfolds Smith adds three additional dimensions to the capital-accumulation argument.

First, in Book II Smith talks about capital accumulation in personal rather than impersonal socio-historical terms—which is to say, in Book II he begins to sketch for us the profile of *the* "person" who, in his capacity as an "undertaker" (i.e., entrepreneur), creates capital by saving money and then investing that money in productive labor. Thus, one of the consequences of the restructuring of the argument of the *WN* that begins in Book II is that the principal agent of economic development assumes a human form (even if only as an ideal type).

Secondly, and this is especially true of Book II, Chapter 3, Smith provocatively singles out "the principle of frugality" as the most important factor in economic growth. Accordingly, in Chapter 3 the "person" who saves money for the purpose of investing in productive labor becomes the "frugal man." That man is now designated as the main agent of economic progress. Thus, whereas in Book I the division of labor drives society toward opulence independent of what Smith calls "human wisdom," in Book II the "character" and "conduct" (not to mention the long-term planning) of the frugal man become instrumental to the process and progress of economic development.

Thirdly and finally, the language Smith uses in Book II, especially in Chapters 2 and 3, to explain capital formation is simultaneously normative and moralistic. That becomes evident once we realize that, throughout Book II, Smith systematically limits how capital can be employed—or how money can be spent for it to qualify, by definition, as a capital investment. In this respect, the point of Smith's notorious distinction between productive and unproductive labor is to emphasize the view that fostering and sustaining economic growth hinges on frugal men making prudent investments of their savings in productive labor. So, at the end of Chapter 3, after having belittled "selfish" and "prodigal" people for spending their money imprudently on themselves rather than electing to invest it in productive labor, Smith has no qualms either about linking economic growth to "private frugality" or about drawing connections between "public capital" and the quantity of productive labor produced by investing capital properly. Smith even uses the religious word "destination" to explain why money was meant to be used as capital for employing productive labor. It is not, therefore, the selfish acts of individuals that create public benefits. Rather, it is the frugality of private individuals that creates a fund of public capital that ultimately employs productive labor to society's benefit. Hence the meaning of Smith's seldom commented upon statement that

> . . . every prodigal appears to be a public enemy, and every frugal man a public benefactor.

The upshot of all this restructuring, then, is that by the time we reach the end of Book II, the figure of the frugal man bulks very large in Smith's view of economic growth. Indeed, from all Smith says in Book II about frugality, saving, capital, and investment in productive labor, it would seem to follow that in order to foster and sustain economic growth a society must create frugal citizens whose destiny in life is to maintain as much productive labor as possible. More specifically, and here is where the Turgot-Smith parallel becomes so obvious, this means that frugal men, besides saving money, automatically—Smith's preferred word is "naturally", Turgot's "immediately" (Turgot 1973, p. 182)—invest it in productive labor. Thus, Smith uses highly moralistic language to censure the conduct of prodigals, spendthrifts, and projectors, while using the same language to endorse the "good conduct" of those who accept the high social responsibility of prudent and proper money management. That Smith does this under the guise of talking about "natural" behavior hardly conceals the fact that what he is doing throughout Book II is moralizing about how people should spend their money.

Economists as well as many students of the history of economic thinking refer to Smith's theory of capital as the "saving is investment" thesis (Hutchison 1988, p. 366; Blaug 1968, p. 58; Coats 1962, p. 28). In that form, it has often been argued that market forces themselves (e.g., competition, technological innovation, the sheer industriousness of people) ensure that savings will be created and automatically invested in productive labor (Rosenberg 1990, pp. 1–17). On these terms, of course, the "saving is investment" thesis is taken to be part of the business process itself. As such, it can be said to operate more or less independently of other social, political, and cultural considerations. In keeping with this, it is customary to invoke the idea of the "invisible hand" of market competition to explain Smith's theory of how capital resources are allocated in society.

But is this what Smith says in Book II? Does his use of moral language not make character and choice key factors in the employment of capital? Is the economists' version of the "saving is investment" thesis not overly optimistic about the investment imperative among businesspersons? Moreover, does Smith's recourse to moral language not suggest that, in the long run, capital can serve the public only if the habit of frugality becomes a socio-cultural measure of good conduct, one that can be "depleted" only at great risk to society? And does all this not mean—as M. Blaug has noted (1968, p. 58)—that something like a "Protestant ethic" (or a Stoic ethic) is hidden in Smith's so-called "system of natural liberty"? For is that ethic, especially in its frugal mode, not instrumental to the process that makes saving and investment, rather than pleasure and enjoyment, the "natural" driving force of economic development?

These are not anachronistic questions. Some eighteenth-century readers of the *WN* criticized Smith for having articulated a "backward"-looking view of how capital formation and expenditure worked (e.g., Bentham 1952, pp. 167ff.). Bentham especially was outraged by Smith's moral strictures on the speculative endeavors of "projectors"—along with merchants, a much-maligned group in the *WN*. James Lauderdale, another important early-nineteenth-century economic thinker, castigated Smith for overemphasizing the role of frugality in economic development (Blaug 1986, pp. 119–21). Conversely, when J. S. Mill and Alfred Marshall wished to give English political economy a more human face later in the nineteenth century, both reminded their readers of how Smith had organized much of his economic thinking around broadly social and ethical considerations. Indeed, to their way of thinking, Smith was part of what A. Sen has recently called the "ethics-related tradition of economic thinking" (Sen 1987, pp. 1–28).

In the end, then, insertion of Book II into the *WN* profoundly altered

Smith's view of how to foster and sustain economic growth. For that reason, it is of the utmost importance for readers of the *WN* to decide exactly what Smith was trying to do in Book II with the frugality-saving-investment sequence. If Smith meant for that sequence to be construed in terms of impersonal market mechanisms, then we can talk about a self-regulating market, spontaneous order, and so on (e.g., Rosenberg 1990, pp. 1–17). But if Smith is read as having offered that sequence as an "as if" ethico-economic imperative, which hinges on the character and conduct of frugal men, who themselves mirror the ethico-social value priorities of their culture, then the "saving as investment" thesis must be talked about in much broader terms.

APPENDIX II. ON BOOK III:

"The Nature of Things" and the Monetarization of History in Smith's Discussion of Feudalism

Book III is at once the simplest and most complicated part of the *WN*. According to W. R. Scott, it also represents the oldest part of the *WN*—dating back, perhaps, to the lectures Smith gave in Edinburgh in the late 1740s (1937, p. 56). On the whole, Book III is quite short, articulating a broad-brush view of Europe's transition from feudalism to commercialism that will be familiar to many modern readers. As the great economic historian E. Heckscher observed, Book III has long been viewed (by Marxists as well as liberals) as a testimony to the relentless quest for economic progress in human history (Heckscher 1955, v. 2, pp. 24–25). And yet, because Book III is such a part of what K. Boulding has called "our extended present" (1971, p. 231), it has not received the critical attention it deserves—which is to say, we tend to take the argument of the book for granted, seldom scrutinizing it as we would other writings. In addition, it does not help matters any that economists (from J.-B Say on) by and large have regarded the book as irrelevant to "scientific" economics.

On the other hand, Book III occupies a structural position in the *WN* toward which and out of which many of the *WN*'s more important themes run. There are, for example, at least three anticipations of Book III in the *WN*'s first two books. Book I, Chapter 3—where Smith discusses both how the size of a market sets limits to the division of labor and how access to the sea facilitates the division of labor by encouraging foreign trade—clearly anticipates a similar line of argument in Book III, Chapter 3. In Book II, moreover, there are two additional lines leading to Book III. The end of Book II, Chapter 3, prefigures Smith's examination in Chapters 3 and 4 of Book III of how the feudal barons' "mode of expence" hampered economic development. And Smith's explanation, at the end of Book II, of how the "policy of Europe" since the collapse of Rome had hindered capital formation and investment in productive labor, especially in agriculture, sets the scene for the argument of Book III in the round.

In addition, Book III, as Schumpeter appreciated (1954, p. 187), is an historical "prelude" to the criticisms of mercantilism and physiocracy that Smith unveils in Book IV. There are also direct textual parallels between parts of Book III and the opening pages of Book V, Chapter 3.

Given Book III's strategic position, then, Smith's task therein was to develop an argument—one that Schumpeter (1954, p. 187) has characterized as an historical sociology of economic life—that demonstrated two things: first, how the "policy of Europe" discouraged economic growth; and, second, how the almost accidental (because unexpected and unplanned) expansion of European commerce during the later Middle Ages not only triggered economic growth but, in the process, undermined the hold the feudal barons had on European civilization as well. To achieve this twofold purpose, Smith developed a view of feudal society in which, relative to a set of abstract "natural" norms, feudal conditions, institutions, and values were identified as "unnatural." As a consequence of this maneuver, the narrative line Smith follows in Book III moves on two different but related levels at once: One line traces the movement of European civilization toward things natural; the other line accounts for the supersession of the unnatural elements of feudal life. Much of the challenge of reading Book III involves explaining the various connections between the two levels of the narrative.

Just as challenging—at least for first-time readers—is the odd use Smith makes of the terms "natural," "naturally," and "natural order of things" in the opening chapter of Book III. The argument Smith develops there is clear enough, and from it he derives a conclusion that permits him to characterize as "unnatural" and "retrograde" a period of European history that stretches for over a thousand years—no mean feat for a thinker reputed to be historically minded. At several points in that chapter, moreover, Smith blames "human institutions" for the deplorable conditions of feudal Europe, denigrating those institutions for having "thwarted" man's "natural inclinations" as well as for having delayed realization of "the natural order of things" in Europe. Furthermore, it is easy to produce evidence from this chapter that Smith thought that, had these inclinations not been thwarted, European society would have enjoyed commercial opulence and civilization much sooner than it did. In the argument of Book III, then, things natural stand to things commercial and civilized as things unnatural stand to things feudal and barbarian. Most of the other binary linguistic oppositions Smith deploys in Book III are meant to be homologous with this basic set of terms (e.g., war/peace, anarchy/order, poor/rich, power/profit, retrogressive/progressive, and so on).

If we examine these oppositions more closely, however, we discover that Smith's understanding of unnatural and natural has less to do with feudal and commercial life per se than with "logical" assumptions Smith has made about how "most men . . . employ their capital." Here Smith operates with a threefold premise: (1) that in the "nature of things" securing one's subsistence precedes developing interests in comforts and luxuries; (2) that, as a consequence of this, investment opportunities in agriculture have priority in men's minds relative to similar and more risky investment opportunities in manufacturing and foreign trade; and (3) that, in calculating one's investment opportunities, it was natural to measure risk along a scale that ran from agriculture, to manufactuing, and on to foreign trade. Time and again, Smith tells us that this scheme of capital employment is "so very natural" that it should constitute the very "order of things" in decisions about capital employment.

Now, there were precursors in English and Scottish thought for thinking about economic activity in history in terms of natural and unnatural behavior. In the seventeenth century, for example, the idea of the unnatural was used by Harrington and the neo-Harringtonians to characterize irrationalities in the relation between power and property in the feudal world. Lord Kames, Smith's mentor in Edinburgh in the late 1740s, used similar language to point up the absence of commercial agriculture in the feudal world. And Hume, in his 1752 essay "Of Commerce," employed the natural/unnatural distinction to underpin his differentiation of ancient martial and modern commercial social systems. Traces of these meanings can be detected in the opening chapters of Book III of the *WN*.

Most interesting of all, however, are the uses Turgot made of the natural/unnatural distinction in his *Reflections*, a work which Smith had in his library and which, we argued earlier (Appendix I), influenced him as he wrote Book II (Turgot 1973, pp. 119–82). In the *Reflections*, published in three parts between 1766 and 1769, Turgot constructed a typology of capital employment on the basis of what he called "physical necessity" and the "natural order of things" (Turgot 1973, pp. 122, 153). As Turgot made clear, his strategy for the allocation of capital resources gave priority first to agricultural investment, then to manufacturing, and finally to foreign trade. On those terms, of course, the laws of "physical necessity" and the rules governing investment operated according to the same "natural" logic, with the result that the natural process of investment and the natural order of things could be correlated. Turgot even admitted at one point in the *Reflections* that his decision to discuss the activities of the "manufacturing entrepreneur" before those of the "agricultural entrepreneur" had "reversed the natural order of things" (Turgot 1973, p. 153), a remark that speaks volumes about the opening chapter of Book III of the *WN*.

Given this language, it would be hard to deny Turgot's relevance for Smith's handling of the feudalism-to-commercialism transition in the *WN*. And if, as was argued in Appendix I, the Turgot-Smith connection represents a relatively late development in Smith's thinking, then the opening of Book III may have been written the way it was in order to complement the capital-accumulation argument of Book II. Since there are two notable anticipations of Book III in Book II, it is not unreasonable to draw this conclusion—which means, of course, that Book III is not only the oldest part of the *WN* but also one of the newest.

The implications of the natural/unnatural distinction for our understanding of what Smith is doing in Book III become clearer when we recall that Smith considered the investment opportunities of the feudal world as "inverted" because incessant feudal "violence" made investment in foreign trade more attractive than equal investment in agriculture (or manufacturing)—the opposite of the natural investment scheme set down in Chapter 1 of Book III. Thus, the logic of the Turgot-Smith investment typology obliged Smith to measure historical change in the feudal world against the standard of a "natural" investment pattern. Accordingly, profits derived from foreign trade in the feudal world had to be characterized as coming from an unnatural source (Since mercantilism—at least in Smith's rendering of it—was an economic system that depended on money derived from favorable balances of trade to fund domestic economic activity, it too could be characterized with the same language—which is precisely why Schumpeter speaks of Book III as a "prelude" to the critique of mercantilism Smith undertakes in Book IV. For more on this, see Appendix III).

One other aspect of the capital-employment argument of Book III warrants our consideration. In the *Reflections* Turgot placed great emphasis on the frugality-savings-investment sequence (See Appendix I). For him, economic development begins with thrift and with the enterprise exhibited by the "landed proprietor" qua fledgling "agricultural entrepreneur" (Turgot 1973, pp. 125, 146, 159, 169). Through the agency of the entrepreneur, Turgot contended, land became an "object of commerce" and a source of "profit" rather than an all-too-human institution for perpetuating the power of feudal lords (Turgot 1973, p. 126). Profits derived by these entrepreneurs from the commercialization of agriculture then move, according to Turgot (1973, p. 169), naturally throughout society under the auspices of various other manufacturing and trading entrepreneurs.

In Book III, Smith's feudal barons, who had long ignored their "real [economic] interest" for the sake of "power," use their land to advance their martial ambitions. Given the martial disposition of the barons, which accounts for the anarchy and violence of feudal life, as well as for the lack of improvement in agriculture, Smith had to find a way to dislodge the barons from the land so that their property could be put to commercial purposes. If that "revolution" could be scripted into Smith's narrative, then the logic of the Turgot-Smith investment typology could come into play as a real historical force.

In Book III, Smith accomplishes this by designating city-dwelling merchants, whose residence near the sea gave them access to foreign markets, as the agents of this change. As Smith tells it, these merchants derive profits from foreign trade and then gradually entice the feudal lords into participation in a money economy with the lure of luxury. The long-term result of this, of course, is the gradual transfer of land from the latter to the former.

Needless to say, this change in land ownership constitutes the silent revolution experienced by the feudal world just before its demise. By the same measure, history is now primed to receive the full force of the Turgot-Smith investment strategy. It can be no surprise, therefore, that Book III ends with a call for investment in agriculture, the assumption being that circumstances in Europe now conform to a natural order of things that dictates use of this investment policy.

It would be quite wrong, of course, to think that the explanation Smith offers in Book III of the transition from feudalism to commercialism was dependent on Turgot. After all, there were countless discussions of the land-ownership issue in the decades preceding the publication of the *WN* (Defoe, Fletcher, Cantillon, Kames, Harris, and Hume come immediately to mind). Yet Smith alters these discussions about the decline of the barons by working them into an explanatory structure which is governed by the logic of the investment typology—which is to say, the meaning of unnatural and natural in Book III is governed by capital considerations. And since these terms are homologous with feudalism and commercialism as social systems and as historical ages, we might well say that what Smith has done in Book III is periodize European history in terms of a capital-investment logic. He has, as it were, monetarized history.

A final point about the argument of Book III: It has always struck me as quite odd that Smith used the feudal lords' pent-up desire for "luxury" as the agency of their destruction—at least of the leveling down of their power to the point where they become, in his words, as "insignificant as any substantial burger or tradesman in a city." As is well known, and as F. Bacon among others had argued, one of the reasons the lords lost control of their estates was because of the debts they had incurred while funding and fighting in the Crusades. For the most part, Smith is silent about that aspect of feudal history. But, while underplaying that argument in his narrative, he allows the luxury argument to emerge full blown—to the point that it becomes a decisive theme in the destruction of the barons' power and the collapse of the entire feudal world.

A key question in interpreting Book III, then, is: Why does Smith proceed this way? Does he wish to depict the barons as the victims of an acquisitive instinct that is so natural and powerful to human beings that even tough martial barons were incapable of resisting it? Or is Smith offering the barons' demise as an object lesson for what happens to the worldly fortunes of people who, lacking the power of self-command, indulge in the kind of selfish consumption of luxury items that brought the barons to ruin? I think the latter, for three simple reasons: (1) Nowhere in the *WN* does Smith say the desire for luxury is a natural instinct; (2) at every point in the *WN* where he has an opportunity to do so, Smith moralizes against such indulgence; and (3) the moralization argument is the corollary of the productive-labor argument that Smith displays so conspicuously in Book II.

The larger irony, of course, is that, had the barons not indulged themselves the way they did, the transition from feudalism to commercialism might not have taken place when it did.

APPENDIX III. ON BOOK IV:

Smith's Critique of Mercantilism and the Problems of the "Automatic Mechanism" and Agricultural Investment

Immediately upon its publication in 1776, the *WN* was recognized as an attack on monopolies, especially as they related to trade with the British colonies in North America. From that day to this, it has always been a basic premise of Smith scholarship that Smith's indictment of monopolies was central to his criticism of "mercantilism" as a "commercial system." And since free trade was the antithesis of monopoly, it was seen as the key both to Smith's "system of natural liberty"—or to what D. Stewart in 1793 called Smith's "liberal system" (1980, p. 339)—and to his criticism of mercantilism.

It is equally well known that the main thrust against mercantilism occurred in Book IV of the *WN*. And if we read that book in isolation from what Smith has said in Books I–III, it is easy to explain its subject matter in terms of the monopoly/free-trade opposition. Quite clearly, the argument is that unrestricted trade allows the market mechanism rather than the monopolistic mentality of merchants to set the prices consumers pay for goods on the market. But if Book IV is read in light of what Smith said earlier in the *WN* about "nature" and "history" (see Appendix II), we uncover reasons other than inflated market prices for Smith to have discussed mercantilism the way he did.

For over one hundred years, or since the great English economic historian W. Cunningham tried in the 1890s to rehabilitate mercantilist thinking by historicizing it (1891, pp. 88–90), modern scholarship has known that Smith was anything but "fair-minded" in his deliberately one-sided (mis)representation of mercantilist thinking. In this vein, several scholars have even suggested that mercantilism was never thought of as an economic "system" by anyone until Smith succeeded in convincing readers that it was indeed a system and a pernicious and illogical one at that (e.g., De Vries 1976, p. 239; Coats 1962, p. 28). At the outset, therefore, readers of the *WN* need to be aware of the polemical intentions at work in Book IV.

Consider the following. Throughout Book III and in the closing pages of Book II, Smith repeatedly argues that the natural order of investment runs from agriculture, through manufacturing, to foreign trade. On the basis of that natural progression, he called the course of European history from the fall of Rome to his own day "unnatural," an inversion of the natural order of things, and so on (see Appendix II). Not surprisingly, the "system of natural liberty" that Smith begins to allude to in Book IV is a reverse image of this—which is to say, in Smith's natural system investment in agriculture is given the highest priority. For that reason, Smith characterized socio-historical situations that either forced investment of capital into foreign trade (i.e., feudalism) or encouraged government policies which privileged investment in foreign trade, as retrograde and contrary to the natural order of things.

Thus, when Smith begins in Book IV to dissect mercantilism as a commercial system, he is able to do so within a linguistic field in which mercantilism is almost by definition a flawed system of political economy, and in two different senses. First, it is flawed because it is premised on erroneous economic principles (e.g., the preference for monopolies; the mistaken equation of money and wealth; the folly of balance-of-trade theory). And second, it is false because, even if in some relativistic sense mercantilism had been "natural" to a certain period of European history, the economic circumstances of history in the eighteenth century had changed markedly, with the result that the mercantilist system was now irrelevant to modern political economy.

The argument of Book III would seem to confirm these two basic points. On the one hand, it was Smith's view there that, contrary to the natural order of things, the violence and internal disorders of the feudal world forced capital to look abroad for investment opportunities. On the other hand, Smith suggested—as he moved from Book III to IV—that the fixation on deriving wealth from foreign trade had been a policy priority not only for merchants but also for officials of absolutist political regimes throughout Europe.

Against the background of Book III, Smith then proceeded skillfully to work this line of argument into a more broadly focused discussion of how absolutist states in Europe used mercantilist doctrine to advance their own "power" interests. Indeed, it was Smith's view that the power policies of absolutism, while certainly economically oriented, kept capital flowing in unnatural channels, to the overall detriment of the "balance of industry" within the domestic economy. As such, Smith thought, those policies impeded civil society's natural progress toward "opulence." In that respect, what begins in Book III as a critique of feudal anarchy and the martial culture that sustained it gradually expands in Book IV into an all-encompassing critique of mercantilism, absolutism, and the power politics of the states system in early modern Europe.

From W. Cunningham to E. Heckscher, economic historians have made a point of noting how Smith's system of natural liberty offered itself as a corrective both to the mistaken economic notions of mercantilism and to the predatory and militaristic principles that governed the economic policies of the early modern European states system. Thus, as a number of Smith-inspired radical writings of the early 1790s reveal (e.g., T. Paine's), free trade was vital both to liberating industry from the shackles

of feudalism and to ending intrusions of martial and absolutist governments on the liberties of citizens.

Now, it is precisely because mercantilism is talked about in the *WN*
as *the* economic system of a negative and unnatural period of European
history—feudalism—and as *the* economic agent of the power state—absolutism—that Smith is able to paint such an unflattering picture of it as
a commercial system. But to pull this off, Smith has to refrain from
acknowledging certain things about mercantilist thinking as it developed
as a mode of discourse in England's Discourse of Trade literature in
the seventeenth and eighteenth centuries. So, for example, instead of
admitting that striking parallels existed between his own critique of mercantilism and many mercantilist critiques of mercantilism, Smith remained silent about what we now recognize as the pronounced "liberalizing" tendencies within mercantilism itself, many of which made generous
allowances for "freer" trade among nations of the world. Needless to
say, such silence had the self-serving effect of making Smith's liberal
economics look all the more original and mercantilism all the more "illib-
eral." The aim of much recent scholarship on the history of economic
thinking is to rescue mercantilism from this kind of skewed analysis.

One of the more confusing aspects of Smith's critique of mercantilism
arises, however, when we situate that critique in the context of the overrid-
ing importance Smith ascribed to frugality in fostering and sustaining
economic growth. As has been noted (Appendix I), Smith identified
frugality as pivotal to the "progress of England toward opulence and
improvement." Similarly, he regarded frugality as an ordinary virtue of
the everyday prudent man (See Appendix IV). And in Book III it was the
frugality of the city merchants that, according to Smith, positioned them
to buy the estates of the feudal lords when the latter failed to resist the
enticing luxury items provided to them by the merchants themselves.

In England's seventeenth-century Discourse of Trade literature, which
is often taken to be synonymous with the economic thinking of mercantilism, frugality is singled out (along with industriousness) as the key to
economic revival in seventeenth-century England. In 1623, for example,
E. Misselden, the first person to use the phrase "balance of trade" in
a *published* writing, talked about the different roles frugality played in
"ancient" and "modern" commerce (1623, pp. 123ff.). As he saw it,
frugality dominated the commercial policy of the former but had been
banished from the latter by luxury-craving "prodigals." As a result of
prodigality, Misselden went on to say, England had slipped into economic
"decline" as her people lost both their industriousness and their competitiveness vis-a`-vis the Dutch. Referring to the Dutch, as F. Bacon and R.
Vaughan had also done (See Appendix IV), Misselden claimed that simple

balance-of-trade calculations would "scientifically" register the extent of England's economic crisis and, at the same time, identify problem areas in the economy where the exercise of frugality might prove beneficial to all (1623, pp. 134–36). Vaughan, Misselden's contemporary, was just as adamant, writing that a return to the moderate monetary and spending policies of the "ancients" would stem England's economic decline (1856, pp. 97–98). He, too, singled out the Dutch as exemplary in this regard.

It would be easy to multiply the statements from leading seventeenth-century economic tracts that pertain to the importance of frugality in balance-of-trade theory. In almost every instance, moreover, the aim of such declarations is to encourage investment in domestic enterprises that would employ more workers and put more productive industry into motion. Renewed industry, in turn, would generate more exports, which themselves would bring in more money, keeping what Misselden called the world's "circle of commerce" in motion. Thomas Mun, generally acknowledged as the main theorist of balance-of-trade theory, said things like this over and over again, and he did so without making the blunders (e.g., mistaking money for wealth) Smith would later attribute to him (Mun 1952).

The point, however, is that Smith is silent about the role of frugality in the Discourse of Trade literature. This is quite odd because the aim of much mercantilist literature was to persuade merchants to do exactly what Smith has them do in Book III of the *WN*; that is, in Book III Smith has the city merchants, who have derived profits from foreign trade, pursue business opportunities in the domestic economy. In Smith's account, these undertakings gradually led to the commercialization of agriculture and, ultimately, to the collapse of the feudal world. But instead of applauding merchants and merchant capital for exploiting the economic potential of their domestic situation, Smith quite gratuitously concludes Book III (as a prelude to the argument of Book IV!) with a critique of mercantilism that focuses on how much faster "the natural course" toward opulence would have been set in Europe had investment in agriculture not been diverted back into foreign trade by a coalition of selfish merchants and misguided government officials.

With this odd criticism in place, Smith proceeds to chastise merchants for being untrustworthy citizens—for being citizens of the world, as Montesquieu (1949, pp. 328–30) had once called them—whose narrow economic interests militated against the establishment of international peace and the expansion of a nation's domestic prosperity. With regard to the matter of peace, Smith held (like Hume before him) that balance--of-trade theory generated economic jealousies between the world's trading nations, each nation erroneously thinking that by depriving the other of economic gain it would enhance its own power position versus the other. This invariably led to economic rivalry and military confrontation, the result of which disrupted international trade and made economic mutualism impossible. Similarly, on the domestic front, where the merchants' monopolistic mentality, which was abetted and exploited by government policy, pushed the prices of domestic goods to artificially high levels and, in the process, gave merchants excessive profits at everyone else's expense. On both the international and domestic levels, then, Smith faulted merchants for having interests that ran counter, respectively, to the world's and to the public's interest.

On the surface, Smith seems to have hit upon two good reasons for opposing mercantilism as a commercial system. And the often used seventeenth- and eighteenth-century phrase "peace and plenty" well expresses what Smith thought would follow for a nation were it to abandon mercantilism and embrace the system of natural liberty he was recommending as an alternative.

For all that, however, neither of Smith's criticisms of mercantilism was new. It is not just, for example, that Hume and Quesnay had similarly expressed themselves on such matters twenty years before the publication of the *WN*. Rather, the fact is that the language of peace and plenty—indeed, of economic universalism—as well as deep distrust of monopolies had been quite common among mercantilists themselves. Recognition of this obliges us to probe deeper into why the *WN*, especially as a critique of monopolies, became, in D. C. Coleman's words, "the Bible of a new politico-economic era" (1969, p. 93).

Although an answer to this question leads beyond what can be attempted here, a summary of modern scholarship's view of Smith's relationship to mercantilism helps pinpoint the decisive issue.

A common point of departure for all modern discussions of Smith's relationship to mercantilism is the early modern European fixation on the primacy of foreign trade—a topic that, not coincidentally, bulks large in the *WN*, too (e.g., Viner 1937, pp. 1–118). To explain this concern, which pervades all mercantilist thinking, scholars point to the widespread perception among all early modern European nations that the "money supply" in Europe was insufficient to fund expansion of every nation's economy (e.g., Hutchison 1988, pp. 368–69; DeVries 1976, p. 240; Monroe 1923, p. 276). And since from early in the seventeenth century economic growth had been deemed essential to national security—money being the "sinews of war," it was said—a regular, stable, and adequate flow of money to "drive" and "quicken" the economy became a vital concern of "reason of state" in every European nation (Suivranta 1923, pp. 48–51). If uncertainties associated with the international payment system between nations are factored into this perception, it becomes understandable why foreign trade obsessed government officials and businesspeople alike. For a nation without "mines," as the title of A. Serra's important early-seventeenth-century tract on trade had put it (Monroe 1923, pp. 275–76; Schumpeter 1954, pp. 354–55), could only meet the challenge posed by "scarcity of money" by having a foreign-trade surplus (Hinton 1955, pp. 283–85). As a result of this, it came to be thought that success or failure in this endeavor could be measured by calculations of a nation's balance of trade with its neighbors. And so it was that balance-of-trade theory and reason of state became intertwined in seventeenth-century economic thinking—from at least Botero on (Botero 1956, pp. 142–43).

It is widely acknowledged by modern scholarship that David Hume pinpointed the theoretical "fallacy" of this way of economic thinking (e.g., Viner 1937, pp. 74–84)—which explains why Hume is also credited with wrecking "balance-of-trade theory" and "mercantilism" at a "single stroke," as well as with laying the foundation for liberal political economy in the process (Angell 1926, pp. 9–39). Although scholars agree that Hume was not the first to detect the "logical" flaw in mercantilist thinking, he is nevertheless identified as the person who brought the issue of mercantilist irrationality to public attention. He did this, so goes the argument, by revealing what modern economic thinkers still understand today as the "automatic mechanism of specie flows" (e.g., Viner 1937, pp. 74ff.; Schumpeter 1954, pp. 365ff.; Angell 1926, p. 26).

According to Hume (1987, pp. 283–86, 309, 311–14, 328), as well as to members of the so-called "classical" school of nineteenth-century economic thinking, discovery of the automatic mechanism rendered balance-of-trade calculations irrelevant to the science of economics, the reason being, in J. Viner's words,

> . . . that a country with a metallic currency will automatically get the amount of bullion it needs to maintain its prices at such a level relative to the prices abroad as to maintain an even balance between its exports and imports. Should more money than this happen to come into the country, its prices would rise relatively to those of other countries; its exports, consequently, would fall and its imports increase; the resultant adverse balance of payments would have to be met in specie; and the excess of money would thus be drained off (1937, p. 74).

From this insight, Hume drew several additional conclusions about how trade, prices, and money interacted on the international and domestic fronts. He reasoned (1987, pp. 312–14, 309, 290, 327–29): (1) that the "exorbitant desire" of mercantilists to amass money as well as their inordi-

nate fear of losing it was "groundless"; (2) that nations' economic problems stemmed less from "scarcity of money" than from flagging industry
and decreasing production at home; (3) that the increases in domestic
prices which always accompanied (albeit not immediately) growing national prosperity could be mitigated somewhat by maintaining proportionality between price rises and increased production; and (4) that economic
rivalries between nations should never be pushed to the point of warfare,
because the automatic mechanism itself assured every nation an adequate
money supply to drive its industry and fund its trade.

In these formulations, of course, it is easy to see the doctrines of
free trade and *doux-commerce* (i.e., international economic mutualism)
emerging with the automatic mechanism providing the impetus and rationale for a new world order among trading nations. In that regard, the idea
of the automatic mechanism would seem to be central to the line Hume
(and Smith) wished to drawn between mercantile and liberal political
economy (Heckscher 1955, v. 1, pp. 308–23). Our question thus becomes:
How does the automatic-mechanism argument figure in the damning
association of mercantilism with the power politics of absolute states?

But before we can answer that question we again encounter a difficulty
on the level of ideas, for it is well known that the automatic mechanism
was known to and discussed by mercantilists from at least the 1690s on
(e.g., Viner 1937, pp. 79–85). One of the virtues of Viner's work is that
it addresses this point head on (1937, pp. 74). He claims, for example,
that several "moderate" mercantilists had written brillantly about the
automatic mechanism prior to Hume (1937, pp. 19, 22, 34, 42). Indeed,
as Viner (and others before him) noted, writers of the stature of S. Clem-
ent, I. Gervaise, J. Vanderlint, R. Cantillon, and J. Harris had realized
that increases in the quantity of a nation's money supply—whether from
mines (as in Spain) or from foreign trade (as with the Dutch)—would
raise prices to the point where the increase reduced the competitiveness
of domestically produced goods on the international market (e.g., Schumpeter 1954, pp. 311–17, 365ff.). As a result of this alteration, money
would begin to flow out of a country rather than into it until a new point
of equilibrium in the prices between nations had been achieved.

In this context, many of these same writers suggested that steps could
be taken to deal with the "overplenty" of money problem before it triggered economically (and socially) devastating price rises (See Appendix
IV for more on this theme). To that end, moderate mercantilists searched
for ways to "sterilize" or "immobilize" the excess, often hinting that
melting money down to silver plate might do the trick (Vickers 1960, p.
210; Monroe 1923, p. 288, respectively). Their aim, in short, was to keep
the supply of money in a condition of what Bacon and Vaughan had

called "mediocrity" (See Appendix IV for this theme). As a strategy for preserving wealth, they said, the "mediocrity of money" policy was what had enabled the Dutch to maintain their extraordinary commercial property for so long. Dutch frugality, needless to say, helped sustain this policy.

All of this "enlightened" discussion of the relationship among prices, money supply, and foreign trade by moderate mercantilists obliged Viner to offer a more nuanced view of what actually separated mercantile from liberal political economy. Focusing on the fallacy noted by Hume, who had scored points against mercantilists by denying them knowledge of the automatic mechanism, Viner made two claims: (1) that it was a logical contradiction for mercantilists to have held to balance-of-trade theory and to the automatic mechanism at the same time and (2) that, instead of trying to control domestic price rises with sterilization and a mediocrity of money policy, mercantilists should have abandoned controls altogether, putting, in Hume's word, their "trust" in the automatic mechanism (1987, p. 326).

By Viner's own reckoning, then, the matter of the relationship between mercantilism and liberalism turns less on fine points of economic knowledge than on the respective unwillingness and willingness of the two protagonists to abide the long-term implications of the automatic mechanism. As Viner unabashedly maintains (1937, p. 111; 1991, pp. 54–55, 269–74), commitment to the long-term perspective is precisely what allowed the "pacific and cosmopolitan" views of liberal political economy, as distinct from the short-term " 'Machiavellian' " policies of the mercantilists, to triumph in the debate. Viner even uses the words "amoral" and "moral" to characterize the Machiavellian and cosmopolitan views of mercantilists and liberals, respectively (1991, pp. 268–69)

As influential as Viner's argument about mercantilism and the automatic mechanism has been, it has been ably challenged by J. Schumpeter——and in a way that reveals even more unmistakably what is at issue for modern economists in Smith's (and Hume's) critiques of mercantilism. With Viner specifically in mind, Schumpeter begins by setting the scene of the eighteenth-century exchange between mercantilists and liberals with a question (1954, p. 316), namely, "What is the quantity of money that a given country needs [to prosper economically]?" He allows Hume to answer (1954, p. 316), paraphrasing him to the effect that

on the level of pure logic this question has no meaning—on the one hand, any quantity of money, however small, will do in any isolated country; on the other hand, with perfect gold currency all around, every country will always tend to have the amount appropriate to its relative position in international trade.

Aside from the esoteric reference to "isolated country" (i.e., to "Crusoe economics"), Schumpeter's choice of the phrase "pure logic" to characterize Hume's rendering of the automatic mechanism is significant. The phrase is telling because Schumpeter (1954, pp. 336–37, 346–47, 351) proceeds to argue that, at bottom, the success of the liberals' campaign against mercantilism hinged on two self-serving distortions of reality: (1) on representing the practical aspects of mercantilist thinking as if they were theoretical principles about economics rather than about power; and (2) on convincing people that the logic of the automatic mechanism was so compelling and so mutually beneficial for everyone that power politics could be ignored in favor of a new economic order founded on free trade.

As Schumpeter warms to his task, he proceeds to criticize Viner for having denounced mercantilism for approaching economic problems from a short-term rather than a long-term perspective. Calling Viner's criticism "hardly fair" (1954, p. 351n5), Schumpeter relishes reminding us that power politics and war were constant features of the mercantile "age"—a period of time, Schumpeter adds, that would be difficult to characterize as either "temporary" or "short-term" (Viner's words: 1937, p. 111). Having made that point, Schumpeter chides Viner for engaging in anachronistic interpretation; that is, for imposing standards of logic and pure theory on "practical-minded" merchants and administrators who, given the circumstances of the age, did not have the luxury of thinking about economic issues in terms of "long-run equilibria" categories, even when they understood, as Viner admits they understood, how the automatic mechanism worked (Schumpeter 1954, p. 351n5).

On the level of ideas, then, Schumpeter and Viner agree that a moderate mercantilist and a liberal could concur about the automatic mechanism and yet still adopt widely divergent practical reponses to the fact of its existence (e.g., Viner 1991, p. 212). Viner, championing Hume's position, called mercantilists to account for not abandoning the short-term Machiavellian/reason-of-state considerations that permeated balance-of-trade theory. To bolster his own position, Schumpeter is able to quote Viner to the effect that mercantile policy looks a good deal less "absurd" if "approached from the short-term point of view" (Schumpeter 1954, p. 351n5). In turn, Viner insisted to the end of his life that, in order to qualify as theoretically informed, economic policy decisions had to be governed by long-term considerations (1991, pp. 273–74; cf. p. 12).

With the Schumpeter-Viner exchange on mercantile and liberal political economy behind us, we can now circle back to the question we raised previously, namely, How does the idea of the automatic mechanism help Smith implicate mercantilism in the power politics of absolutism? The answer is that with the idea of the mechanism at hand—an idea he used to great effect in developing his criticism of monopolies in what is known as the "Early Draft" of the *WN* (Henceforth "ED"), and an idea he credited Hume with discovering (Smith 1978, p. 576)—Smith could present his own system of natural liberty as economically indifferent to money-supply problems. The implication of that, of course, was that Smith liberated economic policy from reason of state as well as from the restrictive economic policies that selfish merchants and Machiavellian administrators had devised to meet the scarcity-of-money problem.

Without ever telling us that this is what he is doing in the *WN*, Smith nevertheless presupposes the automatic mechanism as a backdrop to his critique of mercantilism. Indeed, it is the logic of that mechanism that allows Smith to decouple economic policy from considerations of political power. Once made, that separation pushes the free-trade issue to the center of the public debate about the restrictive aspects of mercantilist trade policy in the late eighteenth century.

For over two hundred years, readers of the *WN* have more or less thought that Smith was right about all this. Even so, it is important to realize—as D. Vickers has realized (1960, pp. 224, 232)—that what makes questions about money supply irrelevant to economic theory and policy is the willingness to adopt the logic of the long-run perspective. Vickers is quick to point out that that perspective does not offer equally compelling guidance for a nation faced with the task of safeguarding its economic gains against the centrifugal pendulum swing of the automatic mechanism. The difference between mercantilism and liberalism, then, comes down not only to a clash between short- and long-term perspectives but also to one between richer and poorer countries.

For most of the twentieth century, students of the history of economic thinking have gone round and round about this. In the last thirty years, however, there have been some indications that the nature of the argument about the automatic mechanism is on the verge of changing. Vickers (1960, p. 232), for example, made the point that, although Hume may have discovered the automatic mechanism, he himself vacillated as to how to respond to the automatic mechanism on the practical level. S. Hollander (1973, pp. 290–91), commenting on Smith's preference for investment in agriculture, puzzled over Hume's and Smith's differences on how the automatic mechanism practically affected an "advanced" economy's capacity to retain its competitive edge versus low-wage competitors. Still more recently, I. Hont has raised all kinds of pertinent questions about the wisdom of relying so much on the automatic mechanism to separate mercantile from liberal political economy (Hont 1983, pp. 271–315).

To my mind, Hont's path-breaking work forces us to conceptualize differently the impact of the automatic mechanism on eighteenth-century economic thinking. For rather than continue to set the mercantilism-liberalism debate within the somewhat anachronistic framework of short-term versus long-term policy considerations, Hont has refigured the issue so that it fits into what we today call the ideological framework of the "rich country-poor country" debate.

In that debate, which actually took place in the 1750s, and which turned on subtle and elaborate interpretations of the automatic mechanism (Davie 1967, pp. 291–302), we witness English and Scottish thinkers responding to the mechanism in diverse and divergent ways. As Hont points out (1983, pp. 289, 302), how thinkers responded very often depended on whether the mechanism was being viewed from the perspective of a relatively rich country (e.g., England) or from that of a relatively poor one (e.g., Scotland).

Hont's argument begins simply enough, with observations about how the logic of the mechanism might look to economic writers in rich and poor countries. Predictably, in a rich country the response would be either to deny the validity of the mechanism itself or to devise policies that would safeguard the nation's material prosperity against the economic pull of what thinkers like Vanderlint and Cantillon had earlier called the "ordinary course of things." Balance-of-trade theory, especially in the hands of Viner's "moderate" mercantilists, was meant to address this issue—which is to say, the theory by the mid-eighteenth century entailed a defense against the centrifugal pull of the automatic mechanism on the wealth of a prosperous nation. Hume, in most of his economic essays of 1752, and Smith in his "ED" as well as in major sections of the *WN*, regarded such interventions in the natural course of things as signs of "bad government" and "errors" of police, respectively (Hume 1987, p. 330; Smith 1978, p. 579). And while neither Hume nor Smith early on used the word "mercantilism" to denote these errors, the list of mistakes they detailed are exactly those Smith attributes to mercantilism in the *WN*. Thus, the errors associated with mercantilism in the *WN* grow out of rich countries' attempts to evade the economic pendulum pull of the automatic mechanism.

From the poor-country perspective, things look very different. There, the workings of the mechanism hold out a promise of eventual material reward for hard-working and frugal citizens. Indeed, the claim is that an industrious but poor people—as the Scots were often depicted in the Union debate of 1707 (Dickey 1993)—can use its low-wage and cheaper-land advantages to become economically competitive on the international levels.

As Hont translates the mercantilism-liberalism debate into rich country-poor country terms, it becomes clear from the evidence he produces that Hume's contemporaries did not respond to the idea of the mechanism the way, say, Viner would have us believe they did. Using words like "paradoxical" and "ironical" to characterize major aspects of the response, Hont shows that the rich-country position on the automatic mechanism generally entailed steadfast denial that the pendulum swing away from rich countries and toward poor countries would result in growing economic parity among the trading nations of the world (1983, p. 281). Here the counterargument was that once a rich country achieved certain levels of technological proficiency, capital accumulation, scale of industry, and specialized labor skills, it would possess resources of economic resiliency that would enable the nation to shift product lines and gear production to domestic consumption, thereby compensating itself for being undersold *in certain areas* on the international market by low-wage rivals (Hont 1983, pp. 281–90).

It is ironic, as Hont notes, that although this argument was invariably presented as a criticism of Hume, it actually articulated the very argument Hume advanced in the essays of 1752, the exception being the essay "Of Money," in which, Hont argues, some imprecision in Hume's language encouraged readers, especially in rich countries, to draw pessimistic conclusions as to how the automatic mechanism would affect the economies of advanced countries (1983, pp. 279–80). For his part, Hume recognized early on how his argument was being read as a pessimistic forecast of the economic futures of rich countries (Hont 1983, p. 291). To set the record straight on that, he added the essay "Of the Jealousy of Trade" to the 1760 publication of his various essays (Hume 1987, pp. 327–31). In that essay, he clarified his position, reiterating that, while the automatic mechanism created opportunities for poor countries to become competitive on the international market in some industries, the real key to generating wealth and to sustaining economic growth lay in the industriousness and skills of a nation's people (Hume 1987, pp. 288, 291, 312, 327–31). So long as those resources were maximized, Hume thought rich countries could preserve their prosperity, the automatic mechanism notwithstanding.

From that perspective, Hume went on to reason, there was no point for merchant capital to "fly" from country to country, trying all the while to anticipate the push and pull of the economic pendulum of world trade and specie flows (1987, p. 283). As he optimistically pointed out, there seemed to be unlimited opportunities for investment in the domestic economies of rich countries (Hume 1987, p. 264). Furthermore, with that option available, there was no need at all, in Hume's words, for "states which have made some advances in commerce . . . to look on the progress of their neighbors with a suspicious eye, . . . and to suppose that it is impossible for any of them to flourish but at their expence" (1987, pp. 327–28). On those terms, one has to wonder just how essential the discovery of the automatic mechanism really was to development of the free-trade argument. For, as Hont shrewdly points out, it is "in reality . . . the international division of labor," not the automatic mechanism, that provides the nexus of trade between rich countries, which specialize in certain products and services, and poor countries, which exploit low-cost advantages and raw material resources (Hont 1983, p. 283).

Locating the idea of the automatic mechanism in the ideological context of the rich country-poor country debate, which, after all, was the context in which the automatic mechanism was initially discussed, enables us to develop another perspective on the criticisms Smith aims at mercantilism—first in the "ED" and then in the *WN*. In the "ED," for example, Smith develops a criticism of merchants, monopolies, and "errors" of police which is written from a complicated perspective. On the one hand, Smith is optimistic about a rich country's capacity to resist the pendulum swing of the automatic mechanism (1978, pp. 567, 577). On the other hand, and *for that reason*, he charges mercantilists with "errors of police" when they try to finesse the automatic mechanism by restricting business activity in certain areas of the economy. Smith says this because he believes such interventions raise prices, disturb the "balance of industry" throughout the nation, and direct capital investments into unnatural channels. Accordingly, Smith contends that faulty mercantile policy results in a gradual loss of flexibility and innovation in the economy, depriving a rich country of the economic resiliency its advanced status has given it. That, of course, is why in the "ED" (1978, p. 577) as well as in Book I of the *WN* Smith builds so much of his argument around the division and subdivision of labor arguments. But in stressing those advantages, Smith means to draw attention to a rich country's capacity to evade the automatic mechanism.

In the final analysis, then, Smith's criticism of mercantilism, at least insofar as he develops it in the ideological context of the rich country-poor country debate, is paradoxical in that mercantilist errors of police are cited as the principal reason the centrifugal pull of the automatic mechanism on a rich country's wealth works the way it does—and sooner rather than later. By the same measure, Smith's position seems to be that, vis-à-vis the automatic mechanism, the best economic policy is one which ignores the mechanism and concentrates on development of and investment in the domestic economy. In that respect, it is once again not at all clear what the automatic mechanism has to do with Smith's economics other than that the errors it provokes among the mercantilists, who are trying to protect against it, are used by Smith to delegitimize mercantilism as a commercial system.

Since parallels between the "ED" and the *WN* are so evident on the themes of monopolies and the division of the labor, it is easy to establish continuity of development in Smith's thinking between the early 1760s and 1776. But over that period, an important change in Smith's thinking takes place, too. And it has to do with the increasing role capital investment in agriculture plays in his thought.

In the "ED" (1978, pp. 565–66), Smith relates how the principle of the division of labor is best applied to the manufacturing rather than the agricultural sector of the economy. And in the "ED," when Smith discusses agriculture, he does so in terms his Edinburgh mentor Kames had used to talk about it: to wit, land was meant to be commercialized; and the easiest way to commercialize it was to have independent people—renters or small owners—tending to it for their own economic benefit (Kames 1763, pp. 26–27, 128–92, esp. 156–58; Smith 1978, pp. 580ff.). In telling language from the mid-1740s, Kames even said the feudal land-holding system was "unnatural" because it militated against the commercialization of land (1763, p. 26). Like Kames, however, Smith does not at this point in time talk about the need for investment in agriculture—a marked contrast to the line he would later pursue in Book III of the *WN*. And Smith fails to discuss the topic in the "ED" because he had not yet fully appreciated the role capital played in making labor, especially in agriculture, more productive. That was a theme he encountered in the writings of the physiocrats, probably in the mid-1760s.

Is that important? I think so, and for the following reasons. In Appendices I and II, I have argued that, after capitalizing the division of labor at the beginning of Book II of the *WN*, Smith proceeded to develop in Books II–IV a rationale for why investment in agriculture should be an economic imperative. This, Smith said, was consistent with the "natural order of things." I also tried to show in these Appendices that this looked like a physiocratic argument, right down to the nuances of Smith's language. In that respect, the language of "unnatural" and "natural" that Smith uses in Book III might be interpreted as the point where Kames's and Turgot's understanding of what was "unnatural" about a society that lacked commercial agriculture blended in with each other (See Appendix II for this theme).

One could say, of course, that since Kames and Turgot had labor-intensive start-up models of economic growth in mind when they sequenced economic development the way they did, the high priority they gave to agriculture was meant to help a poor country "take off" into development. But in the *WN* there is a pecularity about the argument for capital investment in agriculture that does not square with this interpretation, for the language Smith uses and the basic thrust of his argument there duplicate almost exactly main features of Quesnay's attempt to show a rich country how to protect itself against economic decline and the shortsightedness of what he and Mirabeau called the mercantile system (Quesnay 1965, pp. 100–110).

In the *Tableau*, for example, the fickleness of merchant capital is one of Quesnay's primary concerns. To that end, he wrote, the "monetary fortunes" of merchants know "neither king nor country" (1972, p. 13; cf. 1963, pp. 60–63). Referring to these fortunes as "bourgeois"—because they stemmed from mercantile activity in the cities—Quesnay urged government officials to abandon "unenlightened" policies that permitted "mercantile trade" to advance at the expense of agriculture, the key factor, for Quesnay, in promoting "the wealth of the nation" (1972, pp. 11n, 13n, 16n; cf. 1965, pp. 99–109). Quesnay went on to say that, if a way could be found to bring "[bourgeois] wealth back to the countryside," where it could be productively invested in agriculture, "prosperity and power" would be assured the state (1972, p. 11n). Quesnay even speaks (as Smith does in the *WN*) of capital as being "destined" for investment in productive labor, and especially in agriculture (1972, p. 18n). Just as telling, Quesnay said that wealth held by the bourgeoisie was not really theirs at all—rather it was the state's and was destined to be put to productive use in agriculture through their agency (1973, p. 18n).

In the *WN*, Smith talks about the elusiveness of merchant capital at the ends of Book II and Book III, throughout Book IV, and at the end of Book V, Chapter 2. And in Book IV he blasts mercantilists for spending money indulgently on luxury items, often imported at great expense. What is striking about these discussions of merchant capital and merchant modes of expense is that in each instance Smith blames merchants for not employing their capital for the benefit of "particular" countries. With special reference to the situation of the Scots, and perhaps with questions in mind about the political allegiances of merchant capital in the city of Glasgow (Skinner and Campbell 1982, pp. 62–64), Smith depicts merchants as cosmopolitans who move wealth from place to place (within and without particular countries) as the automatic mechanism shifts business opportunities from rich regions/countries to poor regions/countries and then back again. By contrast, and here Smith and Quesnay seem to concur, capital investment in agriculture is presented to the merchant community of a rich country as an opportunity for it to express its political commitment to the well-being of a particular country.

Needless to say, this does not sound very cosmopolitan. In fact, as G. Davie has shown (1967, pp. 296–97), it sounds like the "responsible patriotism" a Scot would exhibit when confronted with the prospect of Scottish money running south rather than into the Scottish countryside. Scottish merchants in Glasgow, of course, had benefitted greatly from the British mercantile system; and there were fears in Scotland that their wealth would either be spent or invested elsewhere. To a patriotic Scot, therefore, the physiocratic project for drawing mercantile wealth to the countryside had some obvious appeal.

None of this, moreover, speaks to Smith's unwavering confidence in the automatic mechanism or to his faith in the inherently productive power of the division of labor. To that end, Smith's so-called "agrarian bias" (Winch 1978, pp. 139–40), which has befuddled students of Smith's thinking for generations, needs to be seen—as the physiocrats had intended—as a way to avoid the pendulum pull of the automatic mechanism. It is that issue, not one peculiarly associated with "agrarian capitalism" as a stage in the economic development of the West, that explains why agricultural investment is so integral to the argument of the *WN*.

To summarize, then, readers of the *WN* need to bear three things in mind. First, the agrarian argument in the *WN* is quite conspicuous. Second, there are clear indications in the *WN* that one of the major arguments against merchant capital and for investment in agriculture is patriotic, for such investment helps sustain the national economy of a rich country against the pull of the automatic mechanism toward poor ones. Third, if Smith's agrarian-investment recommendation is meant to prop up the national economy of particular countries, it is not at all clear why this should not be viewed as politically expedient. Nor, for that matter, is it clear why such a recommendation could not be interpreted in terms of power politics and economic nationalism. Indeed, Smith's wish (as Vanderlint's, Quesnay's, and Mirabeau's was) was to direct capital investment into agriculture and, by so doing, keep food and labor costs relatively low vis-à-vis low-wage competitor countries. True, such investment also improved and/or sustained the conditions of workers throughout the nation. But given the various textual contexts in which Smith developed the agrarian argument, it seems obvious that his primary concern was to deal with the automatic mechanism on a practical level, not give himself up to that mechanism for the sake of theoretical consistency. There is, to be sure, a long-term economic aspect built into the political expediency of Smith's agrarian argument, but it has as much to do with the long-term *political* viability of "particular" countries as with preserving the long-term *economic* equilibrium among the nations of the world.

The upshot of these considerations is that, in the final analysis, Smith's criticism of mercantilism oscillates between faulting it for failing to grasp the equilibrium argument on a general level and criticizing it for devising wrongheaded policies (e.g., supporting monopolies and discouraging investment in agriculture) to protect particular countries against the mechanism. Since Smith's recommendation for correcting these "errors" aims at facilitating investment in agriculture for economic and political reasons, the core of his criticism of mercantilism must be said to hinge on his objections to the efficaciousness of mercantilist policy for evading the pendulum swing of the automatic mechanism.

On a deep level, in other words, the well-being of the national economy of rich countries seems to weigh heavily in Smith's thinking insofar as his agrarian turn is meant to ensure the long-term political and economic viability of particular nations. Indeed, although it may be difficult to determine whether Smith's agrarian bias derives from overt physiocratic influence or constitutes an independent attempt to "balance" economic forces within a particular nation, as between its urban and rural sectors, the fact is that on these terms it is impossible to say either that Smith severed economics from politics or that the long-term logic of the automatic mechanism governed his position. Thus, if our conception of the ideological context of the *WN* is expanded to include the rich country-poor country debate about the automatic mechanism, as well as the debate about agrarian investment, our evaluation of Smith's criticism of mercantilism will become a good deal more complicated than the free trade versus monopoly opposition suggests.

APPENDIX IV. ON BOOKS I AND V:

Doux-Commerce and the "Mediocrity of Money" in the Ideological Context of the Wealth and Virtue Problem

In some of the Appendices to this volume Smith's conception of frugality was identified as essential to his economic and moral thinking, and on several different levels at once. As we discovered, frugality was instrumental: (1) to his theory of capital accumulation, especially as developed in Book II, and (2) to his explanation in Book III of the historical circumstances whereby feudalism was superseded as a mode of social organization by commercialism. The purpose of this Appendix is to show how Smith's conception of frugality had a historical dimension, too, one which casts an interesting light on Smith's philosophical history of commercial society in general and on the relationship between Books I and V in the argument of the *WN* in particular.

Of the five books in the *WN*, Books I and V are the ones most often related to each other by Smith scholars. In discussions of this matter, it has become customary to adopt one or all of the following positions: (1) to see the "melancholy" perspective Smith sketches of workers in Book V as evidence of his growing pessimism about the prospects of capitalist societies (Heilbroner 1975); (2) to ponder whether Smith's differing perspectives on the division of labor in Books I and V can be reconciled (Rosenberg 1965; West 1964); (3) to argue against the laissez-faire aspects of Smith's economics by noting the numerous allowances he makes in Book V for intervention of government in the affairs of economy and society, and especially through educational initiatives (Viner 1991, pp. 85–113; Rosenberg 1979); and (4) to regard Book V's admissions about the deplorable condition of the working class as an anticipation of the stance Marx would later take against the inhumanity of capitalism (Meek 1967, pp. 34–50).

Although fine work has been done on all these themes, none includes in its assessment of the relationship between Books I and V an account of how the frugality and agrarian-investment arguments (discussed at length in Appendices I–III) might figure in a broader explanation of the relationship between the two books. I want to attempt to do that in this Appendix, with special reference to how these two arguments address the negative social situation Smith discusses in Book V.

First some background information. At the end of the seventeenth and the beginning of the eighteenth century a number of English and Scottish thinkers held that the rise of commerce played an important role in two crucial developments in the history of early modern Europe: in the shift from absolute to free governments and in the delegitimization of the martial virtues that had been celebrated, especially by the aristocracy, in the feudal world and under Europe's various "Gothic" regimes.

Among these thinkers, and in an ideological context that was chronolog-
ically delineated on the one side by the "Standing Army" debate in
England in the late 1690s and on the other side by the English-Scottish
Union debate of 1706–1707, a propagandist like Daniel Defoe reiterated
time and again and in published tract after tract that the rule of law was
a precondition for free government and commercial enterprize (Dickey
1993). On the first count, law provided citizens with security against
encroachments on their persons, property, and liberties by government
or other citizens. On the second count, law assured citizens engaged in
peaceful commerce that they would be allowed to enjoy the fruits of
their industry. As a result of the kind of thinking represented and ably
articulated by Defoe in economic writings published over the course of
his life, ideas about law and commerce became intertwined in discussions
of how "civil societies" differed from "martial" ones. Or, in Defoe's
equivalent terms, how commercial societies differed from "Gothic" (i.e.,
feudal) ones.

As the eighteenth century unfolded, the dovetailing of these legal (i.e.,
jurisprudential) and commercial arguments enabled English and Scottish
thinkers (until after the '45) to launch and sustain attacks on England's
and Scotland's feudal/Gothic heritages. In conjunction with each other,
the jurisprudential and commercial arguments promised citizens not only
economic prosperity but relief from centuries of "violence" and "feudal
anarchy" as well. As the twin agents of historical "progress" (i.e., of
increasing political and economic liberty), law and commerce could be
cited as the forces which had led to the civilizing of Europe, a process
writers in England and Scotland from at least the 1690s on also associated
with the rise of trading cities and their emerging political influence in the
English House of Commons.

Much of the argument of Book III of the *WN* is organized around the
interplay between these various civilizing agents. And when Smith in
Chapter 4 of that book identified industrious and frugal city merchants
as the catalyst of change in the feudal-to-commercial transition, he added
another, more human agent to his explanation of the civilizing process in
European history. Thus, when Smith said,

> . . . commerce and manufacturing introduced order and good government, and
> with them, the liberty and security of individuals, among the inhabitants of the
> country, who had before lived almost in a continual state of war with their
> neighbours,

he was articulating a hundred-year-old commonplace of English and
Scottish thought. (True, he disguises that, somewhat, by claiming that

only Hume before him had ventured such thoughts. But that is a bewildering statement, given what Smith had read and what others before him had written.)

Now, readers of the *WN* have found it difficult to resist interpreting Smith's view of the civilizing process in general and of the transition from feudalism to commercialism in particular as anything other than "liberal" in its inspiration. D. Stewart, in his 1793 *Account* of Smith's life and writings, encouraged us to read the *WN* this way (Stewart 1980, pp. 309–24). In this, Stewart yoked Hume and Smith together as the key proponents of a uniquely modern (because civil and commercial) view of liberty. On this score, of course, there is no denying that *one* of the main lines of argument in Book III of the *WN* is devoted to delegitimizing feudalism as a social system. Smith's language conveys that impression exactly, for throughout Book III he expresses his opposition to feudal values and institutions in binary linguistic terms that abet the "black versus white" argument with which he wishes to confront the reader. Accordingly, it is quite impossible in Smith's (and Hume's) terminology for a nation to be civilized without commerce. Conversely, feudal society, precisely because it was martial, warlike, and violent, could have no commerce. Hence, the overall retrograde character of feudalism as a social system in Smith's thinking.

Given the dynamics of this linguistic field, which A. Hirschman has taught us to appreciate as representative of what he calls the *doux-commerce* perspective on the civilizing process in early modern European history (1977, pp. 55–66; 1986, pp. 106–9), it is difficult for us to avoid interpreting the feudal-to-commercial transition in other than the binary linguistic terms in which Smith framed it. As is well known, radicals in France and England read Book III of the *WN* this way in the early 1790s—as a call for the overthrow of feudalism in Old Regime Europe. And since this was actually accomplished in France in August, 1789, Smith's economics and his philosophical history of civil society have long been seen as crucial ideological factors in the triumph of "liberalism" in France in 1789.

Still, just as there are other ways to interpret the argument of Book III of the *WN*, there are ideological contexts other than the one associated with *doux-commerce* and emerging liberalism in which to locate the overall argument of the *WN*. In what follows, I wish to identify the main features of one such context. It is an ideological context that formed itself around a tradition of discourse that dates from at least the early seventeenth century. After sketching the principal features of this tradition, in which a main theme is how to establish "mediocrity of money" in society, I shall argue that Smith drew on this tradition to reinforce the *WN*'s strictures on how money should (and should not) be spent. In addition, recourse to this tradition provided ideological support for Smith's frugality and agrarian-investment arguments, both of which can be viewed as serving the wider stabilizing purposes implicit in the mediocrity-of-money perspective. In doing this, I take it that Smith was trying to uphold the promise of *doux-commerce*—of wealth as compatible with virtue—by showing how it might be economically realized in history without widespread luxury, corruption, and decadence. Or, to put it in G. Davie's terms, Smith resorted to this tradition because he detected in it a way to reconcile "the old ethics [i.e., frugality, honest industry, and so on] with the new economics" (Davie, quoted in McNally 1988, p. 163).

A surprisingly large number of seventeenth- and eighteenth-century thinkers, many of whom contributed to the economic thinking of that period, and all of whom had written tracts on economics that were in Smith's library when he died, regarded frugality as more than just piling up money (i.e., hoarding). Indeed, many saw frugality as essential to commercial development and to the preservation of civilized values in a commercial environment whose very expansion threatened those values in fundamental ways.

Early in the seventeenth century, for example, F. Bacon said things like this while discussing the role of money in national affairs. In his 1607–8 paper/speech, entitled "Of the True Greatness of the Kingdom of Britain," Bacon held two different (but ultimately complementary) positions on the matter (Bacon 1850, pp. 222–29). First, he enthusiastically invoked the "authority of Machiavelli" to point up the fatal modern "conceit" that "money was the sinews of war" (1850, p. 225). Drawing on the wisdom of the ancients, Bacon posited connections on the one hand between riches and cowardice, wealth and national weakness, commerce and softness, and luxury and effeminacy. On the other hand, he connected valor and greatness, and military virtue and national independence.

Yet, Bacon had a second view of the matter, one that he developed in the "True Greatness" text, too. To wit, instead of simply valuing "valor over treasure" (1850, p. 226), as would be the case of a true Machiavellian, Bacon recognized (as many after him would) that the expense of modern warfare had made money—or the "greatest purse"—vital to the success of any modern military engagement, especially a protracted one (1850, p. 226). Conceding that the unexpected success of the Dutch resistence to Spain had recently confirmed the power of the longest-purse argument, Bacon acknowledged that "treasure and money . . . [do] add to the greatness and strength of a state" (1850, p. 226).

Having recognized the exigencies of modern warfare, Bacon went on to explain what conditions had to be met in order for a state to be wealthy without corruption and to be martial without having rude, hard, and barbaric manners (1850, p. 226). In other words, he went on to explain what it meant to be civilized by declaiming against barbarism on the one hand and decadence on the other, the negative polarities that had governed so much of civic humanist discourse since Machiavelli (Pocock 1975).

Of the three conditions Bacon advances to avoid these twin dangers, two are crucial to our purposes here. First, he states that "treasure does advance [national] greatness where it is rather in mediocrity than in great abundance." As Bacon explains (1850, pp. 226–27), "ordinary discourse" testifies to the fact that "excesses of riches" and "surfeit" of treasure ruin a people, especially if that wealth is concentrated in the hands of a "slothful" few who, by indulging in the "greatest expense and consumption," set poor examples for everyone else (Bacon's target group here is the prodigal "nobility").

Bacon's second condition for maintaining a civil balance between barbarism and decadence, and between poverty and luxury, follows from the first. He contends that, in order to avoid inequality and conspicuous displays of wealth by the few, a nation's money should be in as "many hands" as possible (1850, p. 227). And to underline this point, Bacon says that it is especially important for money to be in the hands of "sparing" (i.e., frugal) "merchants, burgers, tradesmen, freeholders, [and] farmers" who, as the Dutch had demonstrated, tended to employ money in productive rather than wasteful ways (1850, p. 227). By using their money productively, Bacon continued, these groups would ensure that "wealth" would be "dispensed" throughout society, circulating rapidly from consumer to consumer and, in the process, generating increasing industry among the people (1850, p. 228). Later, in a similar vein, Bacon said that the "thrift" of "sober men" would redound to the "public interest" in countless ways. He also stated that for this to happen, the "vanity of the times"—"in apparel" and, above all, in "fashion"—had to be avoided. He punctuated the point by implying that "wise men," versed in the "habit of frugality," would do that naturally—without the prodding of any sumptuary "law" (1850, pp. 386–87).

Bacon's observations on how a nation treads the thin line between barbarism, on the one hand, and luxury, decadence, and corruption on the other, can be explained in terms of what I shall call his "mediocrity of money" thesis. As it turns out, this thesis became integral to English thinking on economic and historical issues throughout the seventeenth century. More specifically, we find the perspective most often articulated in England's "Discourse of Trade" literature, and particularly in ideological contexts in which the Dutch are held up to the English as the "epitome" of how a people can preserve the civilized balance between having too much money and too little. To this end, the English literature from Bacon, T. Mun, and E. Misselden on offers endless praise of Dutch industriousness and frugality as the keys to that nation's successful handling of the wealth-and-virtue problem.

A most telling example of the mediocrity-of-money thesis can be found in R. Vaughan's still highly praised *A Discourse of Coin and Coinage* (1856, pp. 9–119), a tract that dates from the 1620s and, according to Schumpeter, was the "standard" English work on money in the seventeenth century (1954, p. 291). In Chapter 7 of that work, in which Vaughan pursues what he calls a "history of money," he spells out "what proportion of money were fittest for the [preservation of the] common-wealth" (1856, p. 36). Vaughan's contention is that a nation could have "too much" as well as "too little" money in circulation at any given time (1856, p. 36; also consult W. Petty's influential economic writings from the 1660s on). As he explained (1856, p. 36), in terms that clearly monetarize the historical stages of the civilizing process,

> Because that the want of money makes the life of citizens pernurious and barbarous, so the over-great abundance of money makes their lives luxurious and wanton, . . .

According to Vaughan, industriousness solved the first problem; to prevent the latter—a "depravation," he said, rooted in "vain and vicious fancies"—a "mediocrity of money" policy had to be pursued by the state (1856, pp. 36–37). And, like Bacon, Vaughan pointed to the Dutch as experts at "the good government of the course of money" (1856, p. 37).

As a recognizable discourse in seventeenth-century England, the mediocrity-of-money thesis fit in nicely not only with civic humanist arguments about wealth and virtue in commercial society but with much emerging economic thinking as well. For, from Bacon on, the thesis informed countless discussions of the intricacies of "balance of trade" theory. Invariably, the argument had two parts. The first part went like this: (1) nations without financial resources were vulnerable militarily to belligerent neighbors; (2) to ensure access to an adequate money supply nations (without mines!) had to secure a perennially positive balance of payments from their foreign trade; (3) the profits from this trade were perceived as providing the money needed both to drive and quicken industriousness within the nation and to furnish the prince with a store of treasure in the case of war; and (4) increasing domestic production would translate into more exports, which, of course, would return more profits, keeping the economy expanding.

Within this cycle, however, many balance-of-trade theorists detected a problem—one which led to the second part of the argument. That part went like this: (1) as the quantity of money in a nation increased, prices rose; (2) as this happened, ways had to be found to negate price rises, otherwise the nation's goods would lose their economic competitiveness, and jobs ultimately would be lost; and (3) the best way to do this—to keep money in mediocrity—was to prevent the excess from entering into circulation.

On this score, the mediocrity-of-money policy solved all kinds of *practical* problems for seventeenth-century economic thinkers. On the one hand, it recognized the importance of foreign trade for the "plenty" of the people and the "power" of the state. On the other hand, the policy aimed at three things: (1) preserving an equitable diffusion of wealth throughout society; (2) maintaining the circulation of an adequate supply of money to generate increased industry among the people; and (3) establishing some proportionality among production, prices, and the amount of money in circulation. In this way, a nation could be rich and competitive without experiencing luxury, corruption, and social inequality.

Bacon, who was one of the first to use the phrase "balance of trade" in his writings, understood very well how the mediocrity-of-money policy addressed a broad range of policy issues that figured in calculations of national greatness. At the same time, Bacon, Misselden, and Vaughan detected in ancient wisdom about the role of money in the rise and fall of empires lessons for contemporary economic thinking. Sallust, Lucretius, and Seneca, after all, had traced Rome's decline—its demoralization, to paraphrase Sallust (1963, p. 226)—to the burdens of what Seneca called "overmuch prosperity" (1969, pp. 178, 215). Sallust and Seneca even set the issue of demoralization in a chronological framework that began with old Roman frugality and ended with luxury and Roman decadence. And while I cannot go into details here, there is much evidence to show that J. Bodin's and G. Botero's work in the late sixteenth century on the relationship between cycles of empire and fluctuation in money supply influenced Bacon's thinking on these matters. As Botero put it, empires, after having "reached their peak through frugality," invariably "fall away from the height of their prosperity, for valor diminishes with increase of power and virtue with accretion of wealth" (1956, pp. 7, 9–10).

That this way of thinking about the mediocrity of money could easily be coordinated with theses about the role luxury and corruption played in the cycles of empires is one reason balance-of-trade theory persisted in English and then British thought for so long. We find these themes linked together in various ways, for example, in three writers who exercised enormous influence on Smith: namely, G. Berkeley, F. Hutcheson, and R. Cantillon. We cannot, of course, deal in detail here with the thought of these writers, but a careful examination of their work in the 1720s and 1730s reveals a preoccupation with welcoming money—from whatever source—as a stimulus to domestic industry but also with using frugality or mediocrity-of-money policy to check the tendency toward luxury and corruption that accompanies the increase in money supply.

In the case of Berkeley, there is considerable evidence from at least 1713 on that, in addition to being a first-rate philosopher and acclaimed Christian moralist, he was an economic thinker whose prescription for Irish economic development as well as for English economic recovery involved the "moralization of money." Indeed, in *The Guardian* writings of 1713, in which Christian education is proposed as a way to bring "private interest" into line with the "public good" (1871, v. 3, p. 191); through his famous 1721 essay on England's impending "ruin," in which "religion, industry, frugality, and public spirit" were identified as agents of moral renewal (1871, v. 3, p. 195); to the *Querist* in the mid-1730s, in which he began to ground his moralism in economic categories (1871, v. 3, pp. 353–405); Berkeley consistently explained the "ruin" of Britain in terms of its moral inability to curb the "corruption and folly of the present age" (1871, v. 3, p. 208).

Since the highly moral language Berkeley uses in his writings is remarkably similar to that which we find in the *WN*, above all in Book II (see Appendix I), it is worthwhile to take note of the framework within which Berkeley develops it.

He starts his 1721 diatribe against luxury and corruption with a Botero--like declaration (1871, v. 3, p. 200):

> Frugality of manners is the nourishment and strength of bodies politic. It is that by which they grow and subsist, until they are corrupted by luxury; the *natural* cause of their decay and ruin.

Berkeley supports this observation by appealing to history, listing Britain among a select group of nations that have been or were about to be ruined "by the same natural causes" (1871, v. 3, p. 200). The lesson of history, he goes on to point out, should have inclined us to "frugal measures" with which to check the slide into luxury and corruption (1871, v. 3, p. 203). For, according to Berkeley, such measures would put a "timely stop" to the process about to bring Britain to ruin (1871, v. 3, p. 205). As it happened, however, Britains had thus far proved incapable of such self-discipline, with the result that once again it appeared to be "in the order of things that civil states should have, like natural products, their several periods of growth, perfection, and decay" (1871, v. 3, p. 211).

As a moralist, and as one who wished to awaken Britain to the extent of its current corruption, Berkeley did not believe in the inevitability of "natural" cycles (e.g., 1871, v. 3, p. 211). Rather, he regarded corruption as an "natural effect" of a systematic propaganda campaign waged by "free thinkers" against the rules of public morality in Britain (1871, v. 3, p. 209). To that end, Berkeley insisted, in the face of all historical evidence to the contrary, that the reason the cycle of industry, wealth, luxury, and corruption seemed perpetually to run the "natural" course it did, was due more to "human folly" than to the "order of things" (1871, v. 3, p. 211). Through moral exhortation, and with the aid of sumptuary laws, "honest methods of industry and frugality" could be preserved in public life, Berkeley thought (1871, v. 3, pp. 195, 197, 205, 209).

In the "Ruin" essay, Berkeley is undeniably injecting moral considerations into economics. Although chastised by his contemporaries for what was perceived as repeated attempts to compromise religion, Berkeley publicly refused to dissociate his Christian values from his economic work (1871, v. 3, pp. 353–54). For, as he saw it, "moral re-entry"—a phrase often used nowadays by economists to explain what late-twentieth-century capitalist societies must do in order to shore up their "depleting moral legacies" (e.g., Hirsch 1976; Rosenberg 1990)—was as much an economic as a moral necessity. So, in the "Ruin" essay Berkeley recommended reviving "that native spark of British worth and honor" (i.e., "old English modesty") to stave off further moral decline and to revitalize the economy (1871, v. 3, p. 210). Not for nothing does the "Ruin" essay begin with a Latin tag from Sallust.

By the 1730s, especially in *Alciphron* (1732) and in the *Querist* (1735–37), we observe Berkeley beginning to economize/monetarize his moralism. For example, in writings from the 1710s Berkeley had insisted that individuals would promote the "common good" out of (Christian inspired) "sympathy" for their fellows (1871, v. 3, pp. 189–91). His view indeed was that through Christian "enlightenment" (1871, v.3 , pp. 168, 174–75, 185), which taught the lesson that true pleasure lay in the satisfaction of "natural" rather than "fantastical" desires (1871, v. 3, p. 159), people would find their "private" interests realized in the well-being of the whole (1871, v. 3, p. 191). In the more economically focused work of the 1730s, Berkeley adopted a different tack and used a different discourse to express it.

In essence, what Berkeley said comes down to a twofold proposition: (1) that how wealth is spent determines whether it was being employed properly or improperly; and (2) that the measure of the proper use of money entailed calculations of how many "hands" were put to work by spending it one way rather than another. To this end, Berkeley asserted that there are ways to spend money "innocently"—ways that employ as many people as would have been employed had the money been "spent upon vice" (1871, v. 2, p. 66). Still more specifically, Berkeley singled out expenditures on domestic construction projects (e.g., building houses, gardens, and furniture) as spending that employed "smiths, masons, bricklayers, plasterers, carpenters, joiners, tilers, plumbers, and glaziers" (1871, v. 2, p. 66; v. 3, p. 388). And, in order to justify his preferred mode of expence, which required "our gentry" neither to ccasc spending money nor eliminate "reasonable . . . vanity" from their lives (1871, v. 2, pp. 365, 388–89), Berkeley implied that it was in the public interest to spend money so as to increase employment. On these terms, one could show sympathy for one's fellows by providing them with employment opportunities—a point Smith makes several times in the *WN*.

An even clearer sense of what Berkeley is doing here as he moralizes against certain kinds of consumption and, in the process, turns sympathy into an economic category, can be found in the work of F. Hutcheson, Smith's famous teacher in the late 1730s at Glasgow. Like Berkeley in *Alciphron*, Hutcheson had been outraged by the views on luxury expressed by Mandeville in *The Fable of the Bees*. In a series of letters published in 1726 in *The Dublin Journal*, Hutcheson argued that a man of "good sense," a man who lived within the "bounds" of "temperance," "frugality," "moderation," and "humility," would use "saved" money in ways that augmented the "public good" (1971, pp. 385–91). As Berkeley would in the 1730s, Hutcheson rebuked Mandeville for claiming that indulgent luxury consumption was vital to economic development. On the contrary, Hutcheson argued, societies, like individuals, could maintain equal levels of consumption without underwriting vices (1971, p. 388). This could be achieved, he claimed, by engaging in what he called the "retrenchment" of expenses (1971, pp. 389–91).

With this declaration, and especially in the economic context in which it was developed, we arrive at a pivotal moment in the history of eighteenth-century thinking, one that illuminates the Turgot-Smith thesis on capital accumulation and the collateral distinction Smith drew in the *WN* between productive and unproductive labor (See Appendix I). For, according to Hutcheson, "the virtue of this retrenchment" is twofold (1971, p. 391). First, it greatly extends the benefits of wealth to wider and wider circles of people—from heads of family, who (like feudal barons) once spent lavishly and exclusively upon themselves, to family members, grandchildren, friends, and so on (1971, pp. 390–91). And second, retrenched expenses entailed procuring "necessaries" and "convenencies" for the many rather than luxury items for the few. This, Hutcheson insisted, kept the level of employment constant without either encouraging "vice" or corrupting "manners" (1971, pp. 390, 383). For this reason, Hutcheson used the word "humility" to describe the motivation behind economic retrenchment (1971, p. 391). As he pointed out, "all . . . ancient and modern" (i.e., Christian) thinkers recommended "temperance, frugality, and moderation" in consumption for moral men (1971, p. 385). For Hutcheson, that recommendation made good economic sense as well, for it did not, as some ancient cynics would have had it, entail "suppressing" pleasure so much as teaching people how to "regulate" it (1971, p. 374).

Here, in the plain language of Smith's great teacher, we see how old ethics was inserted into the new economics. And as we move closer to the 1750s, the period in which Smith began to mature as a thinker, the number of writers who thought about money and frugality this way can be multiplied. Of special importance in this regard is R. Cantillon's *Essay on the Nature of Trade in General*. Written in the early 1730s, but not published until the mid-1750s, Cantillon's famous essay explored in subtle ways how the interplay between "too great abundance of money" and luxury spending "throws . . . [a state] back imperceptively but naturally into poverty" (1931, p. 185). His view was that a nation can avoid economic decline and moral decadence by deciding to "retrench" (*retrancher*) its expenses (1931, p. 169). That, Cantillon stated, could be done either by persuading the rich to retrench their expenses or by enlisting the government in the management of the circulation of money. To that end, Cantillon wrote (1931, p. 185):

> Thus it would seem that when a state expands by trade and the abundance of money raises the prices of land and labor, the prince or the legislator ought to withdraw money from circulation . . . so as to forstall . . . luxury.

But for the most part Cantillon argued that "according to the natural course of humanity" thriving states collapse under the burden of their own prosperity (1931, pp. 185–87). As he explains (1931, p. 235),

> The wealth acquired by a state through trade, labor and oeconomy will plunge it gradually into luxury. States who rise by trade do not fail to sink afterwards. There are steps which might be, but are not, taken to arrest this decline [declin].

The account Cantillon gives in the *Essay* of what he calls "the great circle" of "capital" (1931, p. 195), and of the rising and falling fortunes of empires, still receives high praise from students of the history of economic thinking. And it would appear that Cantillon deeply influenced Smith's as well as Quesnay's and Turgot's view of capital formation and of what, exactly, constituted a productive expenditure. As is plain, however, Cantillon operates with a mediocrity-of-money perspective which he correlates with the life cycle of empires and with the (in)capacity of government and/or the people to retrench their expenses.

Still closer to Smith, we have the entry on "Commerce" in the first edition of the new Edinburgh *Encyclopaedia Britannica* in 1771. In that entry, a long discussion of the importance of "luxury" as a stimulus to trade is followed by a candid section in which some of the negative ramifications of commerce and consumption are explored (1771, v. 2, pp. 237–40). The theme in that stretch of the text is a familiar one—"luxury" shining "triumphant" everywhere, but "inequality" and "misery" becoming progressively "more striking to the eye." In language that goes back to Bacon, the entry conveys the sense that "the wide door to modern distress" will open unless either (or both) of two things happen: (1) statesmen must find a mechanism to spread the "great domestic circulation" of capital in proportion to the industry of society; and (2) the rich have to think less of hiring "useless servants"—a "dead weight on consumption"—and more about "oeconomy." Citing the Dutch as an example of a "frugal people" who, by dint of their moderation had kept the prospect of "luxury" and "large profits" from "dazzling their eyes," the author of the entry insisted that similar restraint in Britain would blunt the "taste for luxury" and stave off many of the "calamitous consequences" associated with "decline"—consequences of the sort we find outlined in Book V of the *WN*.

Having worked our way forward in the mediocrity-of-money tradition from Bacon and Vaughan to the *Encyclopaedia Britannica*, we can now address the issue of how the division-of-labor argument in Books I and V fits into this set of themes.

Among Smith scholars it is well known that by the 1750s the division-of-labor argument had been discussed rather fully by several of Smith's well-known contemporaries, Hutcheson and J. Tucker among them (Tucker even used the division-of-labor argument to critique monopolies). In a 1757 publication, moreover, a "solid" economic thinker by the name of J. Harris had recognized that the division of labor was the "main source of commerce" (1856, p 356). In elaborating this, Harris made most of the points about the division of labor that Smith makes in the opening chapters of Book I of the *WN*. Harris indeed does not just say that the division of labor qua the specialization of function fosters economic and social mutualism among a people and between nations but also that it lowers prices, providing in the process a "comfortable subsistence" for all (1856, pp. 360–61).

Soon after making this point, Harris emphasizes that the division of labor would advance a nation's well-being *independent* of capital flows either in or out of a country (1856, pp. 399–401). However, since he had read Cantillon (or Cantillon in Postlethwayt) carefully on this issue, Harris conceded that fluctuations in a nation's money supply would generate temporary "disorders" in society, disorders like those discussed by Cantillon with regard to the social problems that arise when certain social groups have more disposable income than others (Harris 1856, pp. 401, 406). After noting some of their "pernicious" effects (1856, p. 401), Harris simply down-plays such disorders, accepting them as part of what he said was the "natural course" of things. For in Harris's view such disorders sooner or later would disappear as the ratios among money in circulation, prices, and the overall industriousness of society found their "due equilibrium" (1856, pp. 402; cf. 366, 407).

Given this long-term perspective, which we have discussed in Appendix III as part of the automatic mechanism, Harris is not unduely concerned either about what he calls the "over-plenty" of money or about luxury spending, both of which he calls "benign" conditions in the wider scheme of things (1856, pp. 406–7, 366). Nor, for that matter, is he alarmed at the hardships inflated prices will create for the poor, a group to which he condescends excessively in his book. And yet, ever mindful of Cantillon's theory of the relationship between money supply, economic cycles, and the rise and fall of empires, Harris confesses that, for patriotic reasons, various measures would have to be taken to postpone the inevitable economic downswing that comes from prosperity and the "over-plenty" of money. In that context, Harris gestures in the direction of the ideas of "frugality" and "public spirit" (1856, pp. 414–15, 365–66), but dismisses both as possible remedies for staving off economic decline by noting—in Hutcheson's and Cantillon's exact language—how difficult "retrenching" one's expenses can be (1856, p. 415).

In Harris's tract on money, then, the themes of division of labor, "over-plenty" of money, and frugality are related and worked into a long-term perspective on economic life. But even if Smith had never read Harris (which he had), the line of argument pursued in the latter's work shows that, almost twenty years before the *WN* was published, someone with interests in the division of labor, the quantity theory of money, and the causes of luxury and social disorders, could have talked about these topics in a serious economic tract that Smith thought enough of to purchase for his library.

Beyond that, Harris's work is also important for the way it contrasts with the *WN*. Indeed, it throws into sharp relief where and over which issues Harris and Smith seem to have disagreed. So, where Smith capitalizes the division of labor, Harris does not; where Smith is sensitive to the "social question," Harris is not; where Smith pushes hard for retrenchment, Harris does not.

Clearly, Harris and Smith have very different strategies for dealing with the dynamics of commercial society once the productive powers of the division of labor are unleashed. Harris, to be sure, avoids having to contend with negative social issues by appealing to the self-adjusting market mechanism to solve the problem of short-term social disorder. Smith, although aware of the self-adjusting mechanism, does not take Harris's line in Books II–V of the *WN*. Rather, like Hutcheson, Berkeley, and Turgot, Smith copes with social injustice by moralizing money and by directing savings towards investment in agriculture.

In this vein, it is surely no accident that we find an instructive parallel for what we have been talking about here in Turgot's *Reflections*, a work whose importance for Smith has already been discussed (Appendices I and II). Turgot, for example, had speculated that, unless there is a "continual advance and return of capitals which constitute *what* ought to be called the *circulation of money*," a nation's economic activity "will be reduced . . . and . . . ordinary workmen, ceasing to find employment, will sink into the most extreme destitution" (1973, pp. 158–59). So, to sustain the "useful and productive circulation [of money] which enlivens all the work of society," Turgot insisted that a "nation" had to cultivate a "spirit of economy" in its people (1973, pp. 158, 169). By so doing, he said, the "habit of luxury" would not arise, and the nation could maintain its economic and moral balance in a way that had previously eluded the world's great empires (1973, p. 169).

Harris, we have just seen, situated his economic work in a very similar framework, sensing, for example, the "disorders" with which "over--plenty" of money threatened prosperous nations. But other than counselling patience, Harris offered few specifics as to how a society might deal with luxury, corruption, and inequality. In his view, nations just grew their way out of such difficulties. Smith, by contrast, avails himself of the frugality argument in Book II of the *WN*. He does this, I think, in order to address the social question, for, like Turgot, he thought social disorders—of the sort we find in Book V—might be averted with the aid of the saving-investment strategy. That is why Smith speaks in Book II of the "frugal man" as a person who realizes that his true "interest" lies in seeing to it that the true "destination" of capital is the employment of labor.

It seems reasonable, therefore, to read the *WN* as an oddly organized attempt to come to terms *economically* with the wealth-and-virtue problem. What makes the organization odd, of course, is that the issue of social injustice raised in Book V is addressed in Book II (and elsewhere) through the frugality argument; and that argument, we have seen in Appendix I, is as much an ethical as an economic argument. Failure to see that the arguments of Books II–IV anticipate some of the problems of commercial societies that are raised in Book V accounts for the oversized importance Smith scholarship has assigned to the relationship between the division-of-labor arguments of Book I and Book V.

A close look at the structure of the argument of the *WN* confirms that the sequence of the books might be out of order. Book I starts off with praise of the productive powers of the division of labor. And like Harris before him, Smith traces many improvements in the conditions of workers to the division of labor (e.g., wage increases and relative price deductions for many goods that workers buy). But while noting these beneficial developments, Smith is careful to ground advances in workers' welfare in the economic circumstances of what he calls a "progressive state." As distinct from what he calls "stationary" and "declining" states, a progressive one has two main features: (1) the economy, driven by the division-of-labor principle, is "advancing" or "increasing" the wealth in society; and (2) the division of labor is expected to continue to expand in circumstances of growing prosperity because the frugality-savings-investment logic discussed in Book II still governs business decisions. Counterfactually, Smith also argues that, if the conditions for continuous expansion of production are not met, then the progressive state will begin the slide toward decline, a condition brought about by spending priorities that focus on buying trinkets rather than on investing in productive labor, especially in agriculture (Since in Smith's scheme investment in agriculture runs against certain aspects of the division of labor principle, there seems to be some uncertainty in Smith's mind as between investment in technology, etc., and in agriculture). In any event, it is the counterfactual argument that we confront in Book V—which means that Book V is written in a conditional discourse: it presents an "as if" scenario that need not develop if certain preventive measures are taken to protect against it.

In this it is instructive that Smith chose not to confront the social question of Book V by counselling patience until a competitive equilibrium is reestablished in the market. On the contrary, he charges human beings—frugal men in Book II; "owners of great mercantile capitals" in Book IV; and "common people" and prudent "statesmen" in Book V—with the responsibility for retrenching expences and for ameliorating debilitating social conditions. In that light, frugality and the ethico-political imperative of agricultural investment are where the moral and the socio-economic lines of Smith's argument come together. That is, it is where the moral teachings of Berkeley and Hutcheson and the economic teachings of Quesnay and Turgot—the old ethical and new economic, in

Davie's sense—converge and find their point of balance and mediation.

In Book V, Smith pushes the frugality argument in an unexpected direction, using some very revealing language to characterize the social dynamics of relations between "men of large revenue" on the one hand and the "common people" on the other. He broaches this topic toward the end of Chapter I by juxtaposing "people of fashion," whose "liberal" or "loose system" of morality leads them to "luxury," "intemperance," "wanton and disorderly mirth," and "dissipation," to the "common people," whose "austere" system of morality inclines them to "censure" and "reproach" the well-to-do for the "vices which are apt to arise [among them] from great prosperity." He closes this section of the text on an equally revealing note, blasting "men of large revenue" for indulging in the kind of "vanity" and "dissipation" that detracts from "sanctity of character."

Between the opening and the closing of this section of Book V, Smith links the "austere" moral system of the "common people" with Protestant religious values in general and with "strict regularity" of "conduct" in everyday life in particular. In explaining this connection, Smith implies that the "mediocrity of church benefices" among certain Protestant groups contributes enormously to the high moral life of those churches' clergy. In Smith's estimation, the humility that is nurtured by that kind of equality legitimizes the clergy in the eyes of church members who, in turn, conduct their lives with those values and the exemplary behavior of the clergy in mind.

This language, which is similar to that used in Books II and III to describe the character and conduct of frugal men and to that used in Book IV to describe industrious and frugal Dutch merchants, appears again in the opening pages of Book V, Chapter III (as well as in the new chapter that Smith added to the 1790 edition of the *TMS*). Here Smith complains about the lack of frugality in the modern world, especially in "commercial" countries in which the court and the nobility continue to indulge "frivolous passions" for the sake of ornamentation and display—words Quesnay often used to describe mercantile capital in French courts (Quesnay 1963, p. 202). As Smith sees it, such behavior eventually leads to debt and "ruin" for all. And, again, he finds the counter for this in the agrarian-investment strategy in general and "in the frugality and good conduct" of industrious individuals among the common people in particular.

I take it, therefore, that in Book V one of Smith's main aims was to identify frugality as an "ordinary" rather than a "superior" virtue (Consult Waszek 1984 for this theme); that is, he describes frugality as a virture that is capable of being realized (i.e., valued) and practiced (i.e., realized) by common people in their everyday lives. And given the importance

Smith has assigned to frugality in the process of producing economic wealth, it would seem to follow that, so long as the habit of frugality persisted among the people as a whole, commercial societies could avoid the cycle of commerce, leisure, luxury, and corruption, even if their governments incurred growing debts and obligations to "monied" interests (Montesquieu [1949, pp. 40–46, 94–99], one of the great figures of the Enlightenment, had said things like this in *The Spirit of the Laws* while discussing the role of commerce in the modern world). Accordingly, it would not be inappropriate to suggest that Smith's interest in frugality entailed a democratization of the habit of frugality for the sake of the long-term economic and moral health of society. With frugality as a cultivated *habitus*, the circumstances of Book V would not be likely to arise. But without frugality as a bedrock value, Smith seemed to think that civil society would eventually succumb to the "liberal" system of morality that, in his judgment, was antithetical to the long-term fortunes of the "progressive state" and to the realization of the true promise of *doux-commerce*.

As I explained at the end of Appendix III, Smith's agrarian bias comes into play here because in his work the accumulated capital that frugality creates is destined for employment in agriculture. He is most explicit about this in Book IV, Chapter VII. There—as Quesnay had done in his work (1965, pp. 105–6, 110)—Smith blames merchants of specific countries, who did not invest their capital in agriculture, for reducing rich nations to "beggerly" conditions. Instead of exhibiting "sober" virtues, these merchants indulged in all manner of "superfluous" expense, thus depriving the agricultural sector of the economy of the capital funds needed for improving its productive powers. Accordingly, I see Smith's artful combination of the frugality and agricultural-investment arguments as simultaneous expressions of the moral quality of his economic thinking and of his economic commitment to the mediocrity-of-money policy, for in both instances the point is to prevent too much money from accumulating in the hands of any specific social group. As we have seen, that was a piece of Baconian wisdom. In the *WN*, Smith produced up-to-date arguments for its perennial relevance to sound economic thinking.

REFERENCES TO CITATIONS IN EDITOR'S COMMENTARY

Angell, J. W., 1926. *The Theory of International Prices*, Cambridge, Mass.

Bacon, F., 1850. *The Works of Francis Bacon*, v. 2, ed. B. Montagu, Philadelphia

Bentham, J., 1952. *Jeremy Bentham's Economic Writings*, ed. W. Stark, London

Berkeley, G., 1871. *The Works of George Berkeley*, ed. A. C. Fraser, Oxford

Blaug, M., 1968. *Economic Theory in Retrospect*, rev. ed., Homewood, Ill.

Blaug, M., 1986. *Great Economists before Keynes*, Sussex

Botero, G., 1956. *The Reason of State*, trans. P. J. Waley and D. P. Waley, New Haven, Conn.

Boulding, K., 1971. "After Samuelson, Who Needs Smith?" *History of Political Economy* 3: 225–37

Cannan, E., 1976. "Editor's Introduction," in Adam Smith, *The Nature and Causes of the Wealth of Nations*, ed. E. Cannan, Chicago

Cantillon, R., 1931. *Essay on the Nature of Trade in General*, ed. H. Higgs, London

Coats, A. W., 1962. "Adam Smith: The Modern Reappraissal," *Renaissance and Modern Studies* 6: 25–48

Coleman, D. C., 1969. "Eli Heckscher and the Idea of Mercantilism," in *Revisions in Mercantilism*, ed. D. C. Coleman, 192–217, London

Cunningham, W., 1891. "The Progress of Economic Doctrine in England in the Eighteenth Century," *Economic Journal* 1: 73–94

Davie, G., 1967. "Anglophobe and Anglophil," *Scottish Journal of Political Economy* 14: 291–301

DeVries, J., 1976. *The Economy of Europe in the Age of Crisis, 1600–1750*, Cambridge

Dickey, L., 1993. "Power, Commerce, and Natural Thinking in Defoe's Political Writings, 1698–1707," in *A Union for Empire*, ed. J. Robertson, Cambridge

Forbes, D., 1982. "Natural Law and the Scottish Enlightenment," in *The Origins and Nature of the Scottish Enlightenment*, ed. A. Skinner and R. Campbell, 186–204, Edinburgh

Harris, J., 1856. "Essay upon Money and Coins," in *A Select Collection of Scarce and Valuable Tracts on Money*, ed. J. R. McCulloch, London

Heckscher, E., 1955. *Mercantilism*, 2v., trans. M. Shapiro, London

Heilbroner, R., 1975. "The Paradox of Progress: Decline and Decay in *The Wealth of Nations*," in *Essays on Adam Smith*, ed. A. Skinner and T. Wilson, 524–35, Oxford

Hinton, R., 1955. "The Mercantilist System in the Time of Thomas Mun," *Economic History Review* 7: 277–90

Hirsch, F., 1976. *Social Limits to Growth*, Cambridge, Mass.

Hirschman, A. O., 1977. *The Passions and the Interests*, Princeton

Hirschman, A. O., 1986. *Rival Views of Market Society and Other Essays*, New York

Hollander, S., 1973. *The Economics of Adam Smith*, Toronto

Hont, I., 1983. "The Rich Country-Poor Country' Debate in Scottish Classical Political Economy," in *Wealth and Virtue*, ed. I. Hont and M. Ignatieff, 271–315, Cambridge

Hont, I. and M. Ignatieff, eds., 1983. *Wealth and Virtue*, Cambridge

Hume, D., 1987. *Essays. Moral, Political and Literary*, rev ed., ed. E. F. Miller, Indianapolis

Hutcheson, F., 1971. *Collected Works of Francis Hutcheson*, v. 7, Hildesheim

Hutchison, T., 1988. *Before Adam Smith*, Oxford

Kames, Lord, 1763. *Essays upon Several Subjects Concerning British Antiquities*, 3rd. ed. Edinburgh

Kristol, I., 1983. "Adam Smith and the Spirit of Capitalism," in *Reflections of a Neo-Conservative*, New York

Letwin, W., 1990. "The Wealth of Nations," in *Adam Smith's Legacy*, ed. N. Elliott, 29–47, London

McNally, D., 1988. *Political Economy and the Rise of Capitalism*, Berkeley

Mazlich, B. and Goodwin, N., 1983. "The Wealth of Adam Smith," in *Harvard Business Review*, 61: 52–65

Meek, R. L., 1967. "The Scottish Contribution to Marxist Sociology," in *Economics and Ideology and Other Essays*, 34–50, London

Misselden, E., 1623. *The Circle of Commerce or the Balance of Trade*, London

Monroe, A. E., 1923. *Monetary Theory before Adam Smith*, Gloucester, Mass.

Montesquieu, C., 1949. *The Spirit of the Laws*, trans. T. Nugent, New York

Mun, T., 1952. "England's Treasure by Foreign Trade," in *Early English Tracts on Commerce*, ed. J. R. McCulloch, Cambridge

O'Driscoll, G., ed., 1979. *Adam Smith and Modern Political Economy*, Ames, Iowa

Peil, T., 1991. "A New Look at Adam Smith," in *Pioneers in Economics*, ed. M. Blaug, v. 12: Adam Smith, 279–99

Phillipson, N., 1981. "The Scottish Enlightenment," in *The Enlightenment in National Context*, ed. R. Porter and M. Teich, 19–40, Cambridge

Pocock, J.G.A., 1975. *The Machiavellian Moment*, Princeton

Pocock, J.G.A., 1983. "Cambridge Paradigms and Scottish Philosophers," in *Wealth and Virtue*, ed. I. Hont and M. Ignatieff, 235–52, Cambridge

Quesnay, F., 1963. *The Economics of Physiocracy*, ed. R. L. Meek, Cambridge, Mass.

Quesnay, F., 1965. "Farmers," in *Encyclopedia Selections*, trans. N. Hoyt and T. Cassirer, 86–113, Indianapolis

Quesnay, F., 1972. *Tableau Economique*, ed. M. Kuczynski and R. Meek, London

Raphael, D. D., 1985. *Adam Smith*, Oxford

Robertson, J., 1983. "The Scottish Enlightenment at the Limits of the Civic Tradition," in *Wealth and Virtue*, ed. I. Hont and M. Ignatieff, Cambridge

Rosenberg, N., 1965. "Adam Smith on the Division of Labor: Two Views or One?" *Economica* 32: 127–39

Rosenberg, N. 1979. "Adam Smith and Laissez-Faire Revisited," in *Adam Smith and Modern Political Economy*, ed. G. O'Driscoll, 19–34, Ames, Iowa

Rosenberg, N., 1990. "Adam Smith and the Stock of Moral Capital," *History of Political Economy* 20: 1–17

Sallust, 1963. *Jugurthine War and Conspiracy of Catiline*, trans. S. Handford, New York

Schumpeter, J., 1954. *History of Economic Analysis*, New York

Scott, W. R., 1937. *Adam Smith as Student and Professor*, Glasgow

Sen, A., 1986. "Adam Smith's Prudence," in *Theory and Reality in Development*, ed. S. Lall and F. Stewart, 28–37, New York

Sen, A. 1987. *On Ethics and Economics*, Oxford

Seneca, 1969. *Letters from a Stoic*, trans. R. Campbell, New York

Skinner, A. and R. Campbell, 1982. *Adam Smith*, New York

Smith, Adam, 1978. "Early Draft of *The Wealth of Nations*," in Adam Smith's *Lectures on Jurisprudence*, ed. R. Meek, D. Raphael, and P. Stein, 562–81, Oxford

Stewart, D., 1980. "Account of the Life and Works of Adam Smith," in Adam Smith's *Essays on Philosophical Subjects*, ed. W. Wightman, 269–351, Oxford

Stigler, G., 1976. "Preface," in Adam Smith's *The Nature and Causes of the Wealth of Nations*, ed. E. Cannan, Chicago

Suivranta, B., 1923. *The Theory of Balance of Trade in England: A Study in Mercantilism*, Helsingfors

Tribe, K., 1977. "The Histories' of Economic Discourse," *Economy and Society* 6: 314–44

Turgot, A.R.J., 1973. "Reflections on the Formation and Distribution of Wealth," in *Turgot on Progress, Society, and Economics*, ed. R. L. Meek, 119–82, Cambridge

Vaughan, R., 1856. "A Discourse of Coin and Coinage," in *A Select*

Collection of Scarce and Valuable Tracts on Money, ed. J. R. McCulloch, 9–119, London

Vickers, D., 1960. *Studies in the Theory of Money, 1690–1776*, London

Viner, J., 1937. *Studies in the Theory of International Trade*, New York

Viner, J., 1991. *Essays on the Intellectual History of Economics*, ed. D. Irwin, Princeton

Waszek, N., 1984. "Two Concepts of Morality," *Journal of the History of Ideas* 45: 591–606

West, E. G., 1964. "Adam Smith's Two Views on the Division of Labor," *Economica* 31: 23–32

Winch, D., 1978. *Adam Smith's Politics*, New York